Spinoza

"An absolutely fantastic book. Della Rocca has succeeded in making Spinoza's notoriously difficult thought accessible to a general audience without sacrificing any of the conceptual complexity and rigor that makes Spinoza such a good philosopher." **Martin Lin, University of Toronto**

Routledge Philosophers

Edited by Brian Leiter
University of Texas, Austin

Routledge Philosophers is a major series of introductions to the great
Western philosophers. Each book places a major philosopher or thinker
in historical context, explains and assesses their key arguments, and
considers their legacy. Additional features include a chronology of major
dates and events, chapter summaries, annotated suggestions for further
reading and a glossary of technical terms.

An ideal starting point for those new to philosophy, they are also essential reading for those interested in the subject at any level.

Hobbes	A. P. Martinich
Leibniz	Nicholas Jolley
Locke	E. J. Lowe
Hegel	Frederick Beiser
Rousseau	Nicholas Dent
Schopenhauer	Julian Young
Freud	Jonathan Lear
Kant	Paul Guyer
Husserl	David Woodruff Smith
Darwin	Tim Lewens
Merleau-Ponty	Taylor Carman

Forthcoming:

Aristotle	Christopher Shields
Hume	Don Garrett
Fichte and Schelling	Sebastian Gardner
Rawls	Samuel Freeman
Heidegger	John Richardson

Michael Della Rocca

Spinoza

Routledge
Taylor & Francis Group

LONDON AND NEW YORK

First published 2008
by Routledge
711 Third Ave, New York, NY 10017

Simultaneously published in the UK
by Routledge
2 Park Square, Milton Park, Abingdon, Oxon OX14 4RN

Routledge is an imprint of the Taylor & Francis Group, an informa business

© 2008 Michael Della Rocca

Typeset in Joanna by
Taylor & Francis Books

British Library Cataloguing in Publication Data
A catalogue record for this book is available from the British Library

Library of Congress Cataloging in Publication Data
A catalog record for this book has been requested

ISBN 10: 0-415-28329-9 (hbk)
ISBN 10: 0-415-28330-2 (pbk)
ISBN 10: 0-203-89458-8 (ebk)
ISBN 13: 978-0-415-28329-8 (hbk)
ISBN 13: 978-0-415-28330-4 (pbk)
ISBN 10: 978-0-203-89458-3 (ebk)

For Ben and Ethan

Preface ix
Acknowledgments x
Editions Used and Abbreviations xi
Chronology xiii

Spinoza's Understanding and Understanding
Spinoza **One** 1

1. Spinoza's Understanding
2. Understanding Spinoza
Summary
Further Reading

The Metaphysics of Substance **Two** 33

1. Descartes on Substance
2. Spinoza Contra Descartes on Substance
3. The Argument for Substance Monism
4. Modes
5. Necessitarianism
6. The Purpose of It All
Summary
Further Reading

The Human Mind **Three** 89

1. Parallelism and Representation
2. Essence and Representation
3. Parallelism and Mind–Body Identity
4. The Idea of the Human Body
5. The Pancreas Problem, the Pan Problem, and Panpsychism
6. Nothing but Representation
7. Representation, Will, and Belief

8. Skepticism
Summary
Further Reading

Psychology: Striving and Self-preservation **Four** 137

1. Conatus
2. Desire, Joy, and Sadness
3. Love, Hate, and All That
Summary
Further Reading

The Ethics of the *Ethics* **Five** 175

1. The Good Notion of the Good
2. The Right Notion of the Right
3. Knowledge and Morality
4. Freedom and Morality
5. Helping Others
6. Lies and Degrees of Freedom
Summary
Further Reading

The State, Religion, and Scripture **Six** 206

1. Rights and Power
2. Religion and the State
3. Scripture
4. Prophecy and the Truth of the Bible
Summary
Further Reading

From PSR to Eternity   Seven   254

Summary
Further Reading

The Aftermath of Spinoza   Eight   275

1.   Leibniz
2.   Bayle and Hume
3.   The Pantheism Controversy
4.   Hegel
5.   Nietzsche
6.   Prospects of Spinozistic Rationalism
Summary
Further Reading

Glossary   314
Notes   318
Bibliography   327
Index   333

Preface

In offering this comprehensive account of Spinoza's philosophical thought, I have in mind those coming to Spinoza for the first time. I hope to be able to kindle in these readers the same joy I felt on being introduced to Spinoza more than 25 years ago. I believe that I have found a key—in the shape of the Principle of Sufficient Reason—that will go a very long way toward making Spinoza's thought both more accessible and exciting. At the same time, I hope that this work will also be of real interest to scholars, philosophers, and advanced students. Because the book is designed to serve as an introduction to Spinoza, I do not engage the secondary literature directly in any extensive way, but my thinking is obviously very much informed by and indebted to recent and not-so-recent scholarly debates. Rethinking Spinoza in light of the Principle of Sufficient Reason promises to be important not only for our understanding of Spinoza, but also for our understanding of the philosophical issues Spinoza deals with and that continue to trouble philosophers today. The contemporary debates over these issues suffer, in my opinion, from a lack of systematic attention to the power of the Principle of Sufficient Reason. This book is not only about Spinoza, but it is in the spirit of Spinoza for it takes one step toward addressing that lack.

Acknowledgments

A portion of Della Rocca 2008b appears in Chapter 7 and is reprinted with the permission of the University of Arkansas Press. A portion of Della Rocca 2007 appears in Chapter 3.

The writing of this book was framed by two very memorable seminars I taught on Spinoza at Yale, one in the fall of 2002 and one in the fall of 2007. I would like to thank all the students and colleagues who participated in these seminars for their encouragement and for their remarkable ability to engage with Spinoza. I am particularly grateful to Brian Leiter for inviting me to take on this project and to Tony Bruce for all his support and insight along the way. I am indebted to four referees for Routledge: Charles Huenemann, Martin Lin, Steven Nadler, and anonymous. Their reports resulted in many improvements. Yitzhak Melamed and Samuel Newlands commented extensively and valuably on the manuscript. As I wrote the book and thought through the interpretive and philosophical issues I take up here, many other friends and colleagues were helpful to me, including (in no particular order): Debra Nails, Ed Curley, Don Garrett, Alan Nelson, Ursula Renz, Larry Jorgensen, Lisa Shapiro, Alison Simmons, Justin Broackes, Fred Beiser, Leslie Wolf, Pedro Stoichita, Noa Shein, Dominik Perler, Robin Jeshion, Johannes Haag, Elliot Paul, Robert Adams, John Carriero, Dan Garber, Omri Boehm, Shelly Kagan, George Bealer, Tony Kronman, Troy Cross, Stephan Schmid, Lilli Alanen, Christian Barth, Calvin Normore, Jim Kreines, Michael Nelson, and Carol Rovane. Apologies to those I may have omitted. Finally, to my wife, Christine Hayes, and to my sons, Benjamin and Ethan, my love and gratitude as ever.

Editions Used and Abbreviations

SPINOZA'S WORKS AND DESCARTES'S WORKS

Charles Adam and Paul Tannery (eds). *Oeuvres de Descartes*. 12 vols. Paris: J. Vrin, 1964–76.

John Cottingham, Robert Stoothoff, and Dugald Murdoch (trans.). *The Philosophical Writings of Descartes*. 2 vols. Cambridge: Cambridge University Press, 1985.

John Cottingham, Robert Stoothoff, Dugald Murdoch, and Anthony Kenny (trans.). *The Philosophical Writings of Descartes*. Vol. 3. Cambridge: Cambridge University Press, 1991.

Edwin Curley (ed. and trans.). *The Collected Works of Spinoza*. Vol. 1. Princeton, N.J.: Princeton University Press, 1985.

Carl Gebhardt (ed.). *Spinoza Opera*. 4 vols. Heidelberg: Carl Winter, 1925.

Samuel Shirley (trans.) *Spinoza: The Letters*. Indianapolis: Hackett, 1995.

Samuel Shirley (trans.) *Spinoza: Theological-Political Treatise*. Second edition. Indianapolis: Hackett, 2001.

ABBREVIATIONS FOR SPINOZA'S WORKS AND DESCARTES'S WORKS

AT   Adam and Tannery (eds), *Oeuvres de Descartes*

CM   *Cogitata Metaphysica*

CSM   Cottingham, Stoothoff, and Murdoch (trans.), *The Philosophical Writings of Descartes*, vols 1 and 2

CSMK   Cottingham, Stoothoff, Murdoch, and Kenny (trans.), *The Philosophical Writings of Descartes*, vol. 3

G   Gebhardt, *Spinoza Opera*

KV	*Korte Verhandeling van God, de Mensch, en deszelfs Welstand* (Short Treatise on God, Man, and his Well-being)
PPC	*Principia Philosophiae Cartesianae* (Principles of Descartes's Philosophy)
TdIE	*Tractatus de Intellectus Emendatione*
TP	*Tractatus Politicus*
TTP	*Tractatus Theologico-Politicus*

ABBREVIATIONS FOR PASSAGES FROM SPINOZA'S *ETHICS*

app	appendix
ax	axiom
c	corollary
d	demonstration
da	definition of the affects
def	definition
expl	explication
le	lemma
p	proposition
pref	preface
s	scholium

1p10s = Part 1, Proposition 10, scholium. Unless otherwise noted, all references in this format are to passages from the *Ethics*.

Chronology

1492	Jews expelled from Spain
1590s	Spinoza's father, Michael, flees Portugal
1619	Jews officially granted right to practice their religion openly in Amsterdam
1632	Spinoza is born in Amsterdam on November 24
1640	Uriel da Costa commits suicide
c.1654	Begins studying at Van den Enden's school
1656	Excommunicated
c.1659	Begins studies at University of Leiden
1660	Begins *Short Treatise*
1661	Begins correspondence with Oldenburg
c.1662	Composes the *Treatise on the Emendation of the Intellect*
1663	Publishes *Descartes's Principles of Philosophy*
c.1670	*Theological-Political Treatise* published anonymously
1672	Johan de Witt and his brother Cornelis are brutally murdered
1673	Receives and declines a professorship at the University of Heidelberg
1676	Meets with Leibniz in November
1677	Dies on 21 February in the Hague
1677	Spinoza's disciples publish *Opera Posthuma*, including the *Ethics* and the unfinished *Tractatus Politicus*

One

Spinoza's Understanding and Understanding Spinoza

1. SPINOZA'S UNDERSTANDING

All philosophers seek explanation. All philosophers seek to make the world and our place in it intelligible. To grasp such explanations is the perennial hope and promise of philosophy. However, almost all philosophers expect explanations to run out at some point, whether because of the limitations of our cognitive faculties or because of the recalcitrance of the world itself which admits of certain brute facts, facts without any explanation. "My spade is turned," as Wittgenstein famously says when explanations reach a limit.[1] This admission is, of course, nothing more than a sober and, perhaps, healthy acknowledgment of our finitude and of the bruteness of reality. And, as I said, almost all philosophers reach this point. Almost all philosophers. But not Spinoza. His spade is never turned. Spinoza's philosophy is characterized by perhaps the boldest and most thoroughgoing commitment ever to appear in the history of philosophy to the intelligibility of everything. For Spinoza, no why-question is off limits, each why-question—in principle—admits of a satisfactory answer.

Spinoza's relentless rational scrutiny extends far and deep. Far: his gaze reaches almost all the traditional and important questions of philosophy. Spinoza offers powerful rationalist accounts of causation, of necessity and possibility, of the way in which our minds and our actions take their place in a world governed by strict causal laws. He offers wonderfully rich theories of the human mind, of morality, of political and religious life, of freedom, and of reason itself.

Deep: Spinoza penetrates to the bottom of each of these issues. He single-mindedly digs and digs until we find that the phenomenon in question is nothing but some form of intelligibility itself, of explicability itself. Thus the causation of one thing by another is nothing but one thing making the other intelligible. Our place in the world simply is the way in which we are explained by certain things and can serve to make intelligible—i.e. explain—certain other things. Our emotions are just different manifestations of our power over, and of our subjection to, other things; they are manifestations of the way in which we explain and are explained by other things. For Spinoza, all philosophical problems bottom out in intelligibility itself.

Spinoza's commitment to intelligibility is extremely ambitious in at least two respects. First, he insists that each thing is intelligible, there are no facts impervious to explanation. Second, he holds that these explanations are—in principle—graspable by us. Our minds are, of course, limited in some ways; there are limits to how many things we can fully grasp. As Spinoza says,

> it would be impossible for human weakness to grasp the series of singular, changeable things, not only because there are innumerably many of them, but also because of the infinite circumstances in one and the same thing.
>
> (TdIE §100)

But this limitation is purely quantitative, not qualitative. While particular things may elude our grasp because of our finite ability to keep many things clearly in mind, no thing is by its nature inaccessible to the human mind. Indeed, as we will see, for Spinoza, our knowledge of the world is of precisely the same kind as the best or highest form of knowledge, the kind of knowledge enjoyed by God (whoever or whatever that is—as we will see, Spinoza has a very non-traditional conception of God).

His ambitions are, of course, not always fully realized, as we will see soon enough, but the boldness of his vision for philosophy, the high-wire act that he performs on each page, makes him a philosopher supremely worth studying. This is so especially because Spinoza's ambitious drive for explanation stands in sharp contrast to so much of previous and subsequent philosophy. Sometimes subsequent philosophy in particular seems to be a concerted effort to deny the pretensions of reason. I'm thinking here of, among others, Locke, Hume, and Kant, each of whom wrote a big book that could easily have been entitled—and in one case actually was entitled—*Critique of Pure Reason*. Perhaps even worse than such clipping of reason's wings is that so much of philosophy in the last century seems simply to take the limitations of reason for granted and complacently operates with diminished aims. All too often we find philosophers resorting to primitives, unanalyzable notions, not subject to further explanation but nonetheless extremely important. Thus we encounter philosophers willingly embracing primitive modality (i.e. primitive necessity and possibility), primitive causation, primitive identity, primitive accounts of reference (i.e. accounts of the way words or thoughts succeed in being about things in the world), unanalyzable notions of the good and the right, inexplicable kinds of agency and freedom—the catalogue of philosophy's self-defeats. And we find these philosophers unashamed to do so. Spinoza was and would be appalled—for him, reliance on philosophical primitives is of a piece with the irrational faith or superstition that he devoted his life to fighting. Spinoza, as we shall see, has no objection to belief in God insofar as it is rational, but a less than rational belief in God is objectionable precisely because it is a refusal to dig deeper for an explanation of our place in the world and of the nature of the divinity. In the same way, reliance on philosophical primitives is an irrational refusal to dig deeper for an explanation. Spinoza's worries about Descartes and other insufficiently rationalist predecessors was—and his worry about so much of philosophy down to the present day would be—that, by appealing to primitives or inexplicable notions, philosophy has not advanced much beyond irrational faith.

Spinoza thus sees his philosophy as a stronghold against irrationalism in philosophy and as a challenge to other more complacent ways of doing philosophy. For these reasons—in other words, because of the purity of his philosophy—Spinoza enjoys a permanent and essential place in the canon of great philosophers and provides a refreshing and needed contrast to other, less ambitious philosophical approaches.

The purity of Spinoza's commitment to explanation can best be articulated in terms of his commitments to the Principle of Sufficient Reason (hereafter, the "PSR") and to his naturalism. Consider first the PSR, the principle according to which each fact, each thing that exists, has an explanation. The explanation of a fact is enough—sufficient—to enable one to see why the fact holds. The explanation of a fact enables us to see the explained fact coming, as it were. If the explanation of a thing were not sufficient in this way, then some aspect of the thing would remain unexplained, unintelligible. The PSR is thus the embodiment of Spinoza's commitment to intelligibility. Versions of this principle go way back in philosophy and can be found in philosophers such as Parmenides, the Stoics, Aquinas, and others, but the philosopher most often associated with the principle is Leibniz. He built his system—as far as he could—around his commitment to the PSR. But—as we will see in due course—Leibniz's commitment to the PSR is not absolute. In Spinoza, unlike Leibniz, the PSR takes on an outsized importance—it's rationalism on steroids, but for the fact that, in Spinoza's eyes, this total commitment to the PSR is completely natural.

Spinoza's commitment to the PSR emerges most clearly in 1p11d2: "For each thing there must be assigned a cause or reason, both for its existence and for its nonexistence." This principle is strong because it requires an explanation not only for existence, but also for non-existence. Consider also 1ax2: "What cannot be conceived through another must be conceived through itself." Here Spinoza says, in effect, that each thing must be conceived through something (either itself or another thing). For Spinoza, to conceive of a thing is to explain it.[2] Thus, in presupposing in 1ax2 that everything can be conceived through something, Spinoza presupposes that everything is able to be explained, he builds the notion of intelligibility into the heart of his metaphysical system.

Spinoza's commitment to the PSR quickly leads to his commitment to his naturalism. Of course, "naturalism" can mean many different things, but by "Spinoza's naturalism" I mean his thesis that everything in the world plays by the same rules; there are no things that are somehow connected with each other but that are not governed by the same principles. To understand Spinoza's naturalism, it will be helpful to focus on a famous contrast Spinoza draws between his account of the emotions—or affects—and those of his predecessors such as Descartes.

> Most of those who have written about the affects, and men's way of living, seem to treat not of natural things, which follow the common laws of Nature, but of things which are outside Nature. Indeed they seem to conceive man in Nature as a dominion within a dominion. For they believe that man disturbs, rather than follows [*magis perturbare, quam sequi*], the order of Nature.
>
> (G II 137)

He goes on, later in the preface, to articulate his own view of the place of man in nature, and in so doing he also gives his clearest statement of what I take to be his naturalism:

> nothing happens in Nature which can be attributed to any defect in it, for Nature is always the same, and its virtue and power of acting are everywhere the same, that is, the laws and rules of Nature, according to which all things happen, and change from one form to another, are always and everywhere the same, namely through the universal laws and rules of Nature.
>
> (G II 138)

Spinoza's problem with Cartesian and other accounts of the affects is that such views introduce an objectionable bifurcation between human beings and the rest of reality. Here we have non-human nature which operates according to one set of laws and here we have another part of reality—human beings—which operates according to a different set of laws or, perhaps, no laws at all.

By contrast, Spinoza's own view is one according to which human beings and the rest of reality are not explained in such different ways, according to which human beings and all else operate according to the same laws. Such a unification of explanatory principles is the heart of Spinoza's naturalism about psychology: human psychology is governed by the same fundamental principles that govern rocks and tables and dogs. Thus no new principles are needed to explain human psychology beyond those principles needed to explain the rest of nature anyway. More generally, Spinoza's naturalism, as I understand it, is the view that there are no illegitimate bifurcations in reality.

What exactly, in Spinoza's eyes, is so bad about such bifurcation? That is, why does Spinoza think that it is illegitimate to have two different kinds of things susceptible to radically different kinds of explanation? A crucial clue comes when Spinoza says that, on the view he rejects, man *disturbs* rather than follows the order of nature. The fact that, on this view, human beings disturb the order in the rest of reality suggests that human beings and their behavior are related in some way to the rest of reality and that these relations between human beings and the rest of reality cannot be understood in terms of the laws at work generally.

How then are these relations to be explained? First of all, it is important to note that, for Spinoza, the relations must be able to be explained. This is simply a requirement imposed by the PSR. But, again, how to explain the relations? If they cannot be explained in terms of laws at work generally, then perhaps they are explained in terms of special, local laws of nature–human interaction, as it were. These local laws could not be derived from general laws at work throughout nature, for then the behavior of human beings would, after all, be susceptible to, explicable in terms of, general laws. So the behavior, insofar as it is explained in terms of local laws, would be explained in terms of irreducibly local laws. But then a version of our question arises again: why do these local laws hold, if they are not derived from more generally applicable laws? Because they would be local, such laws would, in fact, seem anomalous, inexplicable. From the perspective of the general laws, there is no way, as it were, to see these local laws as coming, no way to derive these local laws. And thus the relations explained by the local laws would be, in a way, still brute precisely because brute laws would explain them. For Spinoza, then, disturbances are disturbing because they are ultimately inexplicable, because their occurrence would involve brute, inexplicable facts.

In general, for Spinoza, whenever there is a dominion within a dominion, that is, whenever there are two kinds of things that operate according to different principles and are related to each other in some way, then the ways in which these things are related to each other are disturbances and, ultimately, inexplicable, that is they would violate the PSR. In this way, we can see Spinoza's naturalism as driven by his rationalist denial of brute facts.

In this move from the PSR to the naturalistic rejection of certain bifurcations in reality, we can see that the PSR initiates a drive for unification. The PSR prompts the naturalistic unification of laws by which certain things are governed. The PSR also motivates other strategies of unification, naturalistic rejections of other bifurcations. Thus, to mention just a few examples which we will return to later in more detail: Spinoza's PSR dictates the collapse of any distinction between necessary truths and possible truths (this amounts to Spinoza's necessitarianism, the thesis that all truths are necessary truths). The PSR also dictates that, for Spinoza, causation and explanation and the inherence of a property in a subject all amount to the same phenomenon. The PSR also dictates the reduction of the consciousness of a mental state (that most recalcitrant notion in recent and not-so-recent philosophy of mind) to the simple fact that the mental state is a representation of, is about, something. The PSR dictates, as we will see, that an action's goodness, rightness, and power all come to the same thing. To view any of these phenomena—necessary truths and possible truths, causation and explanation and inherence, consciousness and representation, goodness and rightness and power—as ultimately distinct from one another would, in Spinoza's eyes, be to introduce illegitimate bifurcations into reality in violation of naturalism and the PSR.

Often these unifications that Spinoza introduces manifest a twofold use of the PSR that I see as characteristic of his rationalism. Let me illustrate this twofold use of the PSR by returning to the case of causation. Spinoza demands that we give an account of what causation is; we must be able to explain what it is for one thing to cause another. (Thus he rejects the position of some recent philosophers who claim that no such account of causation is in the offing and that the notion of causation is thus primitive.) This insistence on an explanation of causation, this demand that causation be intelligible, is the first use of the PSR in this case. The account of causation that Spinoza goes on to offer is, as we will see in Chapter 2, roughly this: for *a* to cause *b* is nothing more than for *a* to make *b* intelligible, for *a* to explain *b*. If causation were something over and above explanation then in what would causation consist? How would we explain causation? This analysis of causation in terms of explanation or intelligibility is the second use of the PSR in this case. Thus causation is explained in terms of the notion of explanation itself, it is made intelligible in terms of intelligibility itself. Here we see the notion of intelligibility doubling back on itself: a given phenomenon is explained in terms of explanation itself. This double use of the PSR pervades Spinoza's philosophy. Thus he accounts for consciousness and representation in terms of intelligibility itself; he accounts for goodness, rightness, and power in terms of intelligibility; he accounts for the key phenomena at work in his psychology in terms of intelligibility. Indeed, for him, existence itself is to be explained in terms of intelligibility. For Spinoza, to be is to be intelligible. This is the most fundamental statement of his rationalism, and it is the most fundamental instance of the twofold use of the PSR. Be on the lookout for the twofold use of the PSR throughout this book: it will provide the key to unlocking many of the mysteries of Spinoza's philosophical system.

Perhaps the most concrete manifestation of Spinoza's rationalism is the geometrical method he employs in his most famous and wide-ranging work, the *Ethics*. There he sets about presenting his entire philosophical system in the rigid form—in the "mail and mask" as Nietzsche would say—of the Euclidean apparatus of definitions, axioms, and demonstrations. In a way, Spinoza's use of this method for philosophical purposes is simply an extreme display of the seventeenth-century fascination in philosophy and science with mathematical reasoning. At this time, the conception of the physical world was undergoing a change to a more mechanistic picture, a picture according to which the extended world is one vast machine and its states and changes could be fully characterized in mathematical terms, in terms of quantifiable features such as size, shape, and motion. It was natural to apply a mathematical method of reasoning to purely philosophical topics too. Descartes had done so briefly (albeit somewhat reluctantly) in the second set of replies to the objections to his *Meditations*, and early on, Spinoza himself—in expounding some of Descartes's views—had employed the geometrical method. But his most full-blown use of the geometrical method for philosophical purposes was in the *Ethics*.[3] Thus we find Spinoza treating of God and the mind as well as human psychology "just as if it were a question of lines, planes and bodies" (3Pref). It is this aspect of Spinoza's writing that—more than anything else—intimidates potential readers. The French philosopher Henri Bergson expresses this anxiety well when he speaks of:

the formidable array of theorems with the close network of definitions, corollaries and scholia, and that complication of

> machinery, that power to crush which causes the beginner, in the presence of the *Ethics*, to be struck with admiration and terror as though he were before a battleship of the dreadnought class.[4]

But I would encourage you not to be intimidated by Spinoza. In my experience, those most afraid of Spinoza have never really tried to sit down and read him. Spinoza is surprisingly accessible, and the formal apparatus is an aid to understanding because the previous claims that he relies on in his demonstrations are always (well, almost always) explicitly cited. This makes it easier to tease out the structure of Spinoza's reasoning. Also, it is important to note that scattered throughout the Ethics are less formal passages, so-called scholia as well as lengthy prefaces and appendices, in which Spinoza lays out his themes in more flowing, less formal prose. These passages are often oases in the forbidding landscape of propositions and demonstrations.

Finally, before registering complaints about the geometrical method, one should be aware that it is the method of presenting philosophy that is uniquely well-suited to the character of Spinoza's rationalist system. As we will see in the next chapter, for Spinoza, all things that exist follow from the very nature of God and follow from that nature with logical or conceptual necessity. For Spinoza, if one really understood what the nature of God is, one would see that it's absolutely necessary that God exists and that all the things that we observe in the world exist. All existence is necessary existence, all truth is necessary truth, and the source of this existence and truth is simply God's nature. For Spinoza, the nature of a thing is expressed in its definition, and so, in order to understand the world and the things that occur in the world—i.e. in order to carry out philosophy itself—one needs to grasp the definition of God and investigate what logically follows from that definition. And that is precisely what Spinoza does in the Ethics.[5] He begins with the definitions of God and of related philosophical notions such as substance and attribute, and he goes to town with them, drawing out the implications of these definitions in a series of demonstrations presented with Euclidean flair. Given the structure of reality, as Spinoza sees it, there is, in the end, no better and, indeed, no other way of doing philosophy than in geometrical fashion—drawing out the implications of the definition of God. So the method of Spinoza's major philosophical work is particularly appropriate for the content of that work. This melding of form and content in Spinoza's philosophy is of a piece with the drive toward uniformity that Spinoza's PSR and his naturalism generate. Appreciating the inevitability of Spinoza's geometrical method and the way in which it harmonizes with the content of his philosophy helps to make undergoing Spinoza's Euclidean rigors all the more rewarding.

My way of presenting Spinoza's system in the chapters that follow is—for better or worse—not the geometrical method. Rather, I will endeavor to narrate a story, one not without suspense. We will see the increasing power of the PSR, how more and more of the traditional problems and themes of philosophy begin—in Spinoza's capable hands—to fall under its sway. The story is rich and wonderful, but, as we progress, an obvious question becomes more and more acute: isn't Spinoza's trust in the PSR itself in need of justification? Why, in other words, should we trust reason itself? Without such a justification, Spinoza's confidence in the PSR can come to seem as objectionable as the unreasoned faith and philosophical primitives that he is so fond of railing against. Unless his trust in reason can be justified, Spinoza's entire rationalist project, his way of prosecuting the search for explanations, indeed the purity of his philosophy itself is threatened. This challenge will haunt us more and more as we make our progress though the book, and in many ways it furnishes the narrative arc of this book. I will take up this challenge on Spinoza's behalf only at the very end, once we are in a position to see how much turns on being able to meet this challenge.

Before making explicit the explanatory structure of the world as Spinoza sees it, and in order to see why philosophy and reason are so vital to Spinoza, we need to explore some of the apparently contingent, apparently haphazard obstacles placed before him as he strove to reveal this structure. In other words, let's consider Spinoza's biography.

2. UNDERSTANDING SPINOZA

There is something decidedly odd about trying to sketch details of Spinoza's life. As an arch rationalist, Spinoza always strives to perceive things *sub specie aeternitatis*—under an aspect of eternity. From this perspective, the self and its particular concerns would be dwarfed by the power of nature as a whole. As we will see, for Spinoza, singling out any individual for special attention would, in effect, be to behave arbitrarily, to act in a way not in keeping with the PSR. So any special focus on one particular life—even Spinoza's—must inevitably seem to be to go against Spinoza's principles. Thus we are, as Rebecca Goldstein memorably puts it, in some way betraying Spinoza in directing our attention to the details of his life.[6] But—as Spinoza himself recognizes—finite, not fully rational beings that we are, sometimes we must focus on the particular as a necessary stepping stone to a more purely rationalist perspective. So in that spirit, let's spend a few pages on Spinoza and his life.

Spinoza does his best to hide himself from view in his writings.[7] His rationalism and the impressive apparatus of his geometrical method offer very few hints as to Spinoza the human being. This makes it all the more striking that perhaps his oldest surviving writing begins with a rather candid autobiographical passage. He opens the *Treatise on the Emendation of the Intellect* by writing of his quest for happiness:

> After experience had taught me that all the things which regularly occur in ordinary life are empty and futile, and I saw that all the things which were the cause or object of my fear had nothing of good or bad in themselves, except insofar as [my] mind was moved by them, I resolved at last to try to find out whether there was

> anything which would be the true good, capable of communicating itself, and which alone would affect the mind, all others being rejected—whether there was something which, once found and acquired, would continuously give me the greatest joy to eternity.
>
> (TdIE §1)

Spinoza writes that he realized that the goods ordinarily sought by human beings—chiefly riches, fame, and the pleasures of sense—are in the end deeply unsatisfactory and even dangerous. He writes revealingly that sensual pleasure so enthralls the mind

> that it is quite prevented from thinking of anything else. But after the enjoyment of sensual pleasure is past, the greatest sadness follows. If this does not completely engross, still it thoroughly confuses and dulls the mind.
>
> (TdIE §4)

He goes on to say that indulgence in such bodily pleasure leads to repentance. Spinoza does not, however, austerely suggest that we should deny ourselves all sensory pleasures. Indeed, he recommends bodily pleasures in moderation (TdIE §11). But he also knows that there is the danger that sensory pleasures, in addition to leading to temporary sadness, have a tendency to be over-indulged and often lead to death.

The single-minded pursuit of riches or fame seems equally futile and dangerous. While the pursuit of these objects does not tend to the repentance that sensory pleasure often generates, these pursuits can generate ceaseless competition for more and more such goods, a competition that can only end in frustration and despair.

It's hard not to believe that Spinoza writes here out of some painful experiences of his own, experiences that gave rise to an imperative to act. He came to the conclusion that, by abandoning the exclusive pursuit of riches, fame, and bodily pleasures for the pursuit of the genuine good, he would be giving up certain evils for a certain good. For I saw that I was in the greatest danger, and that I was forced to seek a remedy with all my strength, however uncertain it might be—like a man suffering from a fatal illness, who, foreseeing certain death unless he employs a remedy, is forced to seek it, however uncertain, with all his strength. For all his hope lies there.

(TdIE §7)

To free himself from this almost desperate situation, Spinoza turns not to traditional religion, not to family, not to friends, but to the pursuit of knowledge itself; he seeks, in particular, knowledge of "certain laws of nature" (TdIE §12) and of "the union that the mind has with the whole of nature" (TdIE §13). In other words, in order to save himself and to attain "a joy entirely exempt from sadness" (TdIE §10), Spinoza turns to philosophy, indeed to his naturalistic version of philosophy. Spinoza sees his naturalism as literally saving his life.

This commitment to reason is, for Spinoza, from the start inherently social. The knowledge Spinoza seeks to acquire is knowledge that he endeavors that others attain as well:

it is part of my happiness to take pains that many others may understand as I understand, so that their intellect and desire agree entirely with my intellect and desire.

(TdIE §14)

This striving that others may come to know what Spinoza knows is one of the most admirable aspects of Spinoza's philosophical character. He often returned to the hope and conviction that others would see what he had seen, that they too would be persuaded by the rationalist conception of the world that had saved his life. Thus Spinoza was bold not only in his naturalistic conception of philosophy, but also in his conviction that others could be brought to see its value and that, with sufficient accommodation, ordinary people "will give a favorable hearing to the truth" (TdIE §17).

But this boldness was tempered too. His lifelong motto was *caute*—carefully. Spinoza knew that others would find his naturalism and rationalism dangerous, and although he published some work during his lifetime, he withheld from the public the most radical statement of his naturalistic and rationalistic vision. Spinoza's life, thus, was in many ways marked by a balance between, on the one hand, extreme caution and the dread of public controversy and, on the other, an audacious hope and need that others would come to share in his striking naturalistic conception.

To see how Spinoza carried out this balancing act that was his life, we need to turn from the scant biographical material Spinoza offers to the somewhat richer biographical material available to us now. Steven Nadler has done a wonderful job of bringing together this material, and the following sketch owes a great deal to his efforts. I will also make use—from time to time—of the less reliable short biographies produced not long after Spinoza's death, by Jean-Maximilian Lucas and Johan Colerus.[8]

The thought of each philosopher is shaped in fundamental ways by something over which he has no control—the community into which he was born. And no philosopher was more profoundly affected by his community than Spinoza, whose thought was in so many ways both an assimilation of and a reaction against attitudes at work among the Jews of seventeenth-century Amsterdam. Into this relatively new, prosperous, but still precarious group, Spinoza made his entry on November 24, 1632. Most members of the community were Sephardic Jews—Jews who originated from Spain or Portugal. Let's begin then with some information about the Jews of Spain and Portugal in this period.

In the Middle Ages when Spain and Portugal were under Muslim control, Jews in those countries enjoyed a golden age of tolerance, and they prospered. But after the Muslims were conquered by the Christians, life became increasingly difficult for the Jews. Many were forced to convert to Christianity. But often these new Christians, or *Conversos*, as they were called by the Jews, continued to practice their Judaism secretly. These were the so-called *Marranos* or "swine."

In the Marrano way of life, caution was the watchword, as it would be later for Spinoza himself. If one's secret practice of Judaism was discovered, there would be drastic consequences, for oneself, one's family, and one's friends. As a result, a tradition developed of investing outwardly Christian symbols with radically different, Jewish meaning. As we will see, Spinoza too employed much traditional religious language, but imbued this language with a radically different, naturalistic meaning.[9]

With support from religious authorities in Spain, King Ferdinand and Queen Isabella (of Christopher Columbus fame) in 1492 (also of Christopher Columbus fame) expelled the Jews. Jews either had to convert or leave the country. Many emigrated to Portugal, but in 1496, Portugal as well required the conversion of all Jews, and in 1547 the Inquisition came to Portugal. Eventually many Jews found life in Portugal intolerable and sought to move. In 1537, Charles I of Spain granted the Jews permission to settle in the Low Countries, which were then under Spanish control. The initial settlement of Jews in Amsterdam took place around the turn of the seventeenth century. The Jews were attracted not only by the relative freedom of Amsterdam but also by the economic opportunities to be found there.

In 1619 the Amsterdam city council officially granted Jews in 1619 the right to practice their religion openly, but only on the condition that the Jews observe their own orthodoxy. The idea behind this requirement was that the Jews would stay out of the religious disputes between Calvinists and dissenters (Nadler 1999: 14). Thus, so as not to endanger the way in which it was tolerated in this overwhelmingly Christian nation, the Jewish community sought to keep its house in order, to make sure that its members adhered to Jewish orthodoxy.

But the problem was: just what was Jewish orthodoxy? Jewish practice had been so corrupted by the constraints of Marrano life in

Portugal and Spain that the contours of Jewish life needed to be re-established. Thus the community often sought advice on matters of Jewish practice and on the proper interpretation of the Bible and Talmudic teachings from other, more established non-Sephardic Jewish communities in other parts of Europe.

Because the community was so concerned to enforce Jewish orthodoxy, the leaders sometimes resorted to bans—excommunications—to keep the observances of laws strict and to keep outside religious authorities from interfering. Excommunication was not always as radical as it may sound. The ban would prevent the violator from participating in the liturgical rites of the Jewish community and from interacting with other members of the community. The imposition of the ban was meant to correct problematic behavior—the failure to observe Jewish practices or the expression of certain ideas deemed incompatible with Jewish life or otherwise dangerous to the group. In the Amsterdam Jewish community, bans were not uncommon, and in almost all cases the possibility of repentance and reconciliation was held out. *Almost* all cases, as we will see.

In the first half of the seventeenth century, the most notorious case of excommunication was that of Uriel da Costa. Da Costa was in many ways a tragic figure, one who obviously suffered from mental illness. He was a former Converso born in Porto, Portugal in 1585. His father was a Christian but his mother adhered to Jewish practices. After re-immersing himself in Judaism, he became convinced that the Law of Moses was God's revelation and that the later, Talmudic, extra-biblical development of Judaism was not authentically Jewish. He thus challenged Rabbinic authority and the entire basis of post-Biblical Judaism. His 1624 book, *Examination of the Pharisaic Traditions* (*Exame das Tradiçoes Phariseas*) which presented these views was burned, and he was fined and jailed in Amsterdam for ten days (Nadler 1999: 70).

Among his more controversial beliefs was a denial of the immortality of the soul and a denial of the afterlife and the existence of eternal reward for actions in this life. For da Costa, the soul "is engendered naturally by one's parents. It is not created by God separately" (Nadler 1999: 69). These beliefs are naturalistic in the sense I have outlined: the human soul is not an exception to the order of nature, rather it is a part of nature. Although Spinoza does not believe in the human soul, he does, of course, think that human mental life is thoroughly naturalistic, and Spinoza does think, as we will see in Chapter 7, that there is no life beyond this one. It's hard not to imagine that da Costa's naturalism left its mark on Spinoza.

As Nadler demonstrates, the denial of an immortal soul was particularly unwelcome in the Amsterdam Jewish community of the time. Although there was no definitive Jewish teaching in the Bible on the matter of immortality, the doctrine of the resurrection of the dead had been enshrined as one of Maimonides' 13 principles of the Jewish faith. Also, because many Jews in Amsterdam had imbibed Christian ways of thinking, many members did strongly believe in the immortality of the soul—which, of course, is a tenet of most versions of Christianity. Further, the denial of the immortality of the soul would certainly be seen by the Christian community as a heretical belief, one whose presence in the Jewish community could threaten the relative freedom and independence that the Jews then enjoyed.

Da Costa's ban was harsher than most. When he was banned in 1633, the possibility of atonement was left open, but it was atonement by flagellation that was required. Da Costa refused, but by 1640, after enduring years of isolation, he agreed to go through with the punishment during which he was not only whipped in the synagogue, but, after the display, was forced to lie down at the threshold of the synagogue. Those who exited then stepped on his body on their way out. Unable to bear this humiliation, da Costa shot himself several days later.

It is impossible to know what impression this sad episode made on the young Spinoza, who was eight at the time and must have been aware in some way of these goings-on. Doubtless, though, the harsh treatment of da Costa for his beliefs carried echoes for Spinoza as he went through his own process of excommunication only 16 years later.

Yet at the time of the da Costa episode, there were no signs of such difficulty for Spinoza. His father, Michael, was a merchant and an observant, respected member of the community. Michael and his wife, Hanna, had named their third son Baruch (which means "blessed" in Hebrew—after his excommunication, Spinoza went by the Latin equivalent, "Benedictus"). As a child, Spinoza went to the Talmud Torah school and, though he most likely did not study to become a rabbi, he received a traditional training in the Hebrew Bible and in the Talmud. This learning would suffuse all of Spinoza's philosophical writings.

Despite his immersion in the tradition, Spinoza at some point began to question the most fundamental attitudes of those who raised and trained him. Perhaps the first sign we have of Spinoza's movement away from the world of his upbringing comes to us from around 1654, the year of his father's death. Apparently, during this period Spinoza began studying Latin at the school of Franz van den Enden—a free thinker who had previously studied to be a Jesuit, but who also had a reputation for being an atheist. Spinoza was certainly exposed to more than the Latin language in van den Enden's school. Van den Enden, like Spinoza, a great supporter of democracy and tolerance, held that "religious belief was a personal matter, not to be dictated by any organization or authority" (Nadler 1999: 107). With van den Enden, Spinoza may also have encountered Cartesian philosophy. It's easy to imagine that van den Enden had some influence on the direction of Spinoza's thought, and it's also easy to imagine that Spinoza's association with van den Enden caused some strain in Spinoza's relations with the Jewish community.

Around this period also, Spinoza took over (with his brother, Gabriel) his father's mercantile activities, and through his activities in trade Spinoza may have come into contact with a number of merchants who were dissenting Christians and who would later become Spinoza's disciples. These dissenting Christians belonged to a group called the Collegiants, which promoted a non-hierarchical and tolerant version of Christianity in which an individual "had the right to believe what he or she wanted and no right to harass others for what they believed" (Nadler 1999: 139–40). The Collegiants were often at odds with Calvinist authorities, and, for this reason, Spinoza's association with the Collegiants would certainly have added to the growing tension between Spinoza and the Jewish community. Indeed, Bayle and Colerus report that, during this period, an attempt was made on Spinoza's life.[10]

And then it happened. Spinoza was excommunicated on July 27, 1656 with an official proclamation noteworthy for its vehemence:

> The Lords of the ma'amad [lay governing board], having long known of the evil opinions and acts of Baruch de Spinoza, have endeavored by various means and promises, to turn him from his evil ways. But having failed to make him mend his wicked ways, and, on the contrary, daily receiving more and more serious information about the abominable heresies which he practiced and taught and about his monstrous deeds, and having for this numerous trustworthy witnesses who have deposed and born witness to this effect in the presence of the said Espinoza, they became convinced of the truth of this matter; and after all of this has been investigated in the presence of the honorable chachamim [wise men], they have decided, with their consent, that the said Espinoza should be excommunicated and expelled from the people of Israel. By decree of the angels and by the command of the holy men, we excommunicate, expel, curse and damn Baruch de Espinoza, with the consent of God, Blessed be He, and with the consent of the entire holy congregation. ... Cursed be he by day and cursed be he by night; cursed be he when he lies down and cursed be he when he rises up. Cursed be he when he goes out and cursed be he when he comes in. The

Lord will not spare him, but then the anger of the Lord and his
jealousy shall smoke against that man, and all the curses that
are written in this book shall lie upon him, and the Lord shall
blot out his name from under heaven. ... No one should
communicate with him, neither in writing, nor accord him any
favor, nor stay with him under the same roof, nor come within
four cubits of his vicinity; nor shall he read any treatise
composed or written by him.

(Nadler 1999: 120–21)

The proclamation—unlike other such proclamations issued in this
period—contains no provision for repentance and reconciliation.
What could have led to this drastic outcome? Perhaps it was
because Spinoza was studying unorthodox views at van den Enden's
school and with the Collegiants; perhaps it was because of Spinoza's own heterodox philosophical views which were no doubt
developing at this time, views that would be contrary to the beliefs
of many of the Jews of Amsterdam. Among these views are: the
denial of an afterlife, the denial of a special status for the Jews, the
denial of the divine authorship of the Bible, the rejection of any act
of divine creation, the judgment that all religions were superstitious, the denial of the freedom of the will, the support of
democracy and toleration. Equally significantly, most of these views
would also have been seen as heterodox by Christian authorities.
What do all these beliefs have in common? They stem from Spinoza's naturalism and rationalism, from the denial of any sharp
lines in reality, from the denial of special cases. Spinoza was—it is
no exaggeration to say—excommunicated because of his rationalism and naturalism.

For his part, Spinoza welcomed the excommunication. Lucas
reports him as saying:

All the better; they do not force me to do anything that I would not
have done of my own accord if I did not dread scandal. But since

they want it that way, I enter gladly on the path that is opened to
me, with the consolation that my departure will be more innocent
than was the exodus of the early Hebrews from Egypt.

(Wolf 1970: 51; also in Nadler 1999: 154)

And so he was on his own. During the years following his excommunication, Spinoza continued to study at van den Enden's school
and deepened his contacts with the Collegiants. He also may have
had some association with the Quakers during this period, and he
may have translated into Hebrew a pamphlet written by the Quakers encouraging Jews to convert to Christianity. But there is no
indication that Spinoza himself became a Quaker.

There is a report about Spinoza during this period that—unreli-
able though it is—is still irresistible to mention. While at van den
Enden's school after his excommunication, Spinoza—according to
Colerus—fell in love with van den Enden's daughter, Clara, who
was 12 years Spinoza's junior. Colerus tells us of Clara:

Van den Enden had an only daughter, who understood the Latin
tongue, as well as music, so perfectly that she was able to teach
her father's scholars in his absence. Spinoza having often
occasion to see and speak to her, grew in love with her, and he
has often confessed that he designed to marry her. She was none
of the most beautiful, but she had a great deal of wit, a great
capacity and a jovial humor, which wrought upon the heart of
Spinoza, as well as upon another scholar of van den Enden,
whose name was Kerkring. ... The latter did soon perceive that he
had a rival, and grew jealous of him. This moved him to redouble
his care, and his attendance upon his mistress, which he did with
good success. But a necklace of pearls ... which he had presented
to that young woman, did without doubt contribute to win her
affection. She therefore promised to marry him; which she did
faithfully perform.

(Colerus 1880: 414; see Nadler 1999: 108)

Perhaps this episode serves as a source for Spinoza's striking observations about sexual jealousy, observations that we will discuss in Chapter 4.

By 1659, Spinoza began his studies at the University of Leiden, which was at the time a hotbed of Cartesianism and would have enabled Spinoza to acquire a deep knowledge of Descartes. Descartes's rationalism certainly appealed to Spinoza, especially Descartes's view that the extended world was intelligible and amenable to rigorous mathematical analysis. But, as we will see, for Spinoza, Descartes's rationalism did not go nearly far enough. In Spinoza's eyes, Descartes's system is riddled with bifurcations, dualisms that run counter to naturalism. Thus Descartes endorses, most famously, a mind–body dualism, and also a dualism of will and intellect, of created and uncreated substances, of reason and faith. All of these bifurcations will be eliminated by Spinoza's more thoroughgoing application of naturalism and of the PSR.

Spinoza's engagement with Descartes's philosophy pervades his early writings. First, there is the *Treatise on the Emendation of the Intellect* (*Tractatus de Intellectus Emendatione*) which dates from the early 1660s and is probably Spinoza's earliest surviving work. This unfinished treatise begins with the memorable autobiographical passage I have already quoted, and goes on to explore the proper way to prepare the mind to acquire knowledge of the genuine good. This work contains perhaps Spinoza's deepest grappling with the kind of skepticism with which Descartes was so concerned.

In 1661 and 1662, Spinoza worked on the *Short Treatise Concerning God, Man, and His Well-Being* (*Korte Verhandeling van God, de Mensch, en deszelfs Welstand*) which expressed many of the same naturalistic views that were later to enjoy a more systematic elaboration in the *Ethics* (full title: *Ethics Demonstrated in Geometrical Order*; *Ethica Ordine Geometrico demonstrata*). As with the *Treatise on the Emendation of the Intellect*, Spinoza seeks an understanding of metaphysics—of our place within nature as a whole—as the key to our happiness. This, of course, will be the guiding theme of the *Ethics* as well. Spinoza did not publish the

Short Treatise (in fact, it was not published in Spinoza's *Opera Posthuma* which appeared in the year Spinoza died). Rather, it was discovered in the mid-nineteenth century. No doubt, in withholding publication, Spinoza feared the reaction of theologians who might object to its naturalism (Letter 6, G IV 36).

In 1663, however, Spinoza did publish a philosophical work, his exposition of Parts I and II of Descartes's *Principles of Philosophy* (Spinoza's work was entitled *Parts I and II of Descartes's Principles of Philosophy; Principia Philosophiae Cartesianae*). The work had begun its life as a series of teaching notes for Johannes Casaerius, a student who lived with Spinoza for a period and was eager to learn Cartesian philosophy, on which Spinoza was a known expert. Reluctant to teach Caesarius his own philosophical views (Letter 9), Spinoza gave him a crash course on the Cartesian physics of parts II and III of the *Principles*. Some of Spinoza's other friends persuaded him to expand the notes to cover the more purely metaphysical Part I as well. Spinoza's work is relatively faithful to Descartes's original, except for the fact that Spinoza, unlike Descartes, presents Descartes's views in geometrical form. Spinoza's presenting Descartes's views this way does not indicate that Spinoza agreed with these views. On the contrary, Spinoza had a friend, Lodewijk Meyer, write a preface stressing that the views in this work were not necessarily Spinoza's own and that, indeed, Spinoza disagreed with Descartes on key points. It's noteworthy that on each of these points of disagreement, Spinoza's position stems, as we will see, from his acceptance of the PSR (see G I 132). Spinoza appended to his geometrical exposition of Descartes's *Principles* a short work called *Cogitata Metaphysica* (*Metaphysical Thoughts*), in which he allowed himself to speak more in his own voice. Still, though, he did not reveal the radical nature of his opinions.

Spinoza's friend Jan Rieuwertsz published the work on Descartes together with its appendix. Spinoza allowed the work to be published because he had the hope that it might lead prominent people to want to learn more about Spinoza's own views which he had so far not been able to publish. The PPC was thus meant to prepare the way for the reception of the ideas that were first expressed in the *Short Treatise* and that would later find expression in the *Ethics* (Letter 11; Nadler 1999: 206).

Throughout this period, Spinoza worked as a lens grinder. He engaged in this endeavor no doubt partly in order to support himself, but also because of his own scientific interest in optics. The mathematician Christiaan Huygens praised the craftsmanship of Spinoza's lenses, as did Leibniz (Nadler 1999: 182–84; Letter 45). Spinoza's correspondence contains much evidence of his interest in scientific matters. His surviving correspondence dates from 1661, and a number of the earlier exchanges are between Spinoza and Henry Oldenburg, secretary of the Royal Society which fostered scientific research. Spinoza exchanged letters on a range of topics with a number of other notable thinkers in addition to Oldenburg, for example Tschirnhaus and, toward the end of Spinoza's life, Leibniz. In his letters, Spinoza can be terse and acerbic— particularly when he deals with those whom he does not respect intellectually. But he could be expansive in his letters too, and, in particular, the long letter to Meyer on the infinite (Letter 12) and to Oldenburg on the nature and individuation of finite things (Letter 32) are elegant and enormously philosophically important.

By 1665, Spinoza had in hand a nearly complete draft of the *Ethics*, one that he would rework significantly in the early 1670s. But in 1665, he turned his attention to a rather different project: the *Tractatus Theologico-Politicus*.[11] Spinoza was already being dogged by charges of atheism, charges that he saw were standing in the way of publishing what was to become the *Ethics*. He knew that for his ideas to get any hearing, there would have to be more freedom to philosophize in Holland, and so he set out to write a book making the case for freedom of thought. The biggest threat to such freedom and, indeed, to the state of Holland itself was—in Spinoza's eyes—the power wielded in Holland by Calvinist religious authorities. Spinoza argued that close attention to the proper method of interpreting the Bible would help to put the religious authorities in their place and thus simultaneously ensure freedom of thought and a more stable state. Spinoza writes in Letter 30 to Oldenburg in 1665 about his motives in writing the TTP:

I am now writing a treatise on my views regarding scripture. The reasons that move me to do so are these: (1) The prejudices of theologians. For I know that these are the main obstacles which prevent men from giving their minds to philosophy. So I apply myself to exposing such prejudices and removing them from the minds of sensible people. (2) The opinion of me held by the common people, who constantly accuse me of atheism. I am driven to avert this accusation, too, as far as I can. (3) The freedom to philosophize and to say what we think. This I want to vindicate completely, for here it is in every way suppressed by the excessive authority and egotism of preachers.

Thus, despite his natural caution, Spinoza once again dared to hope that his philosophical views would bring about a major change in people's thought. His caution was, again, entwined with his extreme ambition. The work appeared in late 1669 or early 1670. As with the PPC, this book was published by Rieuwertsz, though this time without Spinoza's name and, indeed, the title page of the work gave a false publisher and falsely listed Hamburg as the place of publication (Nadler 1999: 269).

Soon after its publication, religious authorities throughout Holland denounced the TTP as blasphemous and as dangerous to Christianity. In various places in Holland, steps were taken to prevent distribution of the book. The harsh reaction to the TTP made Spinoza even more cautious about publishing the Ethics, an even more bluntly naturalistic work.

At the time, the leader of the Dutch Republic, the Grand Pensioner of the States of Holland, was Johan de Witt, who was an advocate of freedom of religious belief and of freedom to philosophize. Despite some political differences (Spinoza was a democrat, and de Witt was not), both Spinoza and de Witt ran afoul of Dutch religious authorities, and, for Spinoza, de Witt's embrace of toleration spurred Spinoza's hope for an environment in which Spinoza's ideas could be received and discussed openly. But these hopes were dashed, for de Witt's stay in power came to a violent end in 1672. De Witt was held responsible for military losses in the aftermath of the French invasion of the Netherlands, and de Witt and his brother Cornelis were brutally murdered by an angry mob on August 20.

Spinoza recognized that each finite individual has only limited power and can be overcome by other, more powerful things. Human beings can be overcome by their passions which are due to external causes. As Spinoza says in the Ethics, "man is necessarily always subject to passions" (4p4c). Spinoza was no exception to his own rule, and on this occasion he was so enraged by the mob's shocking actions that—as one report goes—he wanted to post a placard at the site of the murders, a placard that read *Ultimi Barbarorum*—"the most extreme of the barbarians." Luckily, Spinoza's landlord locked the house in which Spinoza was staying, thus, no doubt, saving his life.

In the early 1670s, Spinoza returned to work on the Ethics, still hoping against hope to see it published. During this period also, he worked on his *Compendium of Hebrew Grammar* (*Compendium Grammatices Linguae Hebraeae*) which was, unfortunately, left unfinished at his death. He worked on this book at the urging of his friends who wanted help in approaching the Bible directly, in the original language, and not through the mediation of religious authorities. Thus, in his Hebrew grammar, Hebrew was treated as a natural language to be studied as any other natural language. Hebrew, thus, for Spinoza, enjoys no special status among languages, and this view is entirely in keeping with Spinoza's naturalism.

In 1673, Spinoza received a surprising and in a way welcome letter from Johann Ludwig Fabritius, a professor at the University of Heidelberg, writing on behalf of Karl Ludwig, Elector of Palatine. The letter was a job offer, an invitation to take up a professorship in philosophy at the university. The letter read, in part: "the annual salary will be that currently paid to regular professors. You will not find elsewhere a Prince more favorably disposed to men of exceptional genius, among whom he ranks you" (Letter 47; February 16, 1673). So far, so good, Spinoza must have thought. The letter went on, "you will have the most extensive freedom in philosophizing"—even better, Spinoza must have thought—"which he believes you will not misuse to disturb the publicly established religion." Ah, there's the catch!

Inevitably, Spinoza politely declined the offer, but he also allowed himself to express concern about the invitation's "catch" about the disturbance of the established religion. Spinoza replied to Fabritius:

> I do not know within what limits the freedom to philosophize must be confined if I am to avoid appearing to disturb the publicly established religions. For divisions arise not so much from an ardent devotion to religion as from the different dispositions of men, or through their love of contradiction which leads them to distort or to condemn all things, even those that are stated aright. Now since I have already experienced this while leading a private and solitary life, it would be much more to be feared after I have risen to this position of eminence.
>
> (Letter 48; March 30, 1673)

And so, Spinoza missed the chance to become the first professor of philosophy among the great early modern philosophers.

Having completed the Ethics by 1675, Spinoza—boldly daring to hope despite his innate caution—readied the book for publication. He traveled to Amsterdam in July in order to make the arrangements. Once again Rieuwertsz was to serve as Spinoza's publisher. However, rumors quickly started flying that Spinoza was about to publish a book espousing atheism. He explains his response to this development in a letter to Oldenburg in September 1675:

> This rumor found credence with many. So certain theologians, who may have started this rumor, seized the opportunity to complain of me before the Prince and the Magistrates. Moreover,

the stupid Cartesians, in order to remove this suspicion from themselves because they are thought to be on my side, ceased not to denounce everywhere my opinions and my writings, and still continue to do so. Having gathered this from certain trustworthy men who also declared that the theologians were everywhere plotting against me, I decided to postpone the publication I had in hand until I should see how matters would turn out, intending to let you know what course I would then pursue. But the situation seems to worsen day by day, and I am not sure what to do about it.

(Letter 68)

Spinoza decided, in the end, not to publish the *Ethics* and turned, in the months before his death, to work on the *Political Treatise* (*Tractatus Politicus*) which was intended to explain how states of different kinds can be made to operate successfully. Spinoza planned to discuss the nature of monarchy, aristocracy, and democracy, but unfortunately the treatment of democracy was left largely unfinished: this was the book Spinoza was working on at his death.

It came on a winter's day, February 21, 1677. He suffered from a respiratory ailment, perhaps tuberculosis, perhaps exaggerated by inhaling the glass dust produced by his lens-grinding. He knew that he was in decline, and on July 15, 1676—several months before his death—in the midst of a comment on Descartes's definition of matter, he wrote poignantly in Letter 83 to Tschirnhaus: "But perhaps, if I live long enough, I shall come to discuss this with you more clearly." Spinoza died quietly at his home. His landlord's family went to church in the afternoon, and when they returned, Spinoza was dead. He had directed the landlord to send his writing desk—which contained his writings—to his publisher Rieuwertsz. This the landlord did, and Rieuwertsz published Spinoza's works, including the heretofore unpublished *Ethics*. The uproar was immediate. Let's see what the fuss was all about.

SUMMARY

Spinoza can be seen as a pure philosopher, always seeking explanation, always refusing to be satisfied with primitive, inexplicable notions. This purity is most evident in his commitment to the principle that each fact has an explanation, that for each thing that exists there is an explanation that suffices for one to see why that thing exists. Although Spinoza does not himself use the term, this principle is known as the Principle of Sufficient Reason (PSR). Leibniz is more often associated with this principle, but, as will become apparent throughout this book, Spinoza employs the PSR more systematically, perhaps, than has ever been done in the history of philosophy. His commitment to the PSR generates his commitment to naturalism, the thesis that all things in nature that are related to one another play by the same rules. Each thing—whether rock, dog, or human being—is governed by the same fundamental laws. Spinoza's naturalism and his PSR often manifest themselves in his twofold use of the PSR. Time and again, Spinoza seeks to give an account of a phenomenon—whether it be causation, consciousness, goodness, rightness, etc. This is a demand for an explanation and is the first use of the PSR or the notion of explicability. Spinoza's next move is to explain the phenomenon in terms of explanation itself: causation thus amounts to the connection whereby one thing serves as the explanation for another; consciousness is explained as nothing but the degree of power of a mental state, i.e. its ability to explain other mental states, etc. For Spinoza, things in general are explained in terms of explanation itself, they are made intelligible in terms of intelligibility itself. A characteristic expression of Spinoza's commitment to reason is his use of the geometrical method, whereby he expresses his philosophical arguments and conclusions by means of a formal array of definitions, axioms, propositions, and demonstrations. Spinoza employs this method in his major work, the *Ethics*, and it is uniquely well-suited for the articulation of his philosophical system. According to Spinoza's system, all reality flows with strict necessity from the nature of God. With the geometrical method, Spinoza captures the structure of this reality by deducing philosophical conclusions about reality from definitions which express the nature of God.

Spinoza's life reflects his commitment to intelligibility. Although he offers a brief biographical sketch at the beginning of his *Treatise on the Emendation of the Intellect*, in which he credits his rationalist investigation of the world as promising to lead to unalloyed joy, one must turn to other historical sources to begin to understand the contours of Spinoza's life. Spinoza was a Jew of Marrano heritage, born into a Jewish community that was concerned to enforce Jewish orthodoxy. This concern stemmed not only from a desire to re-establish Jewish identity in Holland after a long period of forced conversion and concealed identity in Spain and Portugal, but also from a need to rein in points of view that endangered the status that the Jewish community enjoyed in the relatively—but not completely—tolerant Netherlands. Spinoza's views were far from orthodox and, in 1656, he was expelled from the Jewish community in Amsterdam. It can be argued that Spinoza's multifarious commitments to the PSR precipitated his excommunication. Throughout his life, Spinoza was never unaware of the controversy his views could cause, and was never without the desire to bring his views into the public sphere with the hope that they would lead to the formation of a more rational state and more rational individuals. The major work he published in his lifetime was the *Tractatus Theologico-Politicus*, a work that articulated a radical theory of biblical interpretation, according to which the Bible is to be treated as any other natural object and interpreted as any other text. On this basis, Spinoza presented a new account of the relation between the state and religion, according to which religious authorities were to be subservient to the rulers of the state and freedom of thought and speech were seen as essential to the well-being of the state. The hostile reception of this work eventually convinced Spinoza that he could not publish his most comprehensive philosophical statement, the *Ethics*, in which he articulates his extremely rationalist system which denies any role for a transcendent creator and denies any sharp separation between human beings and the rest of nature. This work was finally published, together with Spinoza's letters, his *Political Treatise* and other writings, after Spinoza's death in 1677.

FURTHER READING

Pierre Bayle (1991) *Historical and Critical Dictionary*, Richard H. Popkin (trans.). (Some biographical material with influential critiques of Spinoza.)

Jonathan Bennett (1984) *A Study of Spinoza's Ethics*, §§ 8, 10. (Helpful sections on naturalism and rationalism.)

Vincent Carraud (2002) *Causa sive Ratio: La Raison de la Cause, de Suarez à Leibniz*. (Scholarly and historical survey of Spinoza's engagement with the notion of causation and with the PSR.)

John Colerus (1880) *The Life of Benedict de Spinoza*, in Frederick Pollock, *Spinoza: His Life and Philosophy*. (1705 biography of Spinoza.)

Michael Della Rocca (2003a) "A Rationalist Manifesto: Spinoza and the Principle of Sufficient Reason." (Philosophical engagement with some of the uses to which Spinoza puts the PSR.)

Alan Donagan (1988) *Spinoza*. (A reading of Spinoza as a naturalist.)

Aaron Garrett (2003) *Meaning in Spinoza's Method*. (Discusses Spinoza's geometrical method.)

Margaret Gullan-Whur (1998) *Within Reason: A Life of Spinoza*. (Interesting, but sometimes speculative biography of Spinoza.)

Steven Nadler (1999) *Spinoza: A Life*. (Definitive biography of Spinoza.)

A. Wolf (1970) *The Oldest Biography of Spinoza*. (Contains Lucas's biography written soon after Spinoza's death.)

Yirmiyahu Yovel (1989) *Spinoza and Other Heretics*, vol. 1. (Discussion of Spinoza's Marrano background and of its importance to his philosophy.)

Two

The Metaphysics of Substance

How many things are there in the world? Spinoza's answer: one. What might seem to be other things are merely ways in which the one thing exists. In this chapter, I will explain Spinoza's conception of this one thing—which Spinoza calls a substance—and of the ways in which it exists. I will also unpack his powerful argument for this monism—this oneness—of substance. It cannot be overemphasized how the rest of Spinoza's philosophy—his philosophy of mind, his epistemology, his psychology, his moral philosophy, his political philosophy, and his philosophy of religion—flows more or less directly from the metaphysical underpinnings in Part I of the *Ethics*.

Spinoza's understanding of substance is, in many ways, a principled transformation and criticism of Descartes's conception. So it will be easier to understand Spinoza's conception if we first briefly sketch that of Descartes. The main theme here is this: Descartes's conception incorporates some guiding rationalist motivations but—Spinoza can be seen as implicitly saying—Descartes does not carry out these rationalist motivations consistently or far enough. Once you take the rationalist motivations in Descartes and follow through on them clear-headedly, you will arrive at something like Spinoza's more controversial account.[1]

1. DESCARTES ON SUBSTANCE

So let's begin with Descartes.

The leading lights of Descartes's metaphysics are substance, attribute (or principal attribute), and mode. Relying on a conception of substance that has its roots in Aristotle, Descartes sees a substance as a thing in which other things, such as properties or qualities or states, inhere and which does not inhere in anything else. Thus Descartes offers this definition of substance:

> Each thing is called a substance which something is in [*inest*] immediately as in a subject or by means of which we perceive anything that exists, that is, by means of which we perceive any property, quality or attribute of which a real idea is in us.
>
> (CSM II 114/AT VII 161, translation altered)

He also says, "we call the thing which they [attributes] are in [*insunt*] a substance" (CSM II 156/AT VII 222, translation altered). That a substance does not inhere in—is not in—anything else is apparent from Descartes's frequent claim that substances exist through themselves.[2]

Another, related dimension of Descartes's conception of substance is substance's independence of anything else. Descartes offers this characterization:

> By substance we can understand nothing other than a thing which exists in such a way as to depend on no other thing for its existence.
>
> (*Principles* I 51)

I will focus here on the characterization of substance in terms of independence and turn to the chararacterization of substance as that in which other things inhere in the next section.

What kinds of things can meet the requirement of independence? It quickly appears that, for Descartes, only God can meet this requirement: all other things depend for their existence on God and are literally inconceivable without God.

Nonetheless, Descartes does recognize a significant sense in which finite things, such as human minds, human bodies, tables, trees, etc. are substances, for although such things do depend on God, they depend on no other created thing. Of course, a table or a tree may be caused to exist by some other finite thing (a carpenter, another tree), and thus the table or the tree may depend for its existence on something besides God. But for Descartes, this kind of dependence does not spoil the fact that finite things are substances. For while the tree may be caused to exist by another tree, Descartes regards it as conceivable that the tree exists without the other tree. Each finite substance is conceptually independent of any other finite substance. One can understand what it is for the tree to exist, Descartes would say, without presupposing the existence of any other finite thing. However, the finite substance could not, Descartes is saying, be conceived without conceiving of God who brings it into existence and, indeed, for Descartes, sustains it in existence.

By holding that finite things are substances, though they are so by meeting a different requirement from the requirement the substance God meets, Descartes explicitly regards the definition of substance as not univocal:

> there is only one substance which can be understood to depend on no other thing whatsoever, namely God. In the case of all other substances, we perceive that they can exist only with the help of God's concurrence. Hence the term "substance" does not apply univocally, as they say in the Schools, to God and to other things; that is, there is no distinctly intelligible meaning of the term which is common to God and his creatures.
>
> (*Principles* I 51)

There are two fundamentally different kinds of substance for Descartes (and this goes along with two fundamentally different kinds of dependence, as we shall see). Because there is this duality of dependent substances and an independent substance, because there is thus no single standard for being a substance, we have here a violation of naturalism, in the sense of naturalism that I discussed in the previous chapter: Descartes here treats different things as playing by different rules.

But Descartes is quite happy to violate naturalism, and he has his motivations for doing so. This is because the alternative to seeing finite things as substances is to have them be mere modes of a substance. And that, as we will see, would be a truly horrifying prospect for Descartes and almost all other philosophers, but not, of course, for Spinoza. But this is to jump the gun a bit. Let's return to Descartes's notion of substance.

For Descartes, each substance has what he calls a *principal* attribute, i.e. "one principal property [*proprietas*] which constitutes its nature and essence, and to which all its other properties are referred" (*Principles* I 53). These other features of a substance that are explained by its essence Descartes often calls "modes" of the substance (*Principles* I 56). Thus each substance has a fundamental feature—fundamental in the sense that it is that feature which explains or enables us to understand all the other features of the substance and is, for this reason, the essence of the substance. There are only two attributes that can play this fundamental explanatory role for Descartes: thought and extension. Thought constitutes the essence of minds in the sense that for Descartes all the particular properties of minds presuppose thought or must be understood through thought. Thus, my feeling pain and my having the thought that today is Thursday are particular properties of a substance, and to say that the substance has these properties is to presuppose that it is thinking. All other properties of the substance also presuppose thought. In precisely the same way, extension is a principal attribute because any substance that has this property is such that all of its other properties presuppose extension. (Extension is literally the property of having extent, existing spatially. It is one of the most notable features of Descartes's account of the physical world that there is no more to being physical than taking up space.) Thus, for Descartes, extension is the principal attribute of an extended substance such as the table. The table is five feet

long, weighs 50 lbs., has a certain shape. All these properties presuppose, for Descartes, that the table is extended:

> Everything else which can be attributed to body presupposes
> extension and is merely a mode of an extended thing.
> (*Principles* I 53; for an account of weight, in particular, in terms
> of extension, see *Principles* IV 20–23)

But why must *all* the properties of a substance be subsumed under a
fundamental feature? Why can't there be a feature of a substance
that does not presuppose the principal attribute of the substance,
but is nonetheless a feature of that substance? Thus, for example,
why can't an extended substance also have some thinking features,
features that cannot be understood through extension? Descartes
does not, as far as I know, explicitly address this question, but it's
clear what his answer would be: there would be no good account
of what makes this free-floating thinking feature a feature of this
extended substance. What would bind this thinking feature to this
extended substance? For Descartes, the conceptual connection provided by an attribute furnishes the link needed to make a particular
property a property of a given substance. Without the link afforded
by an attribute, we cannot see a property as belonging to a substance. In other words, Descartes insists that there be this overarching feature because otherwise there would be no explanation
of why a given feature is a feature of a particular substance.

Because the principal attribute helps us to understand all the
properties of a substance, it tells us what kind of thing the substance
is, what its essence is. And, for this reason, purely formal features
of a substance do not count as attributes in this sense. Each substance has the features, let us say, of existence and of being powerful to some degree. But existence and power are not principal
attributes for Descartes. This is because these features do not tell us
what kind of thing a substance is and do not tell us what kinds of
more particular properties it has.

In this way, we can see that on Descartes's ontology of substance and attribute, substances are explanatory engines. Each substance has a nature that can be articulated or explained in terms of its principal attribute, and this principal attribute in turn articulates or explains all the particular properties of the substance. Thus, for Descartes, each substance is fully conceivable. Everything about a substance must be capable of being understood and what it is understood in terms of is its principal attribute.

This is, of course, a rationalist dimension in Descartes's ontology, and we can appreciate this dimension by contrasting Descartes's view with a broadly Aristotelian account of substance. On the Aristotelian account (or at least on the Aristotelian account as it is developed by medieval philosophers such as Aquinas), a corporeal substance consists of prime matter and a substantial form. The substantial form is, in some ways, like a Cartesian principal attribute: it tells us the nature of a substance and the kind of properties it can have. But the form is not the only constituent of a substance. The substantial form must somehow inhere in a subject and this subject is prime matter, a featureless, bare subject for a substantial form. The prime matter is a thing in some sense, but, precisely because it is featureless, it cannot be articulated or explained.[3] Literally, prime matter is no kind of thing, and precisely for this reason Descartes rejects this notion as unintelligible (see CSM I 91, 92/AT XI 33, 35). Marleen Rozemond sums up the view here nicely:

> Since Descartes eliminates prime matter from the hylomorphic conception of corporeal substance, the result in Aristotelian terms is that a substance just consists in a substantial form. In Descartes' own terms, the result is that the substance just consists in a principal attribute.
>
> (Rozemond 1998: 11)

But a problem immediately arises: if the substance just is its principal attribute, then how can there be more than one substance that has the same attribute? Let's say that substance A has the attribute of thought and substance B (distinct from A) also has the attribute of thought. Substance A might be my mind and substance B your mind. If each substance just is its principal attribute, then A is identical to the attribute of thought and B also is identical to the attribute of thought. Given the transitivity of identity, it would follow that, contrary to our supposition, A and B are identical or my mind and your mind are identical. This is a major problem, and to avoid it Descartes would have to say that there is something more to a particular substance than its attribute. This something more would then help individuate or distinguish one substance from another. Given that Descartes has eliminated prime matter, what can he appeal to to do this job? I think that Descartes would have to appeal to the modes or the particular properties of a substance. But as we will see, there are grave difficulties, pointed out by Spinoza, in allowing mere modes to perform the important task of individuation.

If, for Descartes, principal attributes are basic features in terms of which other features are conceived, then principal attributes must be conceptually independent of one another. Thus, for Descartes, to understand a thing as thinking does not require us to think of it as also extended, and similarly conceiving of a thing as extended does not require conceiving of it as thinking. By contrast, as we saw, conceiving of a thing as five feet long does require conceiving of it as extended. In this way, being five feet long is a mode (literally, a way) of being extended. If thought itself were conceived through extension, then thought would be a mode of extension and thus thought would not be an attribute after all. For this reason, given that thought and extension are each principal attributes, they must be conceptually independent of one another. Further, thinking features in general are conceptually independent of extended features. We can think of something as having a particular thinking feature without thereby thinking of it as having extension or any particular extended feature. Thus my mind's having the property of thinking about a table does not presuppose that my mind has any extended feature, nor in fact does it presuppose that anything else is extended. Certainly this thought is *about something* extended—namely the table—but it does not presuppose that anything actually exists that is extended. The mere fact that I have the thought of a table is compatible with there being no tables or, indeed, no extended objects. That is, one can, it seems, conceive that I have the thought of a table without presupposing that there are tables or extended objects generally. Thoughts of extension are, for Descartes, conceptually independent of extension, or, as Descartes puts it, "the concept of the one is not contained in the concept of the other" (CSM I 298/AT VIIIB 35). This is one of Descartes's points in his famous skeptical arguments in the *Meditations*.

Despite insisting that attributes be conceptually independent, Descartes allows for causal interactions that cross the boundary between two attributes. Thus Descartes holds that certain mental changes, changes in thought, can cause certain changes in the extended world. And certain extended changes can cause changes in thought. Thus consider my mind which, for Descartes, is a substance separate from my body. My mind can cause changes in my body, and certain changes in my body can cause changes in my mind.[4] Thus, for Descartes, despite there being no *conceptual* connections between mental things and physical things, there can be *causal* connections between them.

There is a final aspect of Descartes's ontology of substance that I want to emphasize, and this is his claim that each substance has only one principal attribute. For Descartes, there is only one fundamental feature in terms of which all the properties of a substance can be explained. Speaking of principal attributes, Descartes says (in a passage part of which I just quoted):

> it cannot be said that those which are different, and such that the concept of the one is not contained in the concept of the other, are present together in one and the same subject; for that would

be equivalent to saying that one and the same subject has two different natures.

(CSM I 298/AT VIIIB 349–50)

Why does Descartes hold this view? He does not make his reason explicit, but he does allude here to the conceptual separation between the attributes. Precisely because thought and extension are conceptually independent, it follows that one can think of a substance as thinking without thereby thinking of it as extended (and vice versa). If a substance had both thought and extension as attributes, then, given this conceptual independence, why would they be together in the same substance instead of present in two separate substances? In the case of an attribute and a mode of that attribute, it is clear why they are in the same substance: being extended and being five feet long are features of the same substance precisely because there is a conceptual link between the essence of that substance (the attribute) and the mode. But in the absence of such a link between two attributes, what could account for their presence in the same substance? Earlier we saw that a property that is not explained in terms of an overarching attribute would be problematic for Descartes because there would be no explanation of the fact that it belongs to the substance it belongs to. In the same way, I believe, for Descartes, if a substance has two attributes, then, given their conceptual independence, there would be no explanation of the fact that they belong to the same substance. So, for Descartes, given the conceptual independence between the attributes and given his demand—which can be seen as a rationalist demand—that there be an explanation of why a substance has the features that it does have, we can see why he insists that a substance can have only one attribute. As we will see, Spinoza denies the Cartesian view that a substance can have only one attribute and, intriguingly, he will do this by strengthening not only the rationalist demand, but also the conceptual separation between the attributes.

2. SPINOZA CONTRA DESCARTES ON SUBSTANCE

In light of its rationalist character, one would expect Spinoza to be quite sympathetic to Descartes's ontology of substance and attribute, and indeed he is. He follows Descartes in developing an account of substance according to which it is independent of other things and an account of attribute according to which it is somehow a fundamental feature of the substance that all of its particular properties presuppose. Further, for Spinoza as for Descartes, one attribute is conceptually independent of another.

The latter two theses (at least) are, as I explained, rationalist theses in Descartes, and so Spinoza happily adopts them. However, he diverges significantly from Descartes in this area, and he does so precisely because of his more thoroughgoing commitment to the PSR.

Spinoza, like Descartes, sees a substance as something that has properties but that itself is not a property of anything else. This is why, I believe, part of Spinoza's definition (1def3) of substance is as that which is in itself. For Spinoza, as for Descartes, things inhere in substance and it, in turn, inheres in nothing else. Spinoza also defines substance in terms of independence. The kind of independence Spinoza, like Descartes, has in mind is conceptual independence, and thus the other part of Spinoza's definition of substance is that substance is conceived through itself.

So far the account is a lot like Descartes's. But the first departure is this: Spinoza does not countenance the kind of escape clause that allows finite substances into Descartes's scheme. Spinoza would agree with Descartes that only God meets the requirements for being a substance, but, unlike Descartes, he does not look for a way to have finite things count as substances as well. Any such exception would be too ad hoc, for Spinoza, or, more specifically it would be a violation of his naturalism and of his PSR. In virtue of what could some beings play by different rules? If the notion of a mode is of a being that is conceptually dependent on another, and if finite things such as the table and chairs are dependent in this way, then one should have the courage of one's convictions and admit that such things are modes of the substance. This is precisely what Spinoza does, and it is what his rationalism demands. I will explore this point in the next section.

The second main departure from Descartes concerns Spinoza's notion of attribute. Spinoza defines attribute much as Descartes does:

> By attribute I understand what the intellect perceives of a substance, as constituting its essence.
>
> (1def4)

One obvious difference—though its significance is not immediately apparent—is that Spinoza qualifies his definition in terms of that which the intellect perceives as constituting the essence of substance. I will return to this difference in the next section. Like Descartes, Spinoza regards thought and extension as attributes. Unlike Descartes, Spinoza holds that there is an "infinity of attributes" including thought and extension. For Spinoza, the other attributes are unknown to human beings (Letter 64). I will not focus on this difference between Descartes and Spinoza in what follows. The difference I want to focus on instead emerges from some of the ways Spinoza applies the definition of attribute. Just as Descartes does, Spinoza rules out any kind of conceptual connection between attributes. He makes this claim most prominently in 1p10: "Each attribute of a substance must be conceived through itself." By this claim, Spinoza means, just as Descartes does, that nothing extended is conceptually connected to anything thinking (and vice versa). However, unlike Descartes, Spinoza also does not allow any *causal* relations between thought and extension. For Spinoza, it is precisely because thought and extension are conceptually separate (one can conceive of one without conceiving of the other) that thought and extension cannot causally interact. For Spinoza, in other words, causal dependence amounts to conceptual dependence (and thus when Spinoza says that a substance is conceptually independent of everything else, he means as well that it is causally independent).

We can see that Spinoza accepts that causation is just conceptual connection by turning to his claim that a substance cannot be caused by another thing. His reason is that in such a case the substance would (contrary to the definition of substance) be conceived through that other thing (1p6c). Thus, for Spinoza, there must be some conceptual connection between two things in order for them to be causally related. Indeed, it is clear from this passage, together with the way he uses 1ax4 in 1p25d, that, for Spinoza, causation is coextensive with conceptual connection. But Spinoza's point here is more than a claim of mere coextensiveness. For Spinoza, causal connections are grounded in and stem from conceptual connections. Consider the fact that Spinoza *defines* substance and mode in terms of conceptual connections and *on this basis* goes on to conclude (e.g. in 1p6c and 2p6) that there cannot be causal connections between substances or between modes of different attributes. Conceptual connections are clearly, for Spinoza, more fundamental than causal connections, and the latter can be derived completely from the former. And thus, for Spinoza, causation is nothing more than the relation whereby one thing explains another or makes it intelligible.

Why does Spinoza assimilate causal and conceptual dependence in this way? One can see him as guided by the drive for unification demanded by his rationalism and naturalism. It's as if Spinoza is saying to Descartes: "you have no good reason to separate these kinds of dependence, and if you do separate them, you are making causal relations unintelligible."

Here's one way to see this point as developing. Let's say that *a* is the total cause of *b*. I want to claim on Spinoza's behalf that in such a case the claim "if *a* occurs then *b* occurs" must be conceptually true. If this is so, then we cannot ask why this conceptual connection holds without betraying a misunderstanding of the concepts involved in that claim or at least a failure to grasp those concepts completely. By contrast, on the Cartesian view which allows for causal relations despite a conceptual gap between the mental and the physical, these causal relations are, at bottom, unintelligible. Given the cause, there is no way to see the effect coming. But on Spinoza's view, according to which causes are conceptually connected to their effects, by understanding the concept of the cause, we can just see that the effect has to occur. There is no mystery about the causal relation, for Spinoza. His assimilation of causal and conceptual connections is thus a manifestation of his rationalism, and Descartes's acceptance of unintelligible mind–body causal relations is a sign of Descartes's failure to be truly a rationalist.

I think that one who appreciates the fact that, if there are to be genuine causal connections, they must amount to conceptual connections, is Hume. Hume, of course, denies that there are conceptual connections among distinct things and so he is unable to come up with genuine cases of causation. But, in a way, Hume does accept the rationalist demand that, if there is to be genuine causation, it must amount to conceptual connection. Spinoza accepts this rationalist demand too. But, unlike Hume, he sees there as being genuine conceptual connections, i.e. causal connections, in the world.[5]

Here we see what I called in the previous chapter Spinoza's twofold use of the PSR. In the first use, he asks what causation is. It cannot be a brute fact: we need an explanation or account of causation itself. In the second use, he accounts for causation by appealing to conceivability or explicability or intelligibility itself.

The final major difference between Spinoza's ontology and Descartes's ontology that I want to focus on is Spinoza's denial of Descartes's view that a substance can have only one attribute. For Spinoza, a substance can have more than one attribute; indeed, for him, the one substance, God, has infinitely many different attributes. How can this be so in light of the Cartesian reasons for limiting each substance to one attribute?

To see why, we need to explore the roots of Spinoza's claim that only one substance—with infinitely many attributes—exists. His argument for this claim—for his monism—is one of Spinoza's most elegant and also intriguing and puzzling arguments. The argument does presuppose that a substance can have more than one attribute, but by seeing the ways in which the PSR undergirds this argument, we will be in a position to see how Spinoza would justify the view that a single substance can have more than one attribute.

3. THE ARGUMENT FOR SUBSTANCE MONISM

So, without further ado, let's investigate Spinoza's argument for substance monism.

In addition to the definitions of substance and attribute, there is one further crucial definition at work in his argument, and that is his definition of mode as "that which is in another through which it is also conceived" (1def5). A mode is thus conceptually dependent on something other than the mode itself, and this is why a mode is a mode and not a substance.

Using these definitions and other claims, the argument travels through four key steps. It is, in outline, rather simple. Spinoza argues first that no two substances can share an attribute (1p5). Second Spinoza argues that "it pertains to the nature of a substance to exist" (1p7). On the basis of 1p7, Spinoza argues that God— defined as the substance with all the attributes—exists. Finally, since God exists and has all the attributes and since there can, by 1p5, be no sharing of attributes, no other substance besides God can exist. Any such substance would have to share attributes with God and such sharing is ruled out.

I want to explain each step briefly and, in some cases, raise potential objections, objections to which Spinoza has, I believe, good answers. Thus let's take 1p5 first: "In Nature there cannot be two or more substances of the same nature or attribute." To prove this proposition, Spinoza considers what is required in order to individuate two substances, i.e. what is required in order to explain their non-identity. For Spinoza, the distinctness between two distinct things must be explained by some difference between them, some difference in their properties. In the case of the individuation of substances, this amounts to the claim that they must be individuated via a difference either in their attributes or in their modes. Thus Spinoza says in 1p4d:

> Two or more distinct things are distinguished from one another, either by a difference in the attributes of the substances or by a difference in their affections.[6]

In 1p5d, he makes clear that such a difference in properties is needed for two things to be "conceived to be"—i.e. explained to be—"distinguished from one another."

In insisting on some difference in properties between two things, Spinoza endorses the Principle of the Identity of Indiscernibles. This is the principle—more often associated with Leibniz than with Spinoza—that if a and b are indiscernible, i.e. if a and b have all the same properties, then a is identical to b. One can see that this principle turns on the notion of explaining non-identity and, as such, one can see its roots in the PSR. Non-identities, by the PSR, require explanation, and the way to explain non-identity is to appeal to some difference in properties.

Thus two substances could be individuated either by a difference in their attributes or in their modes. Spinoza dismisses right away any differentiation of substances in terms of their attributes because he says we are considering whether two substances can share an attribute. Thus a case in which substances might have different attributes might seem to be irrelevant to the case at hand. However, as we will see in a moment, this dismissal might be too hasty. Spinoza then considers whether they can be distinguished by their modes. Spinoza eliminates this possibility as well, offering the following argument.

Since a substance is prior to its modes (by 1p1), we are entitled, and indeed obligated, to put the modes to the side when we take up the matter of individuating substances. Thus, with the modes to one side and with the attributes already eliminated as individuators, it turns out that there are no legitimate grounds for individuating substances with the same attribute, for explaining why they are distinct. Thus, since substances with the same attribute cannot legitimately be individuated, there cannot be any sharing of attributes.

Obviously this argument turns crucially on the claim that we should put the modes to one side. But what justifies this claim? Spinoza appeals here to the notion of priority introduced in 1p1. What exactly what does this priority amount to? For Spinoza, as well as Descartes, it is conceptual priority. One can have the idea of a substance without having ideas of its modes.

Thus, we can see why Descartes would have a problem individuating, say, two extended substances. All Descartes could appeal to in order to individuate the substances is the modes, but given Descartes's own explanatory notion of substance, according to which all of a substance's modes are explained through its attributes, such an appeal is illegitimate.

Of course, Descartes might at this point simply give up the claim that the non-identity of substances is explicable. Fair enough. After all, Descartes does not explicitly assert the Principle of the Identity of Indiscernibles. But Descartes's rejection of prime matter is in the spirit of such a principle. For Descartes, there is no way to articulate what prime matter is precisely because it has no qualities. In the same way, there is no way to articulate what the non-identity of a and b consists in because no qualities are available to do the job of individuation. Thus, even on his own terms, Descartes should feel the force of this Spinozistic argument that rules out a multiplicity of substances sharing the same attribute.

But even if substances that share an attribute are not individuated by their modes, perhaps such substances are individuated by attributes that they do not share. Spinoza does allow, after all, that a substance can have more than one attribute. So why can't we have the following scenario: substance 1 has attributes X and Y and substance 2 has attributes Y and Z. On this scenario, while the two substances share an attribute (i.e. Y) they differ with regard to other attributes and can thus be individuated after all. So perhaps then, contrary to 1p5, there can be some sharing of attributes by different substances. This objection was first raised by Leibniz, one of the most acute readers of Spinoza.[7]

This objection is harder to answer than the charge that substances that share an attribute can be individuated by their modes, but Spinoza clearly has the resources to handle this objection too. To see why, let's assume that Leibniz's scenario is possible. If so, then attribute Y would not enable us to pick out or conceive of one substance in particular. The thought "the substance with attribute Y" would not be a thought of one substance in particular, and thus attribute Y would not by itself enable us to conceive of any particular substance. For Spinoza, such a result would contradict the clause in the definition of attribute according to which *each* attribute constitutes the essence of substance. As Spinoza says in 1p10s, a claim that he clearly sees as following from the definition of attribute, "each [attribute of a substance] expresses the reality or being of substance."[8] So for Spinoza, if a substance has more than one attribute, each attribute by itself must enable us to conceive of the substance, and this can be the case only if each attribute that a substance has is unique to that substance. Thus Leibniz's scenario is ruled out.

But this good result only raises again the question of whether a substance can have more than one attribute. Before we can answer this question, we must delve further into Spinoza's argument for substance monism.

The next crucial stage is 1p7: "It pertains to the nature of a substance to exist." Spinoza means by this claim that each substance is such that its existence somehow follows from its very concept or nature. Other things—i.e. limited things or modes—are not such that their existence follows from their very nature. For such things, their existence is at the mercy of other things, the things that limit them. But a substance is special: its existence is beholden only to its own nature. And so the only way that the existence of a substance could be prevented would be if its essence or nature were somehow internally incoherent. Otherwise, i.e. if the nature of a substance is coherent, then that's what it is for the substance to exist. In this way, we can see that, for Spinoza, the existence of a substance is just the fact that it is coherent or, as I will say, conceivable. This reduction of existence to conceivability holds generally for Spinoza (not just for substance) and this fact will play a crucial role in helping us to understand Spinoza's account of the eternality of the human mind in Chapter 7.

How does Spinoza argue for 1p7? He first cites 1p6c, the claim that no substance can be caused by anything else. For Spinoza, as we have seen, if a substance were caused by something else, it would have to be conceived through that something else. But this would conflict with the self-conceived nature of substance. Since substance cannot be produced by anything else, he concludes (in 1p7d) that substance is produced by itself. Here the PSR plays a role: since substance is not produced by anything else, and, by the PSR, it must be produced by something, it follows that substance is self-caused. Given Spinoza's equation of causation and conceivability, it follows that a substance's existence is simply a function of its concept or definition. That is, as Spinoza says, "it pertains to the nature of a substance to exist."

One might, however, object to the notion of self-causation in the following way: causes must exist before their effects, so for a thing to cause itself it must exist prior to itself, which is absurd. Spinoza, however, simply rejects this restrictive notion of causation, and his assimilation of causation to explanation helps us to see how he can do this: to say that a thing is self-caused is nothing more than saying that it is self-explanatory, and this is indeed how Spinoza views a substance.

In 1p11 Spinoza applies 1p7 to the case of God. To see how Spinoza does this, we should have before us his definition of God:

> By God I understand a being absolutely infinite, that is, a
> substance consisting of an infinity of attributes, of which each one
> expresses an eternal and infinite essence.
>
> (1def6)

By "an infinity of attributes" Spinoza means *all* attributes, as is clear
from his explanation of this definition:

> I say absolutely infinite, not infinite in its own kind; for if
> something is only infinite in its own kind, we can deny infinite
> attributes of it; but if something is absolutely infinite, whatever
> expresses essence and involves no negation pertains to its
> essence.

Spinoza thinks that God must be understood in terms of content-
ful, explanatorily basic features. This is in keeping with his rationalist commitment to the intelligibility of all things, including God.

Given that God is by definition a substance (and indeed a substance with all the attributes) and given that, as 1p7 states, existence follows from the nature of a substance, Spinoza concludes
that God exists. Indeed, Spinoza states here that God exists *necessarily*, and it's easy to see why. Definitional or conceptual truths are
necessary truths (for example, "squares have four equal sides" is a
definitional truth and as such it is necessary.) Because existence is a
part of the concept of God, we can say that the statement that God
exists is a necessary truth.

Spinoza gives expression here to a version of what is known as
the ontological argument for the existence of God. Such arguments,
in one way or another, proceed from the claim that existence is
part of the concept of God to the conclusion that God exists. Such
arguments had already had in Spinoza's day a long history dating
back at least to Anselm (1033–1109) and had recently been
employed by Descartes in his Fifth Meditation. Spinoza's version is,
perhaps, unique in the way in which it relies heavily on the PSR.

Spinoza, in effect, says in 1p11 that God must exist by his very nature for if he did not then there would be no explanation for his non-existence. But, this would be intolerable since, by the PSR, each fact must have an explanation. The PSR thus helps us to see that God must have a definition or nature that is so rich as to generate God's very existence.

But there's a loose end: I said earlier in connection with 1p7 that the claim that existence pertains to the nature of a substance would hold only for a substance whose nature is not somehow internally incoherent. In this light, Spinoza can be said to have proved that God exists by virtue of the fact that God is defined as a substance only if Spinoza can show that the notion of God is internally coherent. (This is a kind of difficulty with the ontological argument that Leibniz was at particular pains to address.)[9] But while Spinoza obviously regards the nature of God as coherent, and, in fact, Spinoza explicitly says that to see God's nature as involving a contradiction is "absurd" (1p11d2), he nonetheless offers no direct argument for the claim that God's nature is coherent. And, as it happens, one can well imagine a Cartesian challenging that Spinoza's definition of God is incoherent precisely because it involves the claim that a substance can have more than one attribute. So again we come up against the problem of a multiplicity of attributes. Is there anything that Spinoza says that can be seen as addressing this important difficulty? We'll see that there is indeed by examining a problem with Spinoza's last step, in 1p14, in his proof of substance monism,

Here Spinoza puts it all together. Precisely because God is defined as having all the attributes, it follows that if another substance were to exist in addition to God, it would have to share attributes with God. (Each substance, for Spinoza, must have at least one attribute—1p10s.) But 1p5 prohibits attribute-sharing. So, given that God exists necessarily (by 1p11), no other substance exists or, indeed, can exist. QED.

But an immediate problem arises here. This problem was originally raised by Don Garrett in his classic paper, "Spinoza's

'Ontological' Argument" (Garrett 1979). Spinoza's proof of monism proceeds via the claim in 1p11 that God exists, and that claim is proved on the strength of the claim that God is a substance and also the general claim that it pertains to the nature of a substance to exist. But consider what would have happened if, instead of using 1p7 to prove in 1p11d that God exists, Spinoza had invoked 1p7 to prove that some different substance, a substance with fewer attributes, exists. For example, call the substance with only the attribute of extension, "ES1." ES1 is, let us say, by nature a substance with only that attribute. Invoking 1p7, we can say that it pertains to the nature of ES1 to exist and thus ES1 does exist and necessarily so. (This would be, as it were, an ontological argument for the existence of ES1.) But now, given that ES1 exists and given 1p5—the thesis that substances cannot share attributes—and also given the fact that if God were to exist he would have all the attributes, it follows that God does not exist after all! God would have to share an attribute with ES1 which we have already proven to exist. So it seems that Spinoza was able to prove that God is the only substance only because he began 1p11 somewhat arbitrarily with the claim that God exists. What reason did he have for starting there instead of starting with the claim that, say, ES1 exists? The answer must be that somehow ES1 has an incoherent nature and God does not. But this just brings us back to the question we have already raised: Is God's nature coherent?

How would Spinoza answer this question? He does not answer this question explicitly, but there is one claim that he espouses and that has an indirect bearing on this question. First, let's assume that for each attribute there must be a substance that has that attribute—given that attributes are conceived through themselves (1p10), nothing could prevent the instantiation of a given attribute. Given that there is no sharing of attributes and given that extension is an attribute, it follows that there is only one extended substance. Now consider the question: does this one extended substance have other attributes as well? In particular, does it have the attribute of thought? Well, let's say that it lacks thought. In virtue of what does it lack thought? This last question is a perfectly natural one, and in fact Spinoza's PSR demands that there be a reason here, that there be an answer to this question. What then could explain why the one extended substance lacks thought?

It's clear what Descartes would say: the fact that it is extended is the reason that the one extended substance lacks thought. Not only would Descartes say this, but it also seems the most natural and plausible way to answer the question. Notice, though, that this approach to the question is absolutely illegitimate from Spinoza's point of view. It is ruled out by his strong understanding of the conceptual barrier between the attributes. For Spinoza, as we have seen, no fact about thought depends on any fact about extension. This is just a manifestation of the self-conceived nature of each attribute. As Spinoza understands this separation, this means, for example, that the fact that a substance is extended cannot explain why it has the attribute of thought and *also* cannot explain why it lacks the attribute of thought. To explain the lack of thought by appealing to extension would be to explain a fact about thought in terms of a fact about extension. And this violates the conceptual barrier for Spinoza. He makes precisely the point in 1p10s. He says immediately after articulating the conceptual independence of the attributes that:

> From these propositions it is evident that although two attributes may be conceived to be really distinct (i.e. one may be conceived without the aid of the other), we still cannot infer from that that they constitute two beings, or two different substances.

Spinoza says here that the conceptual barrier shows that one attribute cannot prevent a substance from having another attribute. No other potential explanation of the one extended substance's lack of thought seems to be available. So if this substance did lack thought, that would be a brute fact and as such ruled out by the PSR. In this way, we can quickly see that every attribute not only must be instantiated but must also, on pain of violating the PSR, be instantiated by a single substance.

This understanding of the conceptual independence between the attributes is particularly strong. It uses the conceptual independence to preclude not only positive trans-attribute explanations (e.g. explanations that *a* is thinking because *a* is extended), but also negative trans-attribute explanations (e.g. explanations that *a* is not thinking because *a* is extended). Descartes obviously does not take the conceptual barrier this far: he is quite happy to say that an extended substance lacks thought *because* it is extended. However, Spinoza seems to be saying, if one has a conceptual barrier at all, there is no good reason not to extend it to preclude negative trans-attribute explanations as well as positive ones. And indeed I think that Spinoza is right here. He seems to be carrying to their logical extreme claims already accepted by Descartes. If Spinoza is right, then he has a good reason, on his own terms, for holding that one substance has all the attributes, and he has a good reason for ruling out ES1—the substance with only extension—because it has an incoherent nature. For Spinoza, there is good reason to hold that the only substance with a coherent nature is God, the substance of all attributes.

So now we have seen two respects in which Spinoza adopts a stronger version of the independence of the attributes than Descartes adopts. As we saw earlier, unlike Descartes, Spinoza rejects not only trans-attribute conceptual relations, but also trans-attribute causal relations. And, also unlike Descartes, Spinoza rejects negative trans-attribute explanations as well as positive ones. In taking the independence of the attributes to its logical extremes, Spinoza seems to be guided by the PSR: there is no reason not to take the independence of the attributes to these extremes.

In this light, we can see the argument for substance monism as generated by Spinoza's PSR as well as by his strong version of the conceptual independence of the attributes. And here at last we have a justification of the general Spinozistic claim that it is possible for a substance to have more than one attribute. The explanation is that it's possible because otherwise there would be a violation not only of the PSR, but also of the conceptual independence of the attributes.[10]

This multiplicity of attributes in a single substance raises a problem about the essence of this substance. We have seen that for Spinoza an attribute constitutes the essence of substance, but could *each* of a multiplicity of attributes constitute this essence? Here we return to the significance of the way Spinoza qualifies the Cartesian definition of attribute. Recall that Spinoza defines attribute this way:

> By attribute I understand what *the intellect perceives* of a substance, as constituting its essence.
>
> > (1def4, my emphasis)

The significance of this qualification is to call attention to the fact that, for Spinoza, what counts as the essence of the substance depends on how the substance is being conceived by the intellect. Considered as extended, the substance's essence is extension (and not thought). Considered as thinking, the substance's essence is thought (and not extension). And so on for all the other attributes. Considered neutrally—i.e. simply as God—the essence of the substance is to have all the attributes. This is precisely what the definition of God specifies (1def6).[11] Thus the significance of the non-Cartesian qualification in Spinoza's definition of attribute is to call attention to Spinoza's non-Cartesian view that a single substance can have more than one attribute.

So by seeing the principled ways in which Spinoza's ontology departs from that of Descartes we can see how he generates his argument for substance monism and against Descartes's claim that one substance cannot have more than one attribute. Precisely because Descartes's ontology of attributes—for him, thought and extension, roughly the mental and the physical—continues to be central to metaphysics and philosophy of mind even today, Spinoza's arguments represent a significant advance in our understanding of the traditional and still raging mind–body problem. Nonetheless, and obviously, there is at least one important question unanswered, and here no amount of drawing a contrast with Descartes will help because Descartes faces precisely the same problem.

The question I have in mind is: Why does Spinoza hold that thought and extension are separate attributes? Spinoza's argument that the thinking substance and the extended substance are one and the same thing (1p14, 2p7s) presupposes that thought and extension are separate attributes, but what justifies this presupposition? Unfortunately, Spinoza does not seem to have a good answer here. Spinoza does argue that thought is an attribute and that extension is an attribute (2pp1–2). His argument that thought is an attribute is just the claim that he can conceive of an infinite and conceptually independent thinking being, i.e. he can conceive that thought has the conceptual independence required to be an attribute. (He gives a similar proof for extension being an attribute.) But while this consideration may carry some intuitive weight, it is obviously unsatisfactory as a proof: even if we do have this conception of an independent thinking being, why does Spinoza think we are entitled to rely on this conception? Perhaps when we conceive—or think we conceive—of an infinite thinking being our thought really contains an unnoticed contradiction. Perhaps it is the case that there is some hidden conceptual dependence of thought on extension (or, alternatively, of extension on thought). Perhaps, in particular, to conceive adequately what it is for there to be a being with the mental life that you have, one must presuppose that there is some kind of physical world with which you are in contact, i.e. perhaps part of the very notion of what it is to be mental is that one bears some kind of relation to physical objects. This kind of conceptual connection seems not obviously absurd or illegitimate, and many philosophers have accepted something like it (e.g. Kant, Wittgenstein, and Davidson). If this is legitimate, then thought is, after all, not self-conceived and so not an attribute. If Spinoza is to say that such a conceptual connection is illegitimate, then he needs to do more than simply assert, as he does in 2p1s, that it is.

Spinoza also asserts that extension does not depend on thought. But here too it is not enough simply to assert that one can conceive that extension is self-sufficient; one must argue for this claim and address the arguments and intuitions that tend in the opposite direction, arguments to the effect that extension conceptually depends on thought, as any number of idealists have held.

None of this is to say that Spinoza is worse off than his physicalist or idealist opponents. Typically they too offer merely intuitive grounds for their assertions of conceptual dependence and their positions require argument just as much as Spinoza's does. Thus the problem of explaining how the mental and the physical are related—the traditional mind-body problem—continues to be at an impasse. Unsurprisingly, then, Spinoza has not solved the mind-body problem. But he has advanced our understanding of it. He has shown how, if one skillfully and consistently wields the PSR and the conceptual barrier between thought and extension, one can construct an argument for the view that there is one substance and one can undermine the Cartesian intuitions that material things and physical things cannot be identical. In later chapters, we will return to further ways in which Spinoza's PSR and his conceptual separation between thought and extension shape his understanding of the mind–body problem.

4. MODES

If God is the only substance, then where does that leave such familiar objects as the table, your body, and your mind? What metaphysical status do such objects have? Spinoza's answer is, of course, that these things are modes of the one substance. But what exactly is it to be a mode? This is a matter we have touched on in passing but now need to address more directly. By seeing how Descartes understands modes, we will begin to see why Spinoza's views on you and the table and ordinary objects generally have often been regarded as among his most exotic views and why some have been reluctant to attribute such views even to so bold a thinker as Spinoza.

Recall that, for Descartes, the attribute (or, as he sometimes puts it, the principal attribute) of a substance is the fundamental feature of the substance that all of its other features presuppose. These other, non-fundamental features are the modes of the substance. On this account, each mode presupposes a particular attribute. Modes of extension would be things such as the shape of the table, its size, and its weight. Such a mode is simply a way in which an extended substance is extended. Modes of thought would be, for example, particular thoughts that a given mind has. Thus my belief that, my thought that, Spinoza was a philosopher is a mode of my mind. Such a belief is simply a mode of thought, a way in which a thinking substance thinks.

Two aspects of the way Descartes conceives the relation between a mode and a substance are important. First, for Descartes, a mode is in the substance of which it is a mode (see, e.g., *Principles* I 53). This does not mean that the mode is a part of the substance, but rather that the mode is a *state* of the substance. The traditional, technical term for such a relation is inherence: modes inhere in substance. Thus roundness inheres in the table just in the sense that this is a state in which the table exists. Inherence is a kind of dependence relation: states of a substance depend for their existence on the substance. There cannot be a state of being round without some thing (a substance, for Descartes) that is round.[12]

Besides being in substance, modes are, for Descartes, conceived through the substance of which they are modes. This is what Descartes is getting at when he says that modes presuppose the attribute of the substance of which they are modes. For Descartes, modes literally cannot be understood except as in a substance (*Principles* I 53). Descartes makes clear that this is a kind of conceptual connection between modes and substance: "the nature of a mode is such that it cannot be understood at all unless the concept of the thing of which it is a mode is implied in its own concept" (CSM I 301/AT VIIIB 355).[13]

One debate about the status of modes is whether they are to be seen as universals or as particulars. An example will help bring out this distinction. When we say that a table is round, we are calling attention to a mode of the table. But is this mode something that not only this particular table has, but also any number of other things may also have? If so, then the mode would be roundness, a universal capable of being instantiated by a number of things. Or, alternatively, is the mode of the table not the general feature of roundness, but instead this instance of roundness, i.e. the table's being round, not roundness in general? On this conception of modes they would be particulars and not universals. They would not be capable of being located in more than one substance. This instance of roundness and that instance of roundness would be numerically distinct even if they are intrinsically exactly alike. It is not clear how Cartesian modes are to be understood, although, for what it is worth, on the traditional understanding of accidents they were seen as particulars.[14] The issue of whether modes are particulars or universals will play a role in the debate about Spinozistic modes, as we will see presently.

For Descartes, objects such as your mind, your body, and the table are not modes of any substance, rather they are substances in their own right. And although such finite substances do, as we saw, depend completely on God, they do not depend on God in the way that states of a substance depend on and inhere in that substance. Thus we can see that Descartes recognizes (at least) two different kinds of relations of dependence: inherence and conceptual dependence generally. For Descartes, finite substances depend on God only in the latter way, but modes depend on substance in both of these ways.

Spinoza was, of course, deeply influenced by the Cartesian account of modes, and the main controversy in this area of Spinoza's thought is the extent to which he tranformed this account. On the interpretation I will be offering, Spinoza does agree with Descartes that modal dependence involves both inherence and conceptual dependence, but he differs from Descartes because Spinoza sees inherence as nothing but conceptual dependence. For Spinoza, there is only one relation of dependence here, and not two as in Descartes.

To begin to see the outlines of this account, the most important point is that, for Spinoza, there is only one substance, God. Because all that exists, for Spinoza, is either a substance or a mode (1p4d), it follows that ordinary objects such as finite minds and bodies are modes of God. If Spinoza is adopting the Cartesian account of modes with all of its deep roots in medieval and ancient philosophy, then it would seem that the table, for example, is a *state* of God, that the relation between God and the table is much like the way that Descartes conceives the relation between the table and its roundness.

But how is this possible? How can a thing such as a table or your mind be a state or a feature of another thing such as God? Such objects are not, it would seem, ways in which God or anything else exists, rather they have an existence of their own. Curley often puts this worry by saying that modes, as Descartes conceives them, are properties or universals, while tables and minds are particulars, and no particular can be a universal. As Curley says,

> Spinoza's modes are, prima facie, of the wrong logical type to be related to substance in the same way Descartes' modes are related to substance, for they are particular things (1p25c), not qualities.
>
> (Curley 1969: 18)

However, as we have seen, modes as Descartes and the tradition conceive them are not necessarily universals; rather, they may be, as it were, particularized properties, such as the table's roundness or this roundness instead of mere roundness in general. On this understanding, modes would be particulars and thus, perhaps, of the right logical type.

But to make this important point (as Carriero does so well) is not to eradicate the intuitive unease that Curley rightly feels at the thought that ordinary objects are modes in the Cartesian sense. This is because it may seem extremely implausible to regard the table, your mind, and your body as simply particularized states of something else. It seems almost as (if not equally) absurd to regard my body as a universal, as a property that God has, as it is to regard my body as a particular, namely God's having that property. Such a view would seem scarcely intelligible; it does not do justice to our sense of the robustness that we and other ordinary objects seem to enjoy. This, I think, is the root objection that Curley and others have to treating Spinozistic modes as modes in the Cartesian sense.

I believe that this concern is a powerful one, and it leads Curley to develop a radically different interpretation of Spinozistic modes according to which Spinoza's understanding of modes is radically different from that of Descartes. For Curley, Spinozistic modes do not inhere in substance at all; they are not states of substance. Rather, they are simply causally dependent on substance. Curley, of course, recognizes that Spinoza does say that modes are in substance (1def5), but by 'in' Curley takes Spinoza to mean not that modes inhere in the substance, but only that they are caused by it. And Curley has good evidence to bolster his case that the in-relation is a causal relation. Not only does Spinoza seem to equate the two in TdIE §92, but also, as Curley emphasizes, Spinoza frequently says that God causes, determines or produces modes (e.g. 1p15d, 1p24, 1p26).

Curley's reading is elegant and, as we will see, there is more than a grain of truth in it. Nonetheless, there is strong evidence that Spinoza does indeed see modes as states of substance. To demonstrate this, I will focus first on the evidence for thinking that Spinoza sees bodies in particular as states of substance, and then I will turn to what I take to be compelling considerations in favor of seeing Spinozistic modes of thought as also states of substance. Finally, I will show how this reading of modes as states emerges from and is required by Spinoza's naturalism.

First, bodies as states. For Spinoza, extension is an attribute of God. This is, of course, a highly controversial theological claim. Traditionally, extension was thought to be unworthy of the divine nature because extension seemed to involve divisibility. And divisibility is bad because, for one thing, if a substance is divisible, then it can be divided into parts and, if the parts are divided and no longer together, then it would seem that the whole, the substance, would go out of existence (1p12). But, of course, God cannot be vulnerable to such untoward changes as division and destruction. So, the argument concludes, God cannot be extended. In response, Spinoza says: don't worry, God is extended but not in such a way as to show that God is divisible or vulnerable to destruction. This is because, for Spinoza, individual bodies are not *parts* into which God could be divided, rather they are literally ways in which the extended substance is affected. Spinoza says:

> matter is everywhere the same, and ... parts are distinguished in it only insofar as we conceive matter to be affected in different ways, so that its parts are distinguished only modally, but not really. For example, we conceive that water is divided and its parts separated from one another—insofar as it is water, but not insofar as it is corporeal substance. For insofar as it is substance, it is neither separated nor divided. Again, water, insofar as it is water, is generated and corrupted, but insofar as it is substance, it is neither generated nor corrupted.
>
> (1p15s)

Why, in his discussion of God's indivisibility, does Spinoza focus on finite things, such as individual quantities of water? This emphasis would be out of place if Curley were right. For if he were right,

God's being extended is no threat at all to God's indivisibility. Even if, per impossibile, individual bodies were capable of existence independently of God and of each other, this would not show that, for Curley, God, the extended substance, is divisible. This is so because, for Curley, God as extended is simply the attribute of extension, and the divisibility of the modes of extension which are, for Curley, somewhat ontologically removed from God would have no bearing on God's indivisibility. But in 1p15s, Spinoza obviously does see individual bodies as having a bearing on God's indivisibility, and this goes against Curley's interpretation.

Attention to modes of thought can bring home this point even more forcefully. Just as particular bodies, for Spinoza, are modes of extension, particular minds are modes of thought. But just what is my mind, for example? Spinoza is quite clear on this point: my mind is the idea of my body and this idea is a complex idea consisting of ideas of the various states or parts of my body. There is nothing more to my mind than a certain collection of ideas in God's mind. And the same holds true for your mind and for all other finite minds: each mind is just God's idea of a particular body. Obviously, there are many complexities in this account, some of which we will explore in the next chapter, but from this sketch we can already see that, for Spinoza, modes of thought (at least finite modes of thought) are ideas in God's mind. Individual ideas are naturally regarded as states of the mind that has these ideas. So it is quite natural to see Spinoza as holding that modes of thought are somehow states of God qua thinking thing. Spinoza regards these modes as caused by God, just as Curley stresses, but the modes of thought are also for Spinoza *features* of the substance. Given the strict parallelism between thought and extension (and other attributes) which Spinoza emphasizes and which I will emphasize too in the next chapter, we can see strong reason to think that, for Spinoza, all modes—of thought, of extension, and of each other attribute—are modes in something like the Cartesian sense: they are features or states of God.

Finally, I would like to point out that there is a deeper point here that transcends anything Spinoza might say about extension or thought in particular. This deeper point is a reflection of Spinoza's naturalism and shows that, in the end, Curley is importantly right in one respect. Return to Curley's interpretation. For him, modes are merely causally dependent on God, they do not inhere in God, they are not states of God. And, while Spinoza does say that modes are in God, by this, for Curley, Spinoza means only that they are caused by God. So, for Curley, there are two different kinds of dependence: inherence and what might be called mere causation or dependence that is not inherence. These are both kinds of conceptual dependence. The states of a thing would be conceived through the thing on which they depend, and Curley-esque modes as mere effects would be conceived through substance.

The question I want to press here is this: in virtue of what are inherence and mere causation different kinds of conceptual dependence? What makes them distinct? This is a pertinent question because, after all, they do have something in common: they are both kinds of conceptual dependence. Wherein do they differ? It's hard to see the difference here as anything other than a brute fact. There seems to be no way to elucidate the difference or to explain what it consists in except to say that mere causal dependence is the kind of conceptual dependence that, for example, bodies bear to God and, perhaps, some bodies bear to other bodies, and inherence is that kind of conceptual dependence that, for example, states of bodies bear to those bodies. Such an answer merely states that there is a difference between inherence and mere causation without explaining what the difference consists in. If the account were to end here, I think Spinoza would regard this account as unacceptably trading in primitive or brute facts.

One can see such a distinction as a violation of Spinoza's naturalism which is, as we saw, the thesis that everything in nature plays by the same rules. There is nothing that operates according to principles that are not at work everywhere. If inherence is found only in some dependence relations but not in others, then that is to see a special kind of principle at work in some cases and not in others. One can put this point by paraphrasing Spinoza: dependence relations are everywhere the same.[15]

The worry here is really just the flip side of the worry that leads Spinoza to reject any kind of Cartesian view which allows for two distinct senses of substance. Descartes holds, as we saw, that we, for example, depend on God, but are nonetheless substances in our own right, albeit in a different sense from the sense in which God, who is absolutely independent of everything else, is a substance. This, as I explained, would be an unacceptable violation of naturalism for Spinoza. The Cartesian account allows different things to play by different rules, to be subject to different sets of requirements when it comes to being a substance. And such exceptions to the rules will seem objectionably ad hoc to Spinoza.

To allow for things that depend on God but are nonetheless substances is already implicitly at least to allow for two kinds of dependence relations. The finite Cartesian substances do not inhere in God or depend on him in that way, yet these finite substances have states that depend on or inhere in those finite substances. Thus, precisely because there are two different kinds of substances in Descartes, there are also two kinds of dependence relations. This duality of kinds of dependence relations seems every bit as objectionable from a Spinozistic point of view as the duality in kinds of substance. There is mere causal dependence and, what might be called, dependence of the inherence variety. But what makes them distinct kinds of dependence? If they are each a kind of dependence and if there is nothing that makes them distinct, then they are the same after all, Spinoza would argue. If there is something that makes them distinct kinds of dependence, then what is it? For Spinoza, the Cartesian has to say that there are these different kinds of dependence relations, but that, just as with the different kinds of substance, such a difference is a brute fact and a violation of the naturalist ideal of a single uniform set of requirements. Thus in arguing for the non-Cartesian interpretation of Spinozistic modes as not states, Curley is making what is in the end a very Cartesian move: he is allowing for an unexplained duality in kinds of dependence.

By contrast, the interpretation of Spinoza according to which bodies and minds are modes of God in the sense that they are caused by God *and* inhere in God preserves the PSR and Spinoza's naturalism. Yes, both inherence and mere causation are kinds of dependence, but, for Spinoza, by virtue of his rationalism, they are ultimately the same kind of dependence, and that is conceptual dependence tout court.

Here we can see that in an important way Curley is right after all. He denies that Spinoza's in-relation (the relation of being in itself or in another) is an inherence relation. In doing so, Curley affirms that the in-relation just is the relation of causation. While I disagree with Curley about inherence, he is, I believe, absolutely right that the in-relation just is causation or, more generally, conception. And here I depart from Carriero's interpretation in a significant way. Although Carriero holds that Spinozistic modes do inhere in substance—and I agree—he also holds that the in-relation is a completely separate relation from the relation of causation. I find such a distinction inimical to Spinoza's rationalism for reasons I have already given. When Carriero says that the relations are different his claim is based partly on the further claim that Spinoza keeps his talk of causation and his talk of inherence on largely separate tracks. But this is not true. Carriero regards 1p16 as a key place in which Spinoza affirms the causal dependence of things on God. (1p16 says in part, "From the necessity of the divine nature, there must follow infinitely many things in infinitely many ways.") But Spinoza argues for 1p16 by invoking the ways in which the properties of a thing depend on that thing. As Spinoza says in 1p16d:

This proposition must be plain to anyone, provided he attends to the fact that the intellect infers from the given definition of any

thing a number of properties that really do follow necessarily
from it (that is, from the very essence of the thing).

So in 1p16, the supposed bastion of causal talk as opposed to talk
of inherence, Spinoza seems to mix the two kinds of locution
effortlessly. This is evidence against Carriero's claim that the relations are separate and it is further positive evidence for taking
causal dependence and inherence to be the same for Spinoza.

In effect, we can see Spinoza as offering an account of the nature
of inherence that embodies another twofold use of the PSR. Spinoza would insist on the legitimacy of the demand that inherence
be explained. "What is inherence?" is a natural question for Spinoza. Some account must be given beyond the unacceptable treatment of inherence as a relation of conceptual dependence that
differs brutely from the relation of mere causal dependence. To
make this demand that inherence be intelligible is the first use of
the PSR in this case.

Spinoza meets this demand by arguing that inherence just is
causal and, ultimately, conceptual dependence. Thus, to say that
one thing inheres in another is to say simply that it is understood
or conceived through or intelligible in terms of this other. This
conclusion is the second use of the PSR or of the notion of intelligibility in this case. For Spinoza, inherence must be intelligible
and it is intelligible in terms of intelligibility itself. Here again
Spinoza is making the characteristic rationalist move, the kind of
move he has already made in treating causation as conception.[16]

To tie the interpretation of modes as states of God to Spinoza's
naturalism and his rationalism in this way is not by itself to display
all the significant features of this interpretation. I will omit most of
these other aspects which have been well discussed elsewhere. But
there is one implication that is worth bringing out here because it
will help us later in understanding Spinoza's account of the eternality of the human mind. If, as I have just argued, for Spinoza causation and inherence are the same, then when A causes B, B must

inhere in or be a state of A. While this may be the right account of the relation between God and the modes of God, it hardly seems to be an intelligible account of the relation between one mode and another. Spinoza does allow, and indeed require, that modes stand in causal relations to one another. Spinoza would allow, for example, that the carpenter causes the chair to come into existence. Given that causation and inherence are the same, it would seem to follow that the chair inheres in or is a state of the carpenter. But how can this be? To paraphrase a related claim of Curley's which we saw earlier: the table seems to be of the wrong logical type to inhere in or be a state of the carpenter. How can the relation between the chair and the carpenter be anything like the relation between the carpenter and what may seem more genuinely to be one of his states, for example the carpenter's height? This is a consequence of Spinoza's view and it is one he embraces, as in this passage from TTP: "knowledge of an effect through its cause is nothing but knowing some property of the cause."[17] He seems here to be equating an effect of a cause with a property of the cause. However, it is important to note that, for Spinoza, inherence comes in degrees, and precisely because the carpenter is only a partial cause of the chair, Spinoza would say that the chair only partly inheres in the carpenter and partly inheres in all the other finite causes of the chair. We will investigate the significance of this notion of degrees of inherence more fully when we turn to Spinoza's account of the eternality of the human mind in Chapter 7.

5. NECESSITARIANISM

What is, perhaps, most shocking about Spinoza's claim that finite particulars are merely states of God is that this thesis seems to make these finite things depend too intimately on God. But that's only part of the story, for the dependence on God is even more extreme than the thesis of modes as states would indicate. For Spinoza, not only do modes depend on God by being mere states of God, their dependence is so complete that it is absolutely impossible for any mode—and thus for the entire series of modes—to be different in any respect from the way it actually is. For Spinoza, there is no contingency and all things are absolutely necessary. This is Spinoza's thesis of necessitarianism, the thesis I will explain and motivate in this section.

For Spinoza, everything must be determined either by itself or by another thing (see 1ax2). As we have seen, this is simply a manifestation of the PSR. And, as we also saw in the previous section, this is equivalent to the claim that everything is either a substance or a mode of a substance. Because God is the only substance, it follows that all things depend on or are determined by God.

This much is uncontroversial. Much less clear, at least initially, is whether the things that depend on God depend on God completely, whether *every* truth about those things can be accounted for simply by appealing to God's nature. This is the question at stake in considering whether Spinoza accepts necessitarianism.[18]

To resolve this matter, we must turn briefly to Spinoza's doctrine of infinite modes. Spinoza says that some things follow from the absolute nature of God's attributes (1p21). He also says elsewhere that such things follow from an attribute of God considered absolutely (1p23d). What is it to follow from an attribute considered absolutely? Spinoza's discussion in 1p21d—while notoriously obscure—does seem to indicate at least this much: Something follows from God's nature considered absolutely just in case it does not follow from God only in virtue of other things' following from God as well. Spinoza discusses in 1p21d whether a finite mode can follow from God's nature considered absolutely, and he rejects this possibility precisely because a finite mode can follow from God's nature only insofar as another finite mode of the same kind also follows from God's nature.

It is important to note that to say that a mode follows non-absolutely from God is *not* to say that it follows only partly from God.[19] For Spinoza, to say that a mode follows non-absolutely from God is to say that it follows from God only as part of a package. To say that it follows non-absolutely carries no implications whatsoever as to whether God is not the complete account of the modes. It is, of course, perfectly compatible with God's causing a mode as part of a package that God completely causes that mode. Consider a complete dance with 16 steps. It may be that I can perform step 12 only in the context of performing all the other steps. Nonetheless, I can be the complete cause of the performance of step 12, as well as of all the other steps. Similarly, God may be the complete cause of the infinitely many modes he causes only as part of a package. And we will see that Spinoza holds precisely this view.

Why, for Spinoza, is it the case that a finite mode cannot follow absolutely from God, that a finite mode must follow from God's nature as part of a package of infinitely many other finite modes? Spinoza's reasoning here can be seen as invoking the PSR. Let's say that an attribute gives rise to a finite mode and nothing else, and thus the finite mode would follow absolutely from God's nature. With regard to this situation, the question arises: what prevents the attribute in question from giving rise to other finite modes as well? Certainly not the finite mode in question: for Spinoza, a finite mode is by nature such that it is always conceivable that it be limited by another finite thing of the same kind (1def2). Certainly not the attribute itself: if the attribute gives rise to one finite mode, its nature would seem to be compatible with other finite modes as well. Certainly not another attribute: there can, of course, be no such causal relation between different attributes. And certainly, for Spinoza, it cannot be a brute fact that the attribute produces only this one mode. It seems that we have exhausted possible answers to the question of why the attribute produces only one mode. And so we must conclude that, on Spinozistic terms, the attribute cannot produce only one finite mode. A similar line of argument would tend to the conclusion that the attribute cannot produce only a finite number of finite modes. So the inevitable conclusion is that a finite mode cannot be produced by God's nature except as part of a package of infinitely many other finite modes (1p28). And, for this reason, for Spinoza, a finite mode cannot follow from the absolute nature of one of God's attributes. Anything that follows absolutely from God must itself be infinite.[20]

To say that a mode of a given attribute is infinite is to say, at least, that it is pervasive in that attribute, that the mode is somehow to be found throughout that attribute. How this could be the case is something we shall explore.

For Spinoza, there are two kinds of infinite modes. First there are those that follow directly from God's nature. These are the immediate infinite modes. Second, there are infinite modes that follow from God, not by following absolutely from God, but by following from the infinite modes that do follow absolutely from God. Such infinite modes, Spinoza says, follow mediately from God's nature. These are the mediate infinite and eternal modes.[21]

Some examples of infinite modes may help to clarify the notion. Let's focus on infinite modes of extension. The attribute of extension is infinite because it pervades the entire realm of extension— all modes of extension are understood through the attribute of extension. But obviously the *attribute* of extension is not an infinite *mode* of extension. Spinoza was pressed by Tschirnhaus to give examples of infinite modes, and the example of an immediate infinite mode of extension that he offers is motion-and-rest (Letter 64, see also KV II Preface §7). Here Spinoza's debt to Cartesian mechanism is apparent. Descartes believes not only that all modes of extension presuppose extension, but also that all variety in the extended world could be accounted for simply by differences in the degree of motion and rest of parts of matter (*Principles* II 23). Spinoza makes a similar point here: every extended thing can be understood not only in terms of extension, but, in particular, in terms of motion-and-rest. If motion-and-rest is explanatorily central in this way, one can see how it pervades the realm of extension and can be called an infinite mode.

Obviously, for Spinoza, the notion of motion and rest will figure into the laws extended nature. He sees such laws as pervasive throughout the realm of extension and in general the laws of nature considered under any particular attribute are pervasive in that attribute. As Spinoza says in 3preface:

the laws and rules of Nature, according to which all things happen, and change from one form to another, are always and everywhere the same.

As this passage makes clear, the pervasiveness of these laws involves the fact that they govern all the changes that occur in a given realm. Thus, change in finite modes would be explained in part by the appropriate laws of nature or infinite modes. Although Spinoza gives a few examples of such laws, such as a principle of inertia for extension (see 2le3c) and a principle of the association of ideas in thought (see TTP, chap. 4, p. 58, G III 57–58), he does not offer any full-blown list of the laws of nature, nor could he. Because these laws are the rules according to which *all* things happen, these laws will obviously be quite detailed and perhaps beyond the capacity of human minds to cognize fully. Further, because of their pervasiveness, it is natural to see the laws of nature as infinite modes.[22]

On this conception of infinite modes as laws, they are pervasive *features* found throughout a given realm. Everything in extension has, for example, the property of obeying the law of inertia. But there is an apparently different strand in Spinoza's thinking about infinite modes according to which infinite modes are not *features* of the extended realm or of the thinking realm, but are instead individuals in their own right. This way of thinking is suggested by Spinoza himself. His own example of an immediate infinite mode of thought is "absolutely infinite intellect." The infinite intellect, for Spinoza, seems to be a thinking individual, the individual constituted by all individual ideas. This collection forms a vast thinking individual made up of all of these infinitely many ideas. (Spinoza says that the human mind—a finite thinking individual—is a part of the infinite intellect of God (2p11c).) Thus this infinite mode of thought seems to be not a feature of thought, a property of the realm of thought, but instead a thinking individual.

This suggestion that at least some infinite modes are individuals and not mere features is strengthened by Spinoza's example of a mediate infinite mode (whether of thought or of extension is not clear): the face (*facies*) of the whole universe. It's not clear what *facies* means, but Spinoza attempts to elucidate this claim by citing 2le7s where he claims that the infinite collection of finite bodies forms one vast extended individual:

> the whole nature is of one individual, whose parts, that is, all bodies, vary in infinite ways, without any change of the whole individual.

I will not attempt to adjudicate these apparently conflicting conceptions of infinite modes, for there may not be, in the end, much difference here. Just as, as we saw in the previous section, finite individuals may just be finite features of substance, a similar point may hold for infinite individuals and infinite (i.e. pervasive) features.

One more point about the infinite modes is needed before we can directly address the issue of necessitarianism. The constituents of the infinitely large group of finite modes are causally related, not only to God, but also to other members of the package. God does not cause a package of otherwise causally unrelated modes. Rather, God causes a collection of modes that are causally related to one another. Precisely because no finite modes can follow from God absolutely, in order for a finite mode to follow from God, there must be another finite mode that follows from God, and in order for that finite mode to follow from God, there must be yet another finite mode, etc. This indicates a dependence of each finite mode on God and on other finite modes: the finite mode exists only because God exists and because God causes other finite modes. (Spinoza argues in just this way in 1p28d.)

This account of causation between modes commits Spinoza to determinism. This is the thesis, as Garrett puts it, that "every event is causally determined from antecedent conditions by the laws of nature" (Garrett 1991: 191). According to determinism, the relevant laws of nature are in some sense necessary. The antecedent conditions are other finite modes, and the laws, as we have seen, are among the infinite modes that follow from an attribute of God. According to determinism, given the past, the future is closed, the future is already, as it were, locked in. This is, of course, quite a controversial thesis, not least because many have thought that it would undermine all freedom and responsibility. We will return to this point in Chapter 5. Although the thesis of determinism is controversial, it is not at all controversial that Spinoza accepts it. Indeed, it is easy to see the PSR as determining that Spinoza accepts determinism: if, given the past, more than one future is nonetheless open and there is more than one possible course for events to take, then whatever course of events actually comes to be would seem to be a brute fact; there would be no way, as it were, to see this particular future coming, there would be no reason in the past that suffices for this particular future.

We are now in a position to argue—controversially—that Spinoza accepts a thesis much stronger in many respects than determinism, namely necessitarianism. To see how necessitarianism is stronger, consider a possibility that determinism does not rule out. According to determinism, given the laws of nature (which are necessary), the antecedent conditions determine the later conditions. But determinism does not require that the antecedent conditions are themselves necessary. Determinism requires that if one of the antecedent conditions were changed, then its causes would have had to have been different, and the causes of these causes would have had to have been different etc., all the way back. But, as far as determinism is concerned, there is nothing in principle impossible about the chain of causes having been different all the way back. The laws of nature are necessary, according to determinism, but the particular series of events governed by these laws is not necessary: there could have been a different series of events. The view that there is more than one possible series of events (or, in Spinozistic terms, one possible series of finite modes) is precisely what determinism allows and necessitarianism denies. According to necessitarianism, there is no sense in which it is possible that I wore a purple polka dot shirt today, whereas determinism can allow that it is possible.

This is an extremely implausible thesis. Even if we grant that determinism is true, what would compel us to accept that it is in no way possible for me to have worn a purple polka dot shirt today? Perhaps my friends would welcome this news, but is this a philosophical conclusion that one can endorse? Almost all philosophers would say not. In addition to its intrinsic implausibility, necessitarianism is even more of a threat to freedom than is determinism. If my stealing money from you is absolutely necessary, then how can I be free in acting that way? Leibniz, for example, is happy to say that freedom is compatible with determinism, but wants to draw the line at saying that freedom is compatible with necessitarianism.

Yes, necessitarianism is extremely implausible, but that would not deter Spinoza—bold philosopher that he is—from accepting it if he sees good reasons for doing so. And Spinoza does see such reasons.

Spinoza claims in 1p16:

> From the necessity of the divine nature there must follow infinitely many things in infinitely many ways [modis] (i.e. everything which can fall under an infinite intellect).
>
> (trans. altered)

For Spinoza, everything can be grasped by the infinite intellect— anything that could not be so grasped could not be conceived, but, according to 1ax2, everything can be conceived. Thus, it follows from 1p16 that God's nature determines *everything*, and there seems to be every reason to think that, for Spinoza, "everything" includes the total state of the world. God seems to determine every last detail of everything that exists. Spinoza develops this point further in 1p29 and 1p33 which explicitly depend on 1p16:

> In nature there is nothing contingent, but all things have been determined from the necessity of the divine nature to exist and produce an effect in a certain way.
>
> (1p29)

> Things could have been produced by God in no other way, and in no other order than they have been produced.
>
> (1p33)

These sound like the claims of a necessitarian. A determinist can allow, as we have seen, that some things are contingent (e.g. the entire state of the world) and that things could have been produced in a different way (though not according to different laws). So, Spinoza's claims seem to be distinctively necessitarian claims.

Fundamental here, obviously, is Spinoza's argument for 1p16 which proceeds this way: the more reality a thing has, the more properties follow from its nature. Since God—as the substance of infinite attributes—has the most reality, the most properties possible follow from his nature, i.e. he has *all* possible properties. Spinoza concludes from this that God determines all things. (Notice here, by the way, the implicit equation of particular things and properties of God. This lends further credence to the interpretation of Spinozistic modes as states of God.) The crucial point in the demonstration is the claim that God has the most reality. For Spinoza, reality is equivalent to power,[23] and, in this light, we can see what he means by saying that God has the most reality: as a self-sufficient and unique substance, God has the most power possible. If such a substance lacked some power, what could prevent it from having that power? There is no other substance to prevent God from having that power, and certainly no mode could prevent God from having as much power as possible, so any such lack would have no explanation and is thus disallowed by Spinoza. Thus God has the most power and reality possible, and, as such, determines everything else. And thus we can see that Spinoza's necessitarianism ultimately derives from his PSR.[24]

If Spinoza is a necessitarian for these reasons, how would he answer the following, and perhaps strongest, challenge to necessitarianism? If, so the objection goes, necessitarianism is true, then why does it seem to us (falsely) that things could have been otherwise than they actually are? What explanation can be given of this massive error on our part? Spinoza would have a ready answer: If one fully understood the implications of the very nature of God, then one *would* see that no particular state of affairs could have been otherwise. But, for Spinoza, although we do have a grasp of God's nature, the finitude of our minds prevents us from drawing out completely and clearly the implications of that essence. We will explore these cognitive limitations of the human mind further in the next chapter.

6. THE PURPOSE OF IT ALL

Spinoza's necessitarianism and the law-governedness of nature are at work in his denial of divine teleology, of the view that God brings about certain things with a purpose, for the sake of some particular end. Spinoza is especially concerned to refute that version of the doctrine of divine teleology according to which God orders the rest of nature to serve the interests of human beings and, in general, has a special concern for human beings that guides his actions. The sources of Spinoza's critique are multifarious and, in this section, I will try to disentangle them and reveal a single fundamental line of thought that is centered on the PSR.

We can begin by asking the question Spinoza asks: Does God act for the sake of an end? The traditional answer—and indeed the prevalent answer still today among people generally and among a considerable number of philosophers—is a resounding "yes!" God acts out of a special concern for human beings, either to aid them, or to punish them, etc. This was and is a prevailing religious view. Even Descartes—whose rejection of appeals to divine purposiveness in explaining changes in the physical world was a deep influence on Spinoza—appeals to divine purposiveness when it comes to explaining our knowledge and also the interaction between mind and body. Roughly, Descartes's view is that, since God is a benevolent non-deceiver, he would not allow our beliefs in general to be false and he also arranges for the kinds of connection between mind and body that are most conducive to the successful maintenance of what he calls the union of mind and body, i.e. of the human being.

This kind of special purposive concern that God is seen as having for human beings is, in some ways, of a piece with other influential views which somehow see human beings as central to the workings of the world. The Ptolemaic conception of the universe according to which the earth is at the center is, in part, a manifestation of the conviction that our position in nature is special. The anti-Darwinian view that the human species did not evolve via a natural process from other species is also a manifestation of this conviction. Both the Ptolemaic and anti-Darwinian views were difficult to dislodge, and, in many quarters, the anti-Darwinian views still haven't been dislodged. The view that God acts out of a special concern for human beings is, if anything, more deeply entrenched, as we can see by considering that many, if not most, of those who happily accept the Copernican, heliocentric view and Darwin's theory still believe in a special divine providence, a special divine concern. In denying that God acts in such a way, Spinoza knew that he faced a difficult fight and, perhaps, that is why his attack is, even more than usual for Spinoza, savage and unrelenting.

For Spinoza, it is clear why we tend to believe that God acts for the sake of human beings. First, because human beings see that they act for the sake of an end—namely for their own advantage (more on this in Chapter 4)—they come to believe that all things have a purpose or, as Spinoza says using the traditional terminology, all things have final causes (1app, G II 78). And because we find that many things in nature are advantageous to us, we come to conclude that all natural things are produced for the sake of our advantage. Spinoza's reasoning here is elegant, compelling, and worth quoting at length:

> men act always on account of an end, namely, on account of their own advantage, which they want. Hence they seek to know only the final causes of what has been done. ... Furthermore, they find—both in themselves and outside themselves—many means that are very helpful in seeking their own advantage, for example, eyes for seeing, teeth for chewing, plants and animals for food, the sun for light, the sea for supporting fish. Hence, they consider all natural things as means to their own advantage. And knowing that they had found these means, not provided them for themselves, they had reason to believe that there was someone else who had prepared those means for their use. For after they considered things as means, they could not believe that the things had made themselves; but from the means they were accustomed to prepare for themselves, they had to infer that there was a ruler, or a number of rulers, of Nature, endowed with human freedom who had taken care of all things for them, and made all things for their use.
>
> (G II 78–79)

It is interesting to note that at work in what Spinoza sees as this deeply mistaken way of thinking is, by Spinoza's lights, a genuine insight, namely that all natural events must be explained in the same way. This is really the core of naturalism—everything plays by the same rules. Spinoza's only problem is that the rules invoked here—which turn on human advantage—are not at all legitimate. But to the extent that there is a naturalistic line of thought here, Spinoza would applaud. Here we can see support for Spinoza's implicit contention that a naturalist approach to the world has significant power and is pervasive, even if it is not always followed through consistently.

Spinoza denies not only that God acts for the sake of human advantage, but also that God acts for any particular end whatsoever. Why does he make this general claim? His reasons seem to turn on the fact that, for Spinoza, God acts from the necessity of his nature. Spinoza says that he has shown that nature has no end set before it partly on the basis of "all those [propositions] by which I have shown that all things proceed by a certain eternal necessity of Nature, and with the greatest perfection" (G II 80). Spinoza thus sees acting for an end as incompatible with acting solely out of the necessity of one's nature. In this light, we can see why, for Spinoza, we act for the sake of an end and that's precisely because our actions are, in keeping with our status as modes, determined not wholly by our own nature. They are instead determined wholly by God's nature which determines our nature as well as the nature of other finite things (1p25). Spinoza obviously sees an end as something set, at least in part, by something external to the nature of the thing that acts for the sake of that end, and this is why Spinoza says that ends involve negation (4pref, G II 207–8). In this sense of "end," God obviously cannot act for the sake of an end since there is nothing external to him to help determine his ends.

Fair enough, but this construal of "end" only raises the question; why we should conceive of ends this way? Can't a thing (i.e. God) by the necessity of its nature privilege some things above others so that the latter (the others) are for the sake of the former? Such a determined, necessary process can be seen to be no less goal-directed and teleological than a process that does not follow from the necessity of the nature of a thing. Spinoza needs a further reason—beyond the fact that God acts out of the necessity of his nature—in order to deny that God acts for the sake of an end.

What could this further reason be? At this point, Spinoza would call attention to something he sees as very disconcerting about using divine ends to explain things. Let's say that a is for the sake of b

(e.g. the existence of plants is for the sake of human nourishment). If this is so, it certainly seems that *b* explains *a*, human nourishment is the reason that there are plants. But, equally, it seems that *a* explains *b*, the reason that human beings are nourished is that there are plants. Certainly human nourishment is caused by plants; how then can plants be explained by human nourishment? Or, given the equivalence of explanation and causation in Spinoza, how can plants (which cause nourishment) be themselves caused by nourishment? Isn't this just a case of a thing causing its causes and wouldn't that be, in Spinoza's memorable phrase, "to turn nature completely upside down" (*naturam omnino evertere*)?

Again, fair enough. But there is a ready answer to Spinoza's charge at this point. Intentional action—though it is directed at a future state of affairs—does not require turning nature upside down. In acting because of an intention, one is acting for the sake of the object of the intention—one is acting with a purpose. But the object that the intention concerns—something that may lie far off in the future— does not mysteriously cause any actions that lead to the desired object. Instead, the intention which occurs before *x* non-mysteriously causes *x*.[25] This is a very natural way to make sense of teleological causation. Spinoza himself is quite willing to account for teleology in our case in precisely this way. Here's his mundane example:

> when we say that habitation was the final cause of this or that house, surely we understand nothing but that a man, because he imagined the conveniences of domestic life, had an appetite to build a house. So habitation, insofar as it is considered as a final cause, is nothing more than this singular appetite. It is really an efficient cause.
>
> (4pref, G II 207)

If final causes can be legitimate causes in this way—and there is every reason to think that they can and that Spinoza recognizes that they can—then why can't we see God as acting in a similar way with prior divine intentions causing certain actions which are performed with the purpose, say, of aiding human beings? Isn't this a way of legitimating divine teleology? What's wrong with such divine intentions or goals, especially if they flow from the necessity of God's nature?

This question really gets to the heart of the issue, and Spinoza has a twofold answer to it.

First, Spinoza says that even those who appeal to divine intentions in this way cannot genuinely explain very much of the detail of God's activity. Such partisans of teleology are quickly forced to appeal to our ignorance of God's will. Here's Spinoza's rather acerbic way of making this point:

> the followers of this doctrine [of divine purposiveness], who have wanted to show off their cleverness in assigning the ends of things, have introduced—to prove this doctrine of theirs—a new way of arguing: by reducing things, not to the impossible, but to ignorance. This shows that no other way of defending their doctrine was open to them. For example, if a stone has fallen from a roof onto someone's head and killed him, they will show, in the following way, that the stone fell in order to kill the man. For if it did not fall to that end, God willing it, how could so many circumstances have concurred by chance (for often many circumstances do concur at once)? Perhaps you will answer that it happened because the wind was blowing hard and the man was walking that way. But they will persist: why was the wind blowing hard at that time? why was the man walking that way at that same time? If you answer again that the wind arose then because on the preceding day, while the weather was still calm, the sea began to toss, and that the man had been invited by a friend, they will press on—for there is no end to the questions which can be asked: but why was the sea tossing? why was the man invited at just that time? And so they will not stop asking for the causes of causes until you take refuge in the will of God, that is, the sanctuary of ignorance.
>
> (G II 80–81)

This is a good point, but at most it shows that we do not know God's purposes. It does not make the stronger claim that there are no such purposes. Yet in his denial that God acts for the sake of an end, Spinoza clearly aims to make the stronger claim.

How then can he do that? One way to reach the stronger claim would be to deny that God has a will and, a fortiori, to deny that God has purposes focused specifically on finite beings. Spinoza is sometimes taken to do precisely this in 1p17s when he says that "the intellect and will which would constitute God's essence would have to differ entirely from our intellect and will, and could not agree with them in anything except the name" (1p17s, G II 62–63). But I do not think that this is accurate because I do not think that Spinoza denies that God has a will. Merely to say that if will constitutes God's essence, it would be completely different from ours is not to say that God does not have a will. After all, Spinoza is quite clear that will does not constitute God's essence (1p31). We will touch on God's will again in Chapter 4. Right now, I want to mount a Spinozistic attack on the claim that God has specific purposes in mind, purposes that favor certain finite beings more than others. This attack does not presuppose that God has no will at all. The following argument is not explicit in Spinoza, but, as I will show near the end of this section, there is evidence that Spinoza was thinking along these lines.

Let's say that a thing x is a finite thing for the sake of which God acts. I will speak of x as a particular finite thing, but the argument would go through if we were to take x as a kind of finite thing, such as human beings. Further, let's say that God wills to bring about other finite things in order to bring about, or to aid, x. Those other finite things are thus, in some way, subordinated to x. Finally, let's add a further point—one that Spinoza clearly accepts: each finite thing is part of an infinite series of finite things with infinitely many causes and effects (see 1p28 and 1p36).

This last claim is, of course, derived from the PSR. By the PSR, each finite thing must have a cause. But finite things cannot, as we have seen, come directly from God (1p23), so each finite thing must have a finite cause. Also, each finite thing must have a finite effect (and that effect must have an effect, etc.). This conclusion—which Spinoza draws in 1p36—also can be seen as derived from the PSR: if causal dependence just is conceptual dependence, and if from the concept of a given thing certain states of affairs must follow, then the thing in question must have some causal power. Because the equation of causation and conceptual dependence stems, as we have seen, from the PSR, Spinoza's claim that each thing has causal power also stems from the PSR. I will explore further—in the chapter on Spinoza's psychology—the causal power that each thing has.

Thus x, the finite mode in question, is necessarily in the midst of a series of finite causes and effects. But, we are supposing, x nonetheless outstrips other modes in importance to God. Why does God privilege x in this way instead of privileging some other finite mode, say, certain of x's causes or x's effects? x is neither the culmination of the series of finite modes, nor is it the starting point. So those natural reasons for privileging are not present. Nor can it be said that God privileges x because x is more like God than other finite modes. (This would be Leibniz's way of explaining why God favors so-called rational souls.) For each divine-like quality that x has (such as power, knowledge, etc.), there will be other, perhaps infinitely many other, finite modes that have those divine-like qualities to a higher degree. Spinoza makes this point with regard to power in 4ax1:

There is no singular thing in nature than which there is not another more powerful and stronger. Whatever one is given, there is another more powerful by which the first can be destroyed.

(4ax1)

And since, for Spinoza, perfection and power are coextensive,[26] we can conclude that there are infinitely many other finite modes that have more perfection than x does and are, as such, more similar to God. For this reason, any privileging of x in particular (or even of any finite collection of finite modes) would seem to be arbitrary, a brute fact. And, as such, Spinoza would reject it.

In this light, I think we should understand Spinoza's rejection of any special status for the Jewish people (TTP, chap. 3), his claim that God is equally gracious and merciful to all (TTP, p. 40), and Spinoza's claim that God does not have sympathy for some things and antipathy for others (Letter 19, G IV 90). Each of these views is a manifestation of Spinoza's naturalistic denial of any special concern on God's part for some things rather than others.

I think that this is a powerful argument on Spinozistic terms for the rejection of divine ends. But does Spinoza actually argue in this way? I admit that he does not explicitly do so, but given his systematic aversion to arbitrariness, such an argument seems to be a plausible reconstruction of his thought. Moreover and more importantly, it is hard to see how, in light of the challenges that I raised earlier to his denial of divine ends, he could offer a different defense on his own terms of that denial. For without this kind of argument, the door seems wide open for Spinoza to allow the legitimacy of privileging one finite mode over others.

We reach the perhaps unsettling conclusion that God is not, as it were, looking out for our interests or, indeed, for the interests of any other finite modes. We might seem to be, for Spinoza, on our own, hapless victims of the inexorable grinding away of Spinoza's one substance. Spinoza calls this substance "God or Nature." And while we can readily see why he would call this substance nature—after all it is the totality of what exists, a totality that is governed by fully natural laws and not supernatural principles—it is far from clear that this substance merits the appellation "God." In previous sections, we have already seen that Spinoza's God has some, to say the least, unusual qualities for a divine being: God is extended, God is the only substance that exists, God determines absolutely everything with absolute necessity, God does not transcend the world for, in some sense, God is the world. All of these characteristics are difficult to take from a traditional theistic perspective, but when one adds to this litany the fact that, for Spinoza, we human beings—both collectively and individually—hold no special place in God's plans or God's purposes, we may seriously doubt the propriety of his use of the term "God." Why should the one substance be called "God"? To begin to see how to answer this question, we need to see how, despite these questionable divine qualities, Spinoza's God is also supremely good, perfect and virtuous, and is capable of love and is the source of the kind of eternality that you and I can enjoy. In this light, the term "God" may seem more appropriate. But how Spinoza can say these things consistently with his naturalism is a story that will unfold in succeeding chapters.

SUMMARY

Spinoza's metaphysics is, in many ways, an effort to tap into the underlying rationalist motivations of Descartes's metaphysics and to follow through on these motivations more consistently than Descartes ever did. Employing the Cartesian notions of substance, attribute, and mode, and wielding strongly rationalist principles only hinted at in Descartes—such as the PSR and the Principle of the Identity of Indiscernibles—Spinoza is able to mount a powerful argument for substance monism, for the view that there is, fundamentally, only one thing in the world. On the same basis he argues for the concomitant view that you and I and the table are merely modes of merely states or properties of this one substance and not, as Descartes would have it, substances in their own right. Spinoza's PSR dictates that he holds not only determinism—the thesis that each event is determined by previous states of the world—but also necessitarianism, the much stronger thesis that all truths are absolutely necessary and that there is only one possible total sequence of events. Spinoza's PSR also generates his rejection of divine teleology, the view that God produces the world for the benefit of certain beings, such as, for example, human beings. On the contrary,

Spinoza says, God acts simply out of the necessity of his nature without singling out for special attention any particular finite beings.

FURTHER READING

Jonathan Bennett (1984) *A Study of Spinoza's Ethics*, chap. 3. (Helpful chapter on Spinoza's theory of substance.)

John Carriero (1995) "On the Relationship between Mode and Substance in Spinoza's Metaphysics." (Powerful argument that modes are merely properties of substance.)

———. (2005) "Spinoza on Final Causality." (Good account of Spinoza's attitude toward teleology in relation to Aristotelian and Scholastic Philosophy.)

Edwin Curley (1988) *Behind the Geometrical Method*. (Contains an accessible account of Spinoza's metaphysics as a development of Cartesian metaphysics.)

———. (1991) "On Bennett's Interpretation of Spinoza's Monism." (Sharp criticism of the view that modes are merely properties of substance.)

Gilles Deleuze (1992) *Expressionism in Philosophy: Spinoza*. (Difficult but useful treatment of Spinoza's metaphysics.)

Michael Della Rocca (2002) "Spinoza's Substance Monism." (Defends Spinoza's argument for monism from prominent objections.)

———. (2003a) "A Rationalist Manifesto: Spinoza and the Principle of Sufficient Reason." (Contains a direct argument for a necessitarian reading of Spinoza.)

———. (2006) "Explaining explanation and the Multiplicity of Attributes." (Defends Spinoza's view that there is more than one attribute.)

Don Garrett (1991) "Spinoza's Necessitarianism." (Fine defense of a necessitarian interpretation.)

———. (1998) "Teleology in Spinoza and Early Modern Rationalism." (Sees Spinoza as more friendly to purposiveness than do most interpreters.)

Martial Guéroult (1968, 1974) *Spinoza*. (Volume 1 is a monumental treatment of Part I of the *Ethics*.)

Yitzhak Melamed (forthcoming) "Spinoza's Metaphysics of Substance: The Substance-Mode Relation as a Relation of Inherence and Predication." (Powerful objections to Curley's reading of modes as not mere properties of substance.)

Marleen Rozemond (1998) *Descartes's Dualism*. (Useful account of Descartes's metaphysics of substance, attribute, and mode.)

Peter van Inwagen (2002) *Metaphysics*, second edition, chapter 7. (Argues for the claim that the PSR entails necessitarianism.)

Three

The Human Mind

Spinoza's philosophy of mind is, in many ways, the richest and most challenging part of his metaphysical system. Here, perhaps, more than anywhere else, Spinoza is ahead of his time: anticipating mind–body identity views that were to become much more popular only much later, anticipating the notion of a science of the psychological, every bit as strict as any science of the physical, and anticipating the representational theory of the human mind that grounds all the mind's properties in its ability to have thoughts about things. All of these positions are much more prominent now than in Spinoza's day, but are still extremely controversial. We will find Spinoza's philosophy of mind brimming with insights that are only now beginning to be understood. In part for this reason, much of Spinoza's philosophy of mind will also seem exotic and poorly motivated. While the appearance of exoticness cannot and should not be dispelled, the appearance of poor motivation can and should be. Here again our chief tool in casting away the obscurity is Spinoza's PSR in its twofold use, and here again the contrast with Descartes's treatment of these issues will be extremely useful.

1. PARALLELISM AND REPRESENTATION

The most fundamental question in the philosophy of mind, for Spinoza, is this: What is it for a thought or idea to represent, to be about, a particular object? This is the crucial question because, as we will see later in this chapter, all features of a mental state just are, or derive wholly from, its representational features. In this way, representation—and not, as Descartes would have it, conscious-ness—is the essence of the mental.[1] But not only is representation constitutive of the mental, Spinoza wants representation to be explained, he wants to give an account of what representation is, and, of course, he accounts for representation in terms of the notion of explanation itself, as we will now see.

To understand Spinoza's theory of representation, we must understand his thesis of parallelism. Here is the master statement of Spinoza's parallelism: "The order and connection of ideas is the same as the order and connection of things" (2p7). What can this possibly mean? Recall that, for Spinoza, there is a causal chain of modes of extension. 2p7 asserts that, for any extended thing, x, which is caused by another extended thing, y, there is an idea of x that is about x or represents x. This idea is caused by the idea of y which, in turn, is caused by the idea of y's cause, etc. Similar claims would hold for each extended thing, and thus there is a causal chain of ideas that is isomorphic with, that parallels, that has the same order and connection as, the chain of extended things represented by these ideas.

This elaborate mirroring between extension and thought is the embodiment, as it were, of Spinoza's explanatory and causal separation between the different attributes: for Spinoza, ideas enter into causal relations only with other ideas, just as modes of exten-sion enter into causal relations only with other modes of extension.

Spinoza's thesis of parallelism holds not just for the relations between modes of extension and ideas of them. The parallelism is more general; it is a parallelism of *things* and ideas. This point has two important implications. First, for modes of attribute 3 (an attribute other than thought and extension and thus unknown to human minds), there are parallel ideas that represent these modes of attri-bute 3. These ideas enter into causal relations that are isomorphic with the causal relations that modes of attribute 3 enter into.

Second, because ideas themselves are *things*, there is, for each idea, an idea of that idea. The ideas of ideas enter into causal relations with, and only with, other ideas of ideas, and these causal relations parallel those of what might be called first-level ideas.

Finally, although this is not strictly implied by 2p7 itself, Spinoza also holds that modes of any two non-thinking attributes are parallel to one another. Thus, for example, modes of attribute 3 are causally isomorphic with modes of extension. In this case, the parallelism is not a representational parallelism—because neither modes of extension nor modes of attribute 3 are representational— but it is a kind of parallelism nonetheless. Spinoza gives expression to this more general parallelism in 2p7s:

> whether we conceive of nature under the attribute of extension, or under the attribute of thought, or under any other attribute, we shall find one and the same order, or one and the same connection of causes, that is, that the same things follow one another.[2]

I will not dwell here on these ramifications of Spinoza's parallelism and will instead focus primarily on the parallelism between ideas of modes of extension and modes of extension themselves. This case by itself is most useful for illuminating Spinoza's philosophy of mind. I will, though, at various points turn to some issues raised by the notion of ideas of ideas.

How can Spinoza argue for this remarkable thesis? The demonstration of 2p7 is short and sweet:

> This is clear from 1ax4. For the idea of each thing caused depends on the knowledge of the cause of which it is the effect.

One can see how the axiom is relevant: it states, in part, that if there is an idea of an effect, then that idea depends on the idea of the cause of that effect. But 1ax4 does not get us all the way to parallelism. One problem is that 1ax4 seems to be merely a conditional claim: if there is an idea of an effect, then it depends on the idea of the cause. But, for parallelism to hold, there must actually be an idea of an effect, and 1ax4, by itself, doesn't guarantee that there is such an idea.

It's not hard to see how Spinoza would close this gap. Prior to 2p7, Spinoza has established that there is an idea of each thing: "In God there is necessarily an idea, both of his essence and of everything which necessarily follows from his essence" (2p3). We can see the PSR as undergirding this claim. Given the PSR, each thing is explainable, i.e. each thing can be conceived. Thus each thing is such that there can be an idea of it. Given necessitarianism—which also stems, of course, from the PSR—it follows that this is actually the case, i.e. there is actually an idea of each thing. In this light, it is instructive that in 2p3d Spinoza invokes 1p16, the core claim behind Spinoza's necessitarianism as we saw in the previous chapter.

This goes some distance toward plugging one of the gaps in Spinoza's argument for parallelism. There are other gaps as well, but I believe that these can be filled in similar fashion.[3] Let's leave these details aside and grant Spinoza that his argument is valid. An even more important question is whether the argument is sound, i.e. whether, in addition to the validity of the argument, the premises are true. This brings us to the crucial question: is 1ax4 true? Unfortunately, commentators have not, in general, been able to motivate this axiom in the way that it needs to be and can be motivated. To this extent, I believe, the grounds of the thesis of parallelism have remained opaque. However, light can be shed by turning to Spinoza's notion of essence and its connections with the notion of representation.

2. ESSENCE AND REPRESENTATION

Why should the idea of a thing depend, as 1ax4 suggests, on the idea of the causes of that thing? The answer to this question can be seen as turning on Spinoza's notion of the nature or essence of a thing, and this is so because, for Spinoza, the representation of a thing is intimately connected to that thing's essence.

So let's focus, for a moment, on what the essence of a thing is. In particular, what is the essence of a certain mode, *x*? It will be helpful here to turn to Spinoza's definition of mode. Recall that, for Spinoza, following in a long tradition, the definition of a thing states its essence. Thus the definition of a mode will help us see what its essence is. Spinoza says in 1def5:

> By mode I understand the affections of a substance, or that which is in another through which it is also conceived.

The key point here is that the essence of a mode is to be a thing conceived through another. By contrast, as the definition of substance (1def3) makes clear, the essence of a substance is to be conceived through itself. Given that, as we saw in Chapter 2, the relation of cause and effect is nothing other than the relation of being conceived through, we can say that the essence of a mode is to be caused by other things. And we find Spinoza saying precisely this in a number of places. Thus he says in Letter 60: "the idea or definition of a thing should express its efficient cause."[4]

The picture, then, is this: by seeing what brings *x* into existence, one will grasp what *x* is most fundamentally, what its nature is and thus what it can do. In this way the causes and the essence of a thing explain the thing's abilities. This is simply a manifestation of the kind of explanatory notion of essence that Spinoza shares with Descartes, as we saw in the previous chapter. In tying the explanatory role of essence to a thing's causes, Spinoza is again following in a long tradition—in this case a tradition of offering genetic definitions of a thing, accounts of a thing's essence in terms of its genesis, its causes.[5]

Of course, once *x* is caused to exist, it will undergo changes that are partly due to its own nature and partly due to other things that are (to some degree at least) separate from the causes that brought *x* into existence. These changes are, in each case, due to the nature of *x* and also to the nature of the things with which *x* interacts.

Thus, for example, when a pin pokes my body, the changes in my body are due partly to the nature of my body and partly to the nature of the pin. Had a balloon—instead of the pin—struck my body, the effect on my body would have been much different (in particular, there would have been far less yelling and screaming), and if the pin had struck the balloon, instead of my body, the effect would (again) have been very different—for one thing, the balloon would be far less likely to scream! Spinoza sums up the point this way:

> All modes by which a body is affected by another body follow both from the nature of the body affected and at the same time from the nature of the affecting body, so that one and the same body may be moved differently according to differences in the nature of the bodies moving it. And conversely, different bodies may be moved differently by one and the same body.
>
> (Axiom 1″ after 2p13s)

Given that the essence of a thing is to have certain causes, we can see that Spinoza is committed to the uniqueness of essences: no two things share the same essence. One can see why this is so in the following way. Let's say that x and a distinct thing, y, share the same essence. Because x and y are different, we can ask: in virtue of what are they different? There must be some feature in virtue of which they differ, otherwise their non-identity would be a brute fact and this, of course, Spinoza will not allow. Let's say that the individuating feature is F and that x has F and y lacks F. This feature will be part of the explanation of x's existence as a distinct thing, distinct, in particular, from y. Thus, given the equivalence between explanation and causation, this feature will be part of the *causes* of x's existence. Given that a thing's causes are, for Spinoza, built in to its essence, we can see that x's being F will be part of the essence of x and, because y lacks F, y's being F will certainly not be part of the essence of y. Thus x and y have different essences after all.

So, given Spinoza's PSR and given the causal notion of essences, it turns out that Spinoza is committed to the uniqueness of essences. We can see this commitment explicitly in 2def2:

> I say that to the essence of any thing belongs that which, being given, the thing is necessarily posited and which, being taken away, the thing is necessarily taken away; or that without which the thing can neither be nor be conceived, and which can neither be nor be conceived without the thing.

Because the essence of a thing cannot be without the thing, Spinoza is saying that if the essence of a thing is present, then the thing is present. If another thing were to have the essence as well, it would seem that the essence could be present without the thing. But this would seem to contradict the definition.

It must be admitted, however, that there are passages in which Spinoza seems not to respect this commitment and to allow that men, for example, "can agree entirely according to their essence" (1p17s).[6] It's not clear how to reconcile such passages with 2def2. One strategy might be to see Spinoza as speaking of essences at different levels of generality and specificity. Thus there is the essence of Peter, insofar as he is a human being, and there is also the essence of Peter insofar as he is Peter. The former essence can be shared, but the latter, perhaps, cannot. In any event, however these passages are to be reconciled, the key point is that, according to one major strand in Spinoza's thinking, essences of individuals are unique.

We can see in Spinoza's notion of essence another twofold use of the PSR. Spinoza first asks for an account of what it is to be a particular thing; he is thus demanding that a thing's essence be made intelligible. This is the first use of the PSR. Spinoza meets this demand by appealing to the fact that a thing is caused, i.e. explained or made intelligible in a certain way. So what it is to be a thing can be explained, and it is explained in terms of the notion of explanation itself. Here again is the characteristic rationalist move. We will see in Chapter 7 that not only the essence of thing but also its existence is intimately bound up with its intelligibility.

Let's return to the connection between essence and representation. For Spinoza, to represent a thing is to grasp its essence. There are different ways to see why this is so. Perhaps the following is the simplest.[7] Let's begin with the claim we wish to argue for, namely that to represent a thing is to represent its essence. Let's say that the thing represented is a mode of extension, x, and its essence is E. What would happen if we denied this claim; if we allowed—as seems initially quite plausible—that one can represent a thing without representing its essence? Perhaps one represents x not by grasping its essence E, but by grasping some feature F, besides E, that x has and that is due to y, separate from x. Thus one might represent Emma Thompson not in terms of her essence, but simply as the lead actress in the film, Howards End. One may thus represent Emma Thompson without grasping her essence.

To see what would, for Spinoza, be wrong with a scenario in which an extended object is represented via a grasp of a feature, F, that doesn't stem simply from x's essence, consider the following question: Given that the idea is about the thing that has F, why is that idea about x in particular? The answer, it seems, is that this is because x is the thing with F. Fine, but this fact—that x is the thing with F—depends, as we stipulated, on some object other than x, namely y. Because x is extended and because extended things interact only with other extended things, y too must be extended. In light of the fact that the idea of the thing with F is about x because x is the thing with F, and in light of the fact that x is the thing with F because of some other object, y, it follows that the idea is of x because of some other object, y. And now we reach a problem that would trouble Spinoza: here a certain mental fact—that an idea represents a certain object—is explained by a certain fact concerning not thought, but extension, namely the fact that y exists. But this explanation of something mental in terms of something physical would violate the explanatory barrier. A similar problem would arise, I believe, for each purported case of representation of a thing in terms of its non-essential features.

By contrast, the same problem does not arise for representation of a thing in terms of its essence. The parallel question here would be: Given that the idea is of the thing with essence, E, why is it of x? Answer: because x is the thing with E. But if we ask the next parallel question, we reach nonsense: Given that E is the essence of x, and given that, for Spinoza, as we have seen, the essence of a thing simply amounts to the very intelligibility of the thing, the way in which that thing must be understood, it follows that to ask why x has E is as silly as asking why squares have four equal sides. It's part of the essence, and indeed part of the concept, of squares to have four equal sides—this is how squares must be understood. In the same way, it's just x's concept or essence to have E. So, for Spinoza, given that the idea is of the thing with E, the reason that the idea represents x in particular does not invoke any dependence on an extended object and thus does not violate the explanatory barrier between thought and extension. For Spinoza, in the case of representation of a thing in terms of its essence, which object is represented is determined simply by the nature of the thought itself and by the features grasped in the thought. No help from any extended object, such as y, is required and so the explanatory barrier is preserved.

Evidence that Spinoza holds the general view that the explanatory barrier precludes factors other than thought from determining the object of representation can be found in 2p5 and its demonstration:

> Ideas, both of God's attributes and of singular things, admit not the objects themselves, or the things perceived, as their efficient cause, but God himself insofar as he is a thinking thing.
>
> [2p5]

> This is evident from [2]p3. For there we inferred that God can form the idea of his essence, and of all the things that follow

necessarily from it, solely from the fact that God is a thinking
thing, and not from the fact that he is the object of his own idea.

(2p5d)

Spinoza here seems to say that the fact that there is an idea of a
particular object is to be explained completely in mental terms and
not in terms of any other attribute. This consideration would rule
out representation of things that does not proceed via a grasp of
their essence.

With this account of representation as grasp of essence, we can
now see why Spinoza also insists on 1ax4 and thus insists on parallelism. Because the essence of a thing is, as we have seen, its
place in an explanatory network, to grasp the essence of a thing is
to explain it, to see it as intelligible. Since, as we have also seen, to
represent a thing is to grasp is essence, it follows that to represent a
thing is to explain it, to find it intelligible, to see how it follows
from its causes. And this is more or less what 1ax4 offers: the idea
of a thing depends on and involves the ideas of its causes.

This motivation for 1ax4 and parallelism helps to resolve a lin-
gering worry about representation that must now be addressed. If
representation of x is to be accounted for in terms of having a grasp
of a certain essence, E, then how are we to account for the grasp of
the essence? In virtue of what does a given idea count as a grasp of
a given essence? Until we answer that question, an old problem
may seem to arise again. For it seems that the natural thing to say is
that the idea of E is about E simply because it has some relation to
E itself. If that's the case, then again it seems we have a mental fact
(namely the fact that the idea is of E) being dependent on something extended, namely E, the essence of an extended mode. And,
here again, despite our best efforts to avoid this result, we have a
violation of the explanatory barrier. A different account of the idea
of E is needed and, in light of the recent argument for parallelism,
this is not hard to find. Recall that, for Spinoza, there is an infinite
chain of modes of extension (1p28). Each of these modes has its

own, distinct essence. The essences in this chain depend on one another; thus E depends on essence E′ (the essence of the cause of x), etc. Because parallelism holds, we can also say that the idea of E depends on the idea of E′, etc. So the idea in question is of E because it is the effect of the idea of E′, etc. There is no dependence here of the idea of E on E itself or on anything else extended and so the explanatory barrier is preserved.

We can see in this account of representation another twofold use of the PSR. First, Spinoza asks for an account of what it is for an idea to represent a certain object. He wants an explanation of what representation consists in. This is the first use of the PSR in this case. The account he offers is that representation of a given object is simply explaining that object, to represent an object is to find it intelligible in terms of its causes. Thus representation is to be explained and it is explained in terms of the notion of intelligibility itself. And so we can see how Spinoza's theory of representation is fundamentally rationalist.

3. PARALLELISM AND MIND–BODY IDENTITY

Spinoza's parallelism embodies in many ways a deeply anti-Cartesian view. By keeping the causal chains of modes of extension somehow separate from the causal chains of modes of thought, Spinoza is guided by his overarching denial of any explanatory connections between the mental and the physical, i.e. of connections of the kind that Descartes, in his account of mind-body interaction, quite happily embraces. But precisely because Spinoza separates the causal chains in this way, there might be thought to be a crucial point of agreement between Descartes and Spinoza on the nature of mind-body relations. Descartes holds, as we saw, that the mind and the body or, more generally, mental things and extended things, are not and cannot be identical. This is Descartes's dualism, and Spinoza's parallelism may seem to put him in the dualist camp as well. 2p7 seems to offer the following picture: here's one set of things—modes of extension—and here's another—ideas or modes of thought—which are connected with one another in the same way that the things in the first set are connected. On this picture, we seem to have mental things and physical things belonging to two separate classes, and this would be a kind of dualism.

But this dualist picture is actually not Spinoza's. For him, each idea and the mode of extension to which it is parallel are, as Spinoza says, "one and the same thing" (2p7s), and thus Spinoza explicitly embraces in Part II a monism of finite mental things and finite extended things that is analogous to the monism of extended substance and thinking substance that he embraces in Part I. While parallelism does imply some kind of dualism, as we will see, it is not a dualism of extended things and thinking things, as in Descartes.

To see what kind of dualism Spinoza is committed to, let's see what supports Spinoza's claim that ideas and modes of extension are identical. This support comes largely from the kinds of consideration that also lead to Spinoza's substance monism and that were canvassed in the previous chapter. So I can be brief here.

Recall that Spinoza accepts the Principle of the Identity of Indiscernibles, and thus there must, for him, be a legitimate way of explaining the non-identity of any two distinct things. Take an idea and its parallel mode of extension, and assume, contrary to Spinoza, that these things are not identical. What difference in properties could explain this non-identity? Notice first that, because of parallelism, these things have very many properties in common. After all, each plays the same role in a system of causes and effects. Given that the order and connection is the same, if a mode of extension has a certain number of immediate effects, if it has a certain degree of power, then the parallel mode of thought—the idea of that mode of extension—has the same number of immediate effects and has the same degree of power. Because parallelism guarantees that all the properties concerning order and connection are shared by parallel modes, these properties cannot do the job of explaining the purported non-identity between the mode of thought and the mode of extension in question.

Are there any properties that *can* explain the non-identity here? Perhaps the fact that the idea is thinking, is mental, and the fact that the mode of extension is extended preclude them from being identical. However, to appeal to the properties of thought and of extension to ground the non-identity would be to violate the explanatory barrier. The reasoning here is the same as in the case of the argument for substance monism. That a mode is thinking cannot preclude it from being identical to a mode of extension because this would make a fact concerning extension, namely the fact that a given mode of extension is not identical to a thinking thing, depend on something mental, on the fact that a given mode is thinking. This dependence would violate the explanatory barrier and so Spinoza would reject it. Thus the facts that a mode of extension is extended and that a mode of thought is thinking cannot legitimately individuate these modes. And, as we saw in the case of parallel modes, these modes share all their properties that concern order and connection. These properties, therefore, also cannot legitimately individuate these modes. So what properties are left in order legitimately to individuate these modes? It seems that there are none, and thus, in the absence of an explanation of non-identity, the Principle of the Identity of Indiscernibles and the PSR dictate that these modes are identical. So, far from entailing the non-identity of modes of thought and modes of extension, Spinoza's parallelism actually leads to the claim that they are identical. It is in virtue of the shared attribute-neutral properties concerning order and connections that there is one thing here and not two.

Given this identity, parallelism may seem puzzling. It's hard to shake the impression that, in stating his parallelism, Spinoza is invoking separate collections of things that are similarly structured. It's hard, in other words, to dispel the appearance of dualism. Quite right, but the dualism here is not, for Spinoza, a dualism of extended things and thinking things. Rather the dualism is a dualism of *ways of conceiving* or *explaining* the same thing. One and the same thing can be explained in terms of thought, as following from the attribute of thought, and also and separately can be explained in terms of extension, as following from the attribute of extension. When we explain a thing as thinking, we must explain it through things considered as thinking, and when we explain a thing—the same thing—as extended, we must explain it through things considered as extended. The things themselves don't run on parallel tracks, for Spinoza, rather the ways of conceiving or explaining the things do. Spinoza vividly expresses this point in 2p7s:

> so long as things are considered as modes of thinking, we must explain the order of the whole of nature, or the connection of causes, through the attribute of thought alone. And insofar as they are considered as modes of extension, the order of the whole of nature must be explained through the attribute of extension alone.

All of these points apply to the human mind and the human body because, as we will see presently, for Spinoza the human mind is the idea that is parallel to the human body. So the identity between parallel modes is a general version of Spinoza's mind-body identity thesis. In developing such a thesis, Spinoza is a clear forerunner of the many modern views that see the mind not as something over and above the body, but as somehow identical to it. Such an identity was very threatening to many in Spinoza's day, as it is in our own. For it might seem that if the mind just is the body, then the hope of some kind of existence after the inevitable destruction of the body would be unfounded. One of Descartes's aims in arguing for mind-body dualism was precisely to preserve the possibility of some kind of continued existence of the mind. As we will see much later, despite his mind-body identity thesis, Spinoza wants to preserve some kind of existence of the mind after the destruction of the body. Whether he can pull this feat off and what the significance of this kind of existence would be remains to be seen, and will be seen in Chapter 7.

But, independently of these concerns with the issue of post-mortem existence, it is important to see that, while Spinoza does anticipate modern identity theories in a striking way, his version of the identity claim is, in some respects, not standard and, for that reason, extremely interesting. It might be helpful to lay out roughly several options in the philosophy of mind. First, there is dualism according to which the mind and mental states are not identical to the body and physical states. This is the Cartesian position. Second, there are non-dualist positions that identify the mind and body or the mind and something physical, such as the brain. Spinoza is clearly such an identity theorist. Among identity theorists, there are those that hold that the mental properties of a thing are to be completely explained by and depend on its physical properties which are in some sense more fundamental. Such a theorist would be physicalist. By contrast, an idealist holds that mind and body are identical and, more generally, that physical things just are mental things, and also holds that the mental properties of a thing explain and are more fundamental than its physical properties.

In terms of these descriptions, Spinoza is, despite being an identity theorist, neither a physicalist nor an idealist. This is because of Spinoza's strict explanatory barrier between the attributes which rules out any mental-physical dependence of the kind that both idealists and physicalists invoke. For Spinoza, neither the mental nor the physical are reducible to the other. Rather, they are two separate ways of explaining the same things.[8] In this respect, within contemporary philosophy, Spinoza's position is very similar to Donald Davidson's. Davidson also rejects at least certain kinds of explanatory connections between the mental and the physical and, like Spinoza, employs the lack of these connections as part of the basis for the identity between mental things and physical things.[9] Nonetheless, there are significant differences between Spinoza and Davidson: Davidson rejects any strict science of the psychological.

For Davidson, there are strict laws governing the physical, but no strict laws governing the psychological. Thus for Davidson, the psychological is special, not governed by the same kinds of principles at work throughout nature. This would be a violation of naturalism, according to Spinoza, and thus Spinoza would insist, contra Davidson, on a science of the mental that is every bit as strict and fundamental as the science of the physical, even though there are no explanatory connections between the mental and the physical.

4. THE IDEA OF THE HUMAN BODY

Let us look more closely at the role of the human mind in Spinoza's parallelism. As always with Spinoza, it is helpful to begin with God. The system of ideas that are parallel to modes of extension constitutes God's infinite intellect. These infinitely many ideas are simply the thoughts that God has and the means by which he knows everything. Spinoza ties his parallelism directly to God's intellect in 2p7c:

> God's power of thinking is equal to his actual power of acting.
> That is, whatever follows formally from God's infinite nature
> follows objectively in God from his idea in the same order and
> with the same connection.

Of course, for Spinoza, not only does God's infinite intellect exist, but also finite minds, including human minds, exist. What is the relation between such a finite mind, say, my mind, and the ideas that make up God's infinite intellect? My mind is obviously a thinking thing, but equally obviously for Spinoza, it cannot be a thinking *substance*. Only God is a thinking substance. Thus, my mind must, for Spinoza, be a mode of thought. And since, as we will see in the next section, all modes of thought are or reduce to ideas, my mind must simply be a mode of the thinking substance, i.e. an idea in God's intellect, or, perhaps, a collection of such ideas.

Further, the content of this idea (or ideas) must, for Spinoza, be a function of the content of the idea as it is contained in God's intellect. That is, whatever the idea that is my mind represents, it must represent because that is what is represented by the idea insofar as it is in God's intellect. As Spinoza says in 2p11c:

> the human mind is a part of the infinite intellect of God. Therefore, when we say that the human mind perceives this or that, we are saying nothing but that God, not insofar as he is infinite, but insofar as he is explained through the nature of the human mind, or insofar as he constitutes the essence of the human mind, has this or that idea.

One can easily see why this is so: if the representational content of the idea that is the human mind could not be derived from the representational content of that idea insofar as it is in God's intellect, then where would this new representational content come from? It would seem to be wholly arbitrary—a brute fact—if the contents of the human mind diverged in this way from the content of the relevant idea in God's intellect. To say this, however, is not to say that there cannot be a difference between representation in the human mind and representation in God's mind. There is a difference, and it is important, as we shall see. But the point here is that representation in the human mind must derive from, be a function of, representation in God's intellect on pain of violating the PSR.

Here is a crucial question: Which of the ideas in God's intellect is the idea that is the human mind? Spinoza's answer turns on two important axioms:

> We feel that a certain body is affected in many ways.
>
> (2ax4)

> We neither feel nor perceive any singular things except bodies and modes of thinking.
>
> (2ax5)

Initially the meaning of these axioms is somewhat obscure, but as is the case with so many of Spinoza's crucial claims, their meaning becomes much clearer once one sees the use to which they are put in Spinoza's demonstrations. 2p13d plays this elucidating role for these two axioms. There Spinoza takes 2ax4 to show that the mind is aware of (feels, *sentit*) a particular body, its own body, and he takes 2ax5 to show that the mind is not aware of any other body in this way. The general point here is rather plausible: we have a kind of awareness of our own bodies that we do not have of other bodies. As we will see shortly, Spinoza also holds that the human mind does represent things other than its body, but it does so only via the representation of its body. In this way, one's body, for Spinoza, provides the point of view from which one represents anything else.

Why does Spinoza accept these axioms understood in this way? It's not clear. After all, they are axioms and thus do not receive any explicit argument. However, I will soon go some way toward developing a Spinozistic motivation for these axioms.

But first, with 2ax4 and 2ax5 in hand, we can see why Spinoza holds that the idea of God's that is my mind must be God's idea of a particular body, the body that I feel, my body. Here's one way to make this point. Call my body "A." Let's say—contra Spinoza—that my mind is the idea not of A, but of some distinct body, B. If so, then how could my mind be aware of, how could it represent, body A, as 2ax4—as clarified by 2p13d—says? Given that my mind is, on this scenario, the idea of something else, B, how could my mind also come to have this other content and represent A? Where would this additional content come from if it is not already part of the content of God's idea? Further, if my mind is the idea of some body other than my own, i.e. if it is of B, then this is not compatible with 2ax5 which rules out such awareness of other bodies in the human mind. So, given 2ax4 and 2ax5, my mind can only be God's idea of my body.

But how, though, can these axioms be motivated? Again, Spinoza does not offer an explicit argument, but we can go some distance toward seeing how he might do so. Let's begin with a basic point about Spinoza's theory of individuals. For Spinoza, a collection of things constitutes a singular thing or individual to the extent to which the members of this collection join together to have certain effects (2def7).[10] This point is also rather plausible. The cells that make up the human body, for example, join together to produce many effects—in my case, they produce the marks on the pages that constitute this book, they produce the bodily motions that led to my buying the latest Paul McCartney CD, etc. By contrast, collections of things that are relatively causally independent do not, to that extent, constitute a singular thing. Thus, intuitively, my right thumb, Bill Clinton's nose and the dark side of the moon don't seem to have many joint effects, and to that extent, this relatively disparate collection of things does not constitute a singular thing.

Here again we have a twofold use of the PSR. Spinoza offers an explanation of what it is for a thing or collection of things to be one thing, and what it is for a thing or collection of things to be one thing is for it to have effects, is for it to have things explained or made intelligible in terms of it. Once again, a key metaphysical notion—in this case, being a singular thing—is explained in terms of the notion of explanation itself.

For Spinoza, obviously, the human mind, as well as the human body, are individuals (actually, they are the same individual). However, this individuality of the human mind would be threatened if the human mind were made up of ideas whose contents were relatively disparate, if these ideas were not all focused around a particular unified thing, such as the human body. To see why this is so, recall that parallelism dictates that the ideas of things will be connected, to the extent that the things represented are connected. It follows that if the ideas that make up my mind were of relatively disconnected things, then those ideas themselves would be relatively disconnected, and so these ideas will not form a unified mental individual, a mind. So, given parallelism, to the extent that the human mind is a single mental individual, the ideas in the mind must be focused on, must represent, a single extended individual, just as 2ax4 and 2ax5 state.

But why must the individual that my mind is focused on be my body and not some other equally unified body? Spinoza doesn't take up this question directly, but it's not difficult to see what his answer might be. If my mind is focused on, represents in some direct sense, not my body, A, but say your body, B, then in what sense is A mine instead of B being mine? After all, my mind—if it represents B instead of A—will be parallel to B and given parallelism, it will, as we saw in the previous section, be identical to B. If my mind is, for this reason, identical to body B, it seems that nothing more is needed for B to be my body and for A not to be, after all, my body.

Thus, for Spinoza, what it is for a body to be my body is simply that my mind represents that body. And, as we have seen, what it is for an idea to represent a body is for the idea to represent the body's place in a causal network, i.e. for the idea to be the explanation of the body in thought. This is another twofold use of the PSR. The mineness of my body must be explained, and it is explained in terms of the notion of representation and ultimately of explanation itself.

5. THE PANCREAS PROBLEM, THE PAN PROBLEM, AND PANPSYCHISM

Let's now explore three further, interrelated problems with the thesis that my mind is God's idea of my body. Each of these problems arises naturally from Spinoza's system which has, I will argue, the resources to provide answers to them. These solutions will lead us to see even more clearly how fundamentally rationalist Spinoza's philosophy of mind is.

I call the first problem "the pancreas problem." For Spinoza, my mind is the idea of my body. And just as the body is a complex individual made up of many parts and with many states and which undergoes many changes, so too—given parallelism—the mind is a complex individual made up of many parts (2p15) and with many states and which undergoes many changes. In each case, the ideas parallel to the parts, states or events represent those items.[11] This means, for example, that my mind contains ideas that represent changes going on in my pancreas right now and, indeed, ideas that represent all the changes going on in my other internal organs. Spinoza makes this point in 2p12:

> Whatever happens in the object of the idea constituting the human mind must be perceived by the human mind, or there will necessarily be an idea of that thing in the mind; that is, if the object of the idea constituting a human mind is a body, nothing can happen in that body which is not perceived by its mind.

As Spinoza makes clear in 2p12d, this claim is forced on him by the logic of his parallelism. And it does seem that Spinoza has a real insight here, one that turns on the PSR. Why should some of my bodily states be represented by my mind and others not? Where can one draw the line in a principled way? Spinoza would refuse, of course, to draw an unprincipled line, so he draws no line at all: for him, all my bodily states are represented in my mind, even individual states of my pancreas (whatever they might be). As with so many principled conclusions, this one seems very hard to swallow. How could I perceive in any way all the changes that occur in my body? Yes, I am certainly aware of some of the changes occurring in my body (just consider hunger or pain), but it seems absurd to say that I represent *all* the states of my body. Margaret Wilson presses this worry, and suggests that a view that allows this much scope to the mental will "simply fail to be a theory of the mental."[12] Is there any way to make Spinoza's claim less unpalatable? This is the pancreas problem.

A related problem: Just as there is in God's mind an idea of my body, so too there is in God's mind an idea of each extended mode. And just as the idea of my body is my mind, so too the idea of each extended mode is, in some way, the mind of that mode. Thus *all* extended objects, no matter how apparently unthinking and inanimate, do indeed have minds. Not only I, but the rock, the plant, the kitchen clock, and the pan on my kitchen stove have minds. Mentality, for Spinoza, extends everywhere. Such a view is known as panpsychism. And although Spinoza doesn't use this term, he gives expression to this thesis in 2p13s:

> the things we have shown so far are completely general and do not pertain more to man than to other individuals, all of which, though in different degrees, are nevertheless animate. For of each thing there is necessarily an idea in God, of which God is the cause in the same way as he is of the idea of the human body. And so, whatever we have said of the idea of the human body must also be said of the idea of any thing.

One advantage of this doctrine is that Spinoza—in contrast to Descartes—readily accords a mental life to animals. Descartes saw animals as mere machines, without thought or consciousness, a view that Spinoza directly inveighs against (3p57s). Further, in extending mentality so broadly, Spinoza does seem to have a real insight based on the PSR. If thinking were to be associated with only some physical objects, then where could one draw the line in a principled way? Why does my body have a mind, but the pan does not? For Spinoza, there would be no principled line to draw, and so there is no line to draw at all.[13] Despite this insight, however, the view that pans and clocks have mentality may—once again—seem to disqualify Spinoza's position as a genuine theory of the mental. The challenge here, again, is to make more palatable the view that mentality extends even to objects such as the pan.

In approaching both the pan and pancreas problems, we can perhaps take our cue from something Spinoza says in the passage just quoted from 2p13s, namely that all extended things are animate "though in different degrees." If we can make sense of greater or lesser degrees of animation, then perhaps we can make sense of Spinoza's panpsychism and the mindedness of the pan. Similarly we might, in that case, be able to make sense of the claim that I represent all the changes in my body: if such representation need involve awareness only to a very small degree, then perhaps it wouldn't be so bad to say that I represent changes in my pancreas. More generally, if Spinoza can articulate a view according to which consciousness comes in degrees in this way, then perhaps we can make headway on our two problems.

In this regard, it is helpful to note that Spinoza's immediate successor Leibniz, who was also a panpsychist and believed that I represent all changes in my body, does appeal to varying degrees of consciousness for precisely this reason.[14] Spinoza doesn't have a theory of consciousness nearly as well worked out as Leibniz's. And, in fact, some of the things Spinoza says about consciousness seem to make an appeal to consciousness unable to help resolve the pancreas and pan problems. I have in mind here the passages in which Spinoza seems to think that consciousness is simply having ideas of one's ideas.[15] This theory of consciousness as higher order thought is fairly common (and there are strands of it Leibniz too), but such a theory doesn't by itself seem to give us a handle on degrees of consciousness: either one has an idea of one's idea or one does not. There doesn't seem to be a middle ground when it comes to ideas of ideas, and thus there doesn't seem to be an entry here for the notion of degrees.

However, there is another strand in Spinoza's thinking about consciousness which is potentially very helpful in approaching our two problems. I will elicit this line of thought indirectly by introducing the third in our trio of problems. For Spinoza, as we have seen, my representation of things is a function of the content of those ideas of God's that are contained in my mind. Those ideas of God's that are in my mind are simply God's ideas of states of my body. Nevertheless, it certainly seems as though we represent external bodies—such as the pan!—all the time. Is this yet another deliverance of common sense that Spinoza is prepared simply to deny? Not exactly. Spinoza does want to preserve the intuitive view that we represent external things, but how can he do so consistently within the strictures imposed by his parallelism and his theory of the human mind? This is what I call the external-object problem.

Spinoza happily grants that we perceive external bodies, but he claims that we do so only by perceiving states of our own body. Recall that crucial axiom: "the knowledge of an effect depends on, and involves, the knowledge of its cause" (1ax4). As we saw, for Spinoza this axiom amounts to the claim that we represent things as the effects of certain causes. To grasp an object is already and thereby to have some grasp of its cause. Consider a state of my body that is caused by some external object. Let's say my trusty pan interacts with my body. Perhaps it reflects light in a certain way that affects my eyes and leads to changes in my brain. These changes are, ultimately, caused by the pan. Of course, there will be—as our discussion of the pancreas problem showed—an idea in my mind of those changes in my brain. Since any representation of a thing involves representation of its causes, it follows that in having the idea of the brain change, I am having also an idea of the cause of that change, i.e. an idea of the pan. Spinoza's point is the fairly commonsensical one that we perceive external bodies because of their effect on our body. He is simply adding the point that when we perceive the external body we are doing so in virtue of *perceiving* its effects on my body. Spinoza argues in precisely this fashion in 2p16 and its corollaries.

It is crucial to note that when we perceive external bodies in this way, we are inevitably *confused*. This is indicated by 2p16c2:

> the ideas which we have of external bodies indicate the condition
> of our own body more than the nature of the external bodies.

Here Spinoza seems to say that we confuse the external object with the state of my body that object causes. Indeed, he stresses that whenever we perceive things through the common order of nature, we can have only confused ideas not only of external objects but also of our own bodies and of our own minds (2p29s). Why are all these ideas inevitably confused?

Spinoza's general account of confusion seems to be the following. (This is apparent in his discussion in 2p40s1 of certain universal notions which for him are highly confused.) For Spinoza, an idea is confused when it represents, is about, two separate things and yet the mind is unable to distinguish these things by having an idea that is just of one of the objects and an idea that is just of the other of the objects. In a case where more than one thing is represented, lack of confusion requires being able to perceive the things separately. I think that this is a fairly plausible condition to place on being free of confusion.

When the body is affected by an outside object and the mind perceives the bodily effect as well as the outside object, all the ingredients for confusion are in place. Thus the idea in question is of two separate things: the bodily effect and the external cause. Further, the mind is unable to have an idea that is just of that effect and an idea that is just of the external object; for consider that each idea in the human mind is of its extended counterpart in the body. This follows from Spinoza's parallelism. Thus, since a given idea is of a bodily state, E1, and of the external cause, C1, of that state, no idea will be available in the mind to be just of E1 or just of C1. Each other idea is already committed, as it were, to being (at least) of some other bodily state. So the human mind can never catch up: because of its limited resources, it can never succeed in having an unconfused idea of C1. For the same reason it can never succeed in having an unconfused idea of its own state, E1. And now we can begin to see why, as Spinoza says in 2p29s, our ideas not only of external objects, but also of our own bodily states are confused. (By a similar line of reasoning it can be shown that our ideas of our own minds or mental states are also confused.)

The culprit behind all this confusion is the fact that the body is affected from without by external bodies just as the mind is determined externally by other ideas that are in God but are not contained in the human mind. It is this external determination of the mind that leads the mind to represent external bodies in a way that must always be tainted by confusion, because any idea that represents external bodies also has to represent a state of one's own body in such a way that one is unable to separate the contribution to the idea's content made by the external body and the contribution made by the bodily state. Thus Spinoza says that:

> the mind has, not an adequate, but only a confused knowledge, of itself, of its own body, and of external bodies, so long as it perceives things from the common order of nature, that is, so long as it is determined externally. ... For so often as it is disposed internally, ... then it regards things clearly and distinctly.
>
> (2p29s)

As Spinoza indicates here, such confused ideas are inadequate. For Spinoza, "inadequacy" is a technical term referring to ideas a given mind has but that depend on ideas not contained in that mind (2p11c). Here it is instructive to note that Spinoza explicitly links adequate ideas to the mind's being the complete cause of such ideas (3p3).

In this light, we can see two important points. First, God's ideas are never confused, they are always adequate. This is because God's mind is not subject to external causes; God's mind is always determined internally. In fact, the very same idea that is caused from outside my mind is not caused from outside God's mind. Thus that idea is confused and inadequate relative to my mind (see, for example, 2p28), but unconfused and adequate relative to God's mind.

Second point: for this reason also, it seems difficult, if not impossible, for the human mind to have genuinely unconfused and adequate ideas. How could any of our ideas fail to be caused—at some remove or other—from outside the mind? This is an important problem, but whether or not we can make sense of human ideas that are adequate simpliciter for Spinoza, he is, as we will now see, certainly entitled to appeal to—and he does appeal to—human ideas that have a greater degree of adequacy, but may not be fully adequate.[16]

Let's return now to the issue of degrees of animation. Spinoza's account of the perception of external objects gives us a new means of making sense of such degrees. The crucial notion Spinoza invokes in accounting for perception of outside objects is that of dependence on outside causes. Such dependence can come in degrees. That is, while most, if not all, of our ideas depend, at some remove, on ideas that are not contained in our mind, nonetheless some ideas may be less dependent on outside ideas than others. These ideas will be due more wholly to one's own mind and will, to that extent, be less confused and have a greater degree of adequacy.

It will be helpful to illustrate the notion of degrees of dependence on outside causes before turning to the case of the mind. (This is in keeping with Spinoza's own stated method, for he says in 2p13s that we can—and indeed have to—get at the differences among minds by looking at the differences among the corresponding bodies.) Let's say that the frying pan on my stove is so heavy and that I am so weak that I am unable to lift it without help from someone else. However, imagine that, after taking the right vitamins, I am able to lift the pan without assistance from anyone else. In this case, I become less dependent than I was previously on outside causes in the production of a certain effect. In the same way, one can envisage that a Spinozistic mind might gain greater independence from external causes in the production of certain ideas. These ideas would thus be relatively less confused and more adequate. Of course, neither my body nor my mind will achieve complete independence from outside causes, but one can, I believe, make sense of increasing independence in these cases.

Spinoza's notion of degrees of animation can usefully be understood in terms of degrees of independence of outside causes and thus in terms of degrees of confusion and adequacy. Spinoza makes this clear in 2p13s soon after making his point about degrees of animation:

> in proportion as the actions of a body depend more on itself
> alone, and as other bodies concur with it less in acting, so its
> mind is more capable of understanding distinctly.

Spinoza similarly ties degrees of consciousness to a mind's degree of independence of outside causes in 5p39s:

> he who, like an infant or child, has a body capable of very few
> things, and very heavily dependent on external causes, has a
> mind which considered solely in itself is conscious of almost
> nothing of itself, or of God, or of things. On the other hand, he
> who has a body capable of a great many things, has a mind which
> considered only in itself is very much conscious of itself, and of
> God, and of things.

On this way of seeing things, the problem with the pan is that it is less able to act on its own than are my mind and my body. Simply put, for Spinoza, there are more things that we can do on our own or more completely on our own, and thus more things that we can understand, than a pan can. From this point of view, that pan differs from us not in kind, but merely in degree of independence of ideas, and this difference exhausts the way we are to understand the difference between us and the pan with regard to being minded or animated. This is the way, I believe, Spinoza would approach the pan problem.

Of course, for this response to work, we would need to be confident that we are more able to do things on our own than is the pan. This idea does have some plausibility—after all, the pan just sits there and is not capable of the great variety of movements and activity that we are. Nonetheless, this plausible idea is still quite sketchy and needs more development than Spinoza provides.

A similar strategy may enable us to make some progress on the pancreas problem. For Spinoza, we are aware of changes in our pancreas, but only to a small degree. The reason that we are not more aware of these changes is that they are only to a small degree bound up with the activity of our body, with the ability to do more things on our own. However, this line of thought also is in need of much more development before it can really support Spinoza's position.

Further, even if a precise sense could be made out in which our bodies are more independent than the pan and in which particular pancreatic changes are less central to our bodily activities than other changes, what reason is there for thinking that this kind of independence and activity goes along with animation and consciousness? Here I think that Spinoza would have a ready, though controversial rejoinder: How else are we to understand animation and consciousness but in terms of causal independence in some such way? If animation and consciousness are not to remain inexplicable, a Cartesian mystery, they must be explained in terms of the notion of causal power in the above way. To appeal to something else beyond causal power, beyond what, as we have seen, a thing most fundamentally is, is to threaten to treat animation and consciousness as something merely tacked on to a thing and its essence. This would be a violation of naturalism and, ultimately, of the PSR. So, for Spinoza, any other explanation of animation and consciousness would be no explanation at all. For Spinoza, in effect, unless one wants to give up on these notions altogether, one must treat the degrees of animation and consciousness as simply the degree of causal independence of a mind.

Here again we see the characteristic twofold use of the PSR. Spinoza insists that animation and consciousness be explained. And he believes that they can be explained only in terms of the notion of a thing's degree of causal independence and the degree to which it approximates being the complete cause of other things, including its own states. Of course, for Spinoza, the notion of causation just is the notion of conceiving or explaining something. Thus to say that a thing is to some degree the complete cause of a thing is to say that it is to some degree the complete explanation of that thing. So, for Spinoza, animation and consciousness are to be explained and they must be explained in terms of the notion of explanation itself. Animation and consciousness can be made intelligible only as some form of intelligibility itself.

6. NOTHING BUT REPRESENTATION

In the previous section, we began to see how fundamental Spinoza's notion of representation is to his theory of the mind. But there's much more to the story than representation's role in accounting for consciousness. One might say—and I do say—that for Spinoza every feature of the mind as a mind is to be derived from its representational features, from the fact that the mind represents things. Thus Spinoza holds a thoroughly representational theory of the mind—and in this he anticipates a prominent strand in contemporary philosophy of mind.[17] This is in keeping with Spinoza's overarching rationalism, for not only is the aim of attempting to account for all mental phenomena in terms of a single feature a rationalist move, but also the use of representation for this purpose is thoroughly rationalist given that Spinoza's notion of representation just is, as we have seen, the notion of mental explanation, of giving reasons for things.

In this section, I will first outline briefly Spinoza's argument for the general view that everything in the mind is representational. I will then explore (in Section 7) how Spinoza seeks to show in particular that volition or the will is to be understood purely in representational terms. As we will see, this connection between will and representation will generate Spinoza's representational conception of belief and his trenchant attack on Descartes's theory of belief. Later in this chapter and in the succeeding two chapters, I will show how the representational nature of mind provides Spinoza with his response to skepticism and his account of epistemic justification (Section 8), and also provides him with his account of the emotions (Chapter 4) and of moral obligation (Chapter 5). Throughout all these arguments the twofold use of the PSR will be prominently on display.

First, let's explore Spinoza's argument for the claim that all mental states are representational—i.e. ideas—and that all features of mental states are to be explained in terms of representation. The view that all mental states are representational, are about things, are ideas in Spinoza's sense, is certainly not a commonsense view, the view of the person on the street. To the extent that the average person has a view of such matters, it is likely to be something like the following:[18]

> There are mental states that are not representational or merely representational. For example, fear is a mental state, but involves something more than the representation or idea that something harmful may happen to me. After all, one could imagine having the idea without any affective overlay. Fear may involve a representation, such as the one just mentioned, but it also crucially involves something over and above such an idea: a distinctive kind of feeling beyond anything representational that may be kicking around in the mind. Similarly, emotions such as love, hate and also perhaps other non-emotional states (such as will) also involve a distinctive feeling or other kind of non-representational state.

So much for the view of the person on the street. It's striking that—initially at least—Spinoza seems to agree with this commonsense view. It's striking because, as we have seen, Spinoza is so often not in line with common sense. Thus Spinoza says early in Part II of the *Ethics*:

> There are no modes of thinking, such as love, desire, or whatever is designated by the word affects of the mind, unless there is in

the same individual the idea of the thing loved, desired, and the
like. But there can be an idea, even though there is no other
mode of thinking.

(2ax3)

Here Spinoza seems to give expression to the standard view that
there are ideas, i.e. representations, and there are "other" modes of
thought which may presuppose certain ideas but are something
over and above these ideas. However, it's clear from the way Spinoza uses 2ax3 later in Part II that he sees himself as making a
much bolder claim. In the midst of his argument that the human
mind is God's idea of the human body, Spinoza says this:

The essence of man (by 2p10c) is constituted by certain modes of
God's attributes, namely (by 2ax2), by modes of thinking, of all of
which (by 2ax3) the idea is prior in nature, and when it is given the
other modes (to which the idea is prior in nature) must be in the
same individual (by 2ax3).

(2p11d)

Here Spinoza reveals that, contrary to what 2ax3 might suggest on
its own, he is not merely saying that affects and other similar mental
states somehow require or involve an idea (as the person on the street
would hold). Rather Spinoza is making the much stronger claim that
ideas fully account for modes of thought such as, love, desire, etc.[19]

To see why Spinoza would hold this view, consider what
would be the case if it were false, if there were two radically different kinds of mental states: ideas, i.e. representations, and non-
representational states such as the non-representational states pur-
portedly involved in fear, love, etc. Such a scenario would, I believe,
amount to a violation of Spinoza's naturalism and, ultimately, a
violation of the PSR.

Let's say that A is an idea or representation and that B is a non-
representational state in the same mind. In virtue of what are A

and B both mental states? What feature do these states have in common that enables us to classify each as mental? If there is nothing in virtue of which A and B are both thinking, nothing that explains why A and B are both mental states, then it would seem that there would be no reason why B—the non-representational state—couldn't belong to another attribute, say extension, rather than thought. That B is thinking would thus be a brute fact and this would obviously be unacceptable to Spinoza.

What then is it that makes A and B both thinking? A Cartesian would have a ready answer: consciousness, i.e. A and B are both such that the one who has these states is aware of them in a char-acteristically immediate way.[20]

But one could challenge this answer by asking: In virtue of what are these two, rather disparate, states both conscious? Here again, this fact can, it seems, be nothing other than a brute fact which would be unacceptable to Spinoza.

So let's return to the original question: What is it in virtue of which A and B are both thinking? Perhaps they are both mental in virtue of the fact that they causally interact with mental states. But this won't get us very far. For Spinoza, two things interact only because they belong to the same attribute, for example the attribute of thought.[21]

I know of no other plausibly Spinozistic way to answer the question what is it in virtue of which A, a representational mental state, and B, a non-representational mental state, are both thinking. Thus the existence of such disparate mental states would involve a brute fact for Spinoza and so be unacceptable. For Spinoza, the relation between A and B—their both belonging to the attribute of thought—would be unintelligible in the same way that mental-physical causal relations are, for Spinoza, unintelligible. In each case, two otherwise disparate items do not have enough in common to explain why they stand in these relations. In this way, the distinction between representational and non-representational states in the same mind is a replication of the mind–body problem within the mind itself. We can thus see that Spinoza's PSR forces on him the view—contrary to common sense—that if some mental states are representational, then all must be.

This line of reasoning would also lead to the view that not only are all mental states representational—i.e. ideas—but also all other features of ideas derive from their representational features. For consider: If there were both representational features of an idea and independent non-representational features of an idea, then in virtue of what would these rather different features be features of the same idea? So given that ideas are representational, then all features of ideas must, on pain of violating the PSR, somehow derive from their representational features. Again, this is a fully representational account of the mind and its contents.

It must be acknowledged that the lines of reasoning I have just articulated are not to be found on the surface of Spinoza's texts; yet I think that they are not far below the surface. This is particularly evident in the way Spinoza sees his thesis about the intelligibility of the relations among modes of thought as captured by his thesis of the parallelism between *ideas* and other kinds of modes. Thus, for Spinoza, the intelligibility of relations involving modes of thought is to be captured by relations specifically between ideas:

> the formal being of the idea of the circle can be perceived only through another mode of thinking, as its proximate cause, and that mode again through another, and so on, to infinity. Hence so long as things are considered as modes of thinking, we must explain the order of the whole of nature, or the connection of causes, through the attribute of thought alone.
>
> (2p7s)

Spinoza seems to be saying here that, in the realm of the mental, only ideas—only representations—enter into intelligible relations, relations that are compatible with the explanatory self-sufficiency of thought.[22]

7. REPRESENTATION, WILL, AND BELIEF

Spinoza's account of the will and his famous, but poorly under-stood, critique of Descartes's views on the relation between will and belief turn heavily on his view that all mental states are idea-tional. Here again I will begin with the view of the person (or phi-losopher) in the street.

On a standard reading of Descartes, the mind has two faculties, two basic capacities: intellect and will. The intellect is the mind's faculty of having ideas, representational states, states that are about things. These ideas are purely passive. The causal power or oomph, as it were, in the mind comes from the will, from its volitions which are active but non-representational mental states. Volition and intellect come together in all cases of action. Thus, to put it a bit crudely: I may have the idea that—the representation that—eating ice cream would be good and that there is ice cream nearby in the freezer. These ideas are not enough by themselves to get me to act; if they were, then—given that I have these ideas almost all the time—I would be eating altogether too much ice cream. Instead, a separate kind of mental state—an act of will, a volition—is needed to carry out the action. And, on any given occasion, I may or may not bring to bear an act of will on this matter, but when I do, I will act and get the ice cream or at least try to do so (if someone hasn't padlocked the freezer to save me from myself). On this view which sometimes seems to be at work in Descartes, the volition would be a non-representational mental state and would be just a bit of mental power, as it were.[23]

Spinoza, of course, has no patience for such separate volitions. For him, the power of the mind must come from ideas, from the intellect, alone: "the power of the mind is defined by understanding alone" (Mentis potentia ... sola intelligentia definitur; 5Pref). In denying separate acts of will, Spinoza does not deny that there are volitions. He merely holds that volitions are identical with ideas (2p49 and 2p49c). His reasoning here turns crucially on 2ax3 which, as we have seen, is a key place where Spinoza articulates the representa-tional nature of all mental states.

For Spinoza, ideas as such are active and inherently have a tendency to prompt action. Does this mean that, perhaps, my friends should after all put a padlock on the freezer because I will always be trying to get the ice cream? Not at all. For Spinoza, although each idea has some power, not all ideas are equally powerful. The default position, as it were, is that I will act on each idea I have. If I am to be prevented from acting on that idea, it must not be because an act of will separate from any idea leads me in the other direction; rather it must be because some other idea with greater power leads me in the other direction. Thus, my idea that eating ice cream is good may be overwhelmed by another idea I have, an idea that eating ice cream will lead to poor health. The latter idea may be more powerful and will thus lead me to refrain from going to the freezer. We will explain these matters in more detail in the next chapter when we discuss Spinoza's psychology, but for now the key point is that whether I act is a function solely of my *ideas* and not of any separate act of will.

Some of the most important implications of Spinoza's views on the representationality of volitions emerge when he considers Descartes's theory of belief. Descartes recognizes that there is a difference between merely having an idea and believing it. Thus I may entertain the idea that Emma Thompson is a Martian without *believing* it even for a second. Something more is needed for belief, according to Descartes, and this something is provided by the will. When I join a non-representational volition—in this case an act of assent—to an idea, then, and only then, is the idea believed. In this way, Descartes assimilates belief to ordinary action: *believing* that my stupid friends have locked the freezer and wielding an axe to break the lock are each actions in the same sense: they result from an appropriate combination of intellect and will, of representational and non-representational states.

This role for will in belief is especially important to Descartes because it enables him to get God off the hook for our having false beliefs. Descartes, especially in the Fourth Meditation, famously worries that a truly good God would not allow his creatures—for example you and I—to fall into error, as we obviously do with startling frequency. Descartes's account of the will and belief allows him to exonerate God: our false beliefs are a product of our will, and thus because for Descartes the will is free, these beliefs, these actions, are our fault, not God's. Thus Descartes maintains the goodness of God.

Spinoza, of course, has no truck with this account. For him the idea of a good God who genuinely looks out for his creatures and needs to be gotten off the hook implies a divine purposiveness which, as we have seen, conflicts with the PSR. Similarly, the notion of the freedom of the will is, for Spinoza, incoherent, also because of the PSR. We treated Spinoza's account of freedom briefly in the previous chapter and will return to the topic in more detail in Chapter 5. But the point I want to stress now is that Spinoza denies that acts of will separate from ideas have any role to play in belief formation. Spinoza agrees with Descartes that belief involves the notion of power. In this way, Spinoza would be happy to agree with Descartes in assimilating belief to action generally. However, for Spinoza, the mental power resides not in a separate volition, but in the idea believed itself. If an idea is not to be believed, that is not because I employed an act of will separate from all ideas, but rather because some other, more powerful idea led me to withdraw assent from the original idea. Thus even my idea that Emma Thompson is a Martian has some tendency to be a belief, but I don't actually assent to it because other ideas—for example the idea that no evidence of life, let alone evidence of movie stars has been found on Mars—are more powerful than this idea. Spinoza makes this point with an equally fanciful example:

> I deny that a man affirms nothing insofar as he perceives. For what is perceiving a winged horse other than affirming wings of the horse? For if the mind perceived nothing else except the winged horse, it would regard it as present to itself, and would

not have any cause of doubting its existence, or any faculty of
dissenting, unless either the imagination of the winged horse
were joined to an idea which excluded the existence of the same
horse, or the mind perceived that its idea of a winged horse was
inadequate. And then either it will necessarily deny the horse's
existence, or it will necessarily doubt it.

(2p49s)

One of Spinoza's rare images can help us grasp this point. He
says—on a couple of occasions—that we must not make the mistake
of seeing ideas as "mute pictures" on a panel or tablet. Instead, we
should recognize that "an idea, insofar as it is an idea, involves an
affirmation or a negation" (2p49s). For Spinoza, Descartes's ideas
passively waiting for volitions to bring them to life are mute pictures. But this Cartesian view must be wrong, says Spinoza, because
it would involve two radically different kinds of mental states, in
violation of the PSR. As I mentioned in the previous section, this
kind of view would simply be an objectionable replication within
the mind itself of the mind–body problem and of unintelligible
Cartesian interaction. Instead, we must see ideas as inherently
powerful, inherently active, and even inherently affirmatory. Of
course, other ideas may be more powerful and better able to lead to
affirmation or, as Spinoza might say, more strongly affirmed. Just
as, as we have seen, there are no differences in kind between
conscious mental states and apparently non-conscious mental
states, rather there are only differences in degree of consciousness,
so too ideas may differ in degree of affirmation, but there are
no differences in kind between ideas that are affirmed and ideas
that are not. Rather, all ideas enjoy a degree of power, a degree
of affirmation.

Here again, unsurprisingly, we see a twofold use of the PSR.
Spinoza asks, in effect, for an explanation of belief and mental
activity in general. This is the first use of the PSR. His answer is
that belief and mental activity do not turn on some mysterious

non-representational act of will. Rather these phenomena are to be explained simply in terms of ideas—mental representations—themselves. This is the second use of the PSR because, as we have seen, for Spinoza the notion of representation is just the notion of explaining something in thought. Thus belief and mental action are to be explained and what they are to be explained in terms of is the notion of explanation itself.

8. SKEPTICISM

In the early modern period, interest in skepticism underwent a revival. Much of the fascination was due to the renewed attention to ancient philosophy in which skepticism played a prominent role, but much of it also stemmed from the new science which, unlike the previous, Aristotelian science, refused to take the senses more or less at face value. Descartes explicitly engaged in discussions of skepticism in order to promote, as he puts it, detachment from sense. Spinoza, from early on in his career, was deeply influenced by Cartesian physics and was in many ways in tune with the anti-Aristotelian tenor of the new science. He was thus, like Descartes, motivated to consider skeptical scenarios that called the evidence of the senses into doubt.

Spinoza's attention to skepticism is more explicit and detailed early in his career when the influence of Descartes on Spinoza was strongest. Spinoza's early, unfinished work, the *Treatise on the Emendation of the Intellect*, was wholly devoted to the theory of knowledge and gave serious attention to skepticism. Spinoza's early book on Descartes's *Principles* begins with a long discussion of the so-called Cartesian Circle, of the charge that Descartes, after raising his skeptical doubts, uses illegitimate means to get out of the doubt. Much of the detailed treatment of skepticism drops out in the *Ethics* and, of course, it is not really present in the political writings. But it would be a mistake to think—as some have—that, by the time of the *Ethics*, Spinoza has more or less abandoned the issue of skepticism. There is indeed in the *Ethics* a well worked out and extremely interesting position on skepticism, one that is a consistent development of the views on this matter found in his earlier works, especially the *Treatise on the Emendation of the Intellect*. This underappreciated position constitutes, I believe, a highly unusual and specifically rationalist challenge to skepticism.

Let's begin with a sketch of the skeptic's position, as Spinoza sees it. Consider the skeptical scenario that Descartes concocts in the First Meditation. There Descartes comes to doubt that our sensory ideas—indeed any of our ideas—give us any knowledge, give us any purchase on reality at all. For the Descartes of the First Meditation, ideas, such as that there is a world of extended objects, and even our most coherent and compelling ideas, such as $2 + 2 = 4$, ideas that Descartes famously and obscurely calls clear and distinct, are called into doubt. To do this, he invokes the possibility that there is a maximally powerful deceiver bent on deceiving Descartes. As Descartes says from the abyss of this doubt, "there is not one of my former beliefs about which a doubt may not properly be raised" (AT VII 21/CSM II 14–15).

This kind of skeptic need not deny—and certainly the Descartes of the First Meditation does not deny—that we can have clear and distinct ideas, but for the skeptic these features do not constitute and, indeed, are not even necessarily connected with the certainty of the idea in question. More specifically, while these features may go along with the merely *psychological* certainty of such ideas, i.e. with the fact that such clear and distinct ideas are extremely compelling and perhaps impossible to doubt while one is attending to them, they are nonetheless, for our skeptic, not normatively certain, i.e. certain in a way that meets the standards for genuine knowledge. No matter how clear and distinct the ideas are, the skeptic says, they do not amount to knowledge or genuine normative (and not merely psychological) certainty. In what follows, whenever I speak of certainty I have in mind this kind of normative, not-merely-psychological certainty.

Equally, however, for the skeptic, the fact that such ideas are clear and distinct does not by itself constitute the fact (if it is a fact) that those ideas are not genuinely certain. For the skeptic, these ideas fail to be certain not because they are clear and distinct, but because of some further feature that is independent of clarity and distinctness. Although the lack of clarity and distinctness, i.e. some kind of internal incoherence, may entail that the idea in question is not genuinely certain and does not amount to knowledge, clarity and distinctness by itself does not, for the skeptic, entail lack of genuine certainty. So, for the skeptic, clarity and distinctness do not entail or constitute either certainty or its lack. Clarity and distinctness, on this view, are at most a merely psychological feature of ideas and not an epistemic one, i.e. not a feature having to do with knowledge.

What, then, does constitute the epistemic status of clear and distinct ideas if not their clarity and distinctness? For the skeptic, that epistemic status depends on epistemic features of ideas, typically other ideas. Why, on this view, doesn't a given idea amount to knowledge? Answer: because we cannot rule out a certain possibility, i.e. we do not know or are not certain that, an evil demon (or whatever) is not making it that case that the idea is false despite its clarity and distinctness and despite its seeming to us to be true. For the skeptic, being certain of an idea depends on being certain of such things as that God is not a deceiver. For the skeptic, if, per impossibile perhaps, the idea were to amount to knowledge or certainty, that would only be because we were already certain, for example, that God is no deceiver.

We can see, then, that for the kind of radical skeptic we are considering, there is a sharp divide between epistemic features of ideas (i.e. whether or not they are genuinely certain) and other features such as clarity and distinctness. And it is precisely because of this separation that the skeptic gets his skepticism going. If the epistemic status of ideas—or at least the certainty or positive epistemic status of ideas—were simply a function of their clarity and distinctness, then we would automatically have certainty just by having clear and distinct ideas. (Recall that this skeptic does not deny that we have clear and distinct ideas.) But because the epistemic status of ideas is a feature separate from clarity and distinctness, the door is left open for the skeptic. If the skeptic sees even an inch of daylight here, he will exploit it for all it's worth: for once the distinction is allowed, any putative fact that might be invoked to close the gap between clarity-and-distinctness, on the one hand, and truth, on the other, would itself be called into doubt and so could not legitimately close the gap.

This is, in effect, the problem of the Cartesian Circle alluded to earlier. The worry is that in setting up such a radical skepticism early in the *Meditations*, Descartes has dug himself a hole so deep that he has no way to get out. Any tool—and claim—that he might use to argue his way out of the doubt has already been swept away by the vast doubt.

There has been a bewildering variety of responses to this problem—some proposed by Descartes himself who was pressed on this very point by astute interlocutors. Spinoza's strategy for dealing with the radical skeptic is, I believe, rather distinctive, generally overlooked, and particularly powerful.

Spinoza pounces on the skeptic's basic thesis that there is a sharp divide between epistemic features of ideas and other features of those ideas. This separation would, in Spinoza's eyes, be a brute fact, a primitive, inexplicable separation between two features of a given idea. As we have just seen, on the Cartesian view from the representational features of an idea, in particular from the clarity and distinctness of an idea, we can draw no conclusion either way about the epistemic status of the idea. The epistemic status derives, in general, not from the idea's representational qualities, but from the *epistemic status* of other ideas. In this way, epistemic status cannot be derived from the representational features of ideas. And, obviously, the representational features of an idea cannot be derived from its epistemic status. For the skeptic, just by knowing that an idea does not amount to knowledge, we cannot infer that the idea is or is not clear and distinct or that it represents such-and-such an object in such-and-such a way. Thus we can see that the epistemic status and representational features of an idea are merely tacked on to one another: there is no way to explain the connection between the representational features of an idea and its epistemic status.

We can see this point in the following way: starting just from the representational character of an idea and even presupposing the representational character of other ideas as well, there is no way intelligibly to get to the epistemic status of that (or any other) idea. From the representational character alone, there is just no way to see the epistemic status coming, as it were. And from epistemic status alone there is no way to see the representational character coming.

We have seen this phenomenon already: in the will/intellect case, from intellect alone, from the nature of ideas qua ideas, there is no way to see the distinct Cartesian volitions coming. In the same way, on the Cartesian view from a physical change, there is no way to see a mental change coming. In each case, there is a relation between two things that must remain inexplicable, and in each case Spinoza would rule out this relation for precisely this reason.

Again, I believe, Spinoza would plead with us this way: "Hey, if you feel uneasy about the inexplicable relation, on the Cartesian view, between the mind and the body and, then you should feel equally uneasy about the inexplicable relation between representational character and epistemic status that is at the heart of the skeptical position." Spinoza would point out, in effect, that what's wrong with skepticism is that it conflicts with naturalism by introducing an illegitimate bifurcation between features of ideas, and that, ultimately, it conflicts with the PSR in much the same way that various other Cartesian dualisms do.

Instead of the skeptical primitive separation between features of ideas, Spinoza proposes a rival view according to which ideas are inherently certain and do not need any external help to achieve that status. What provides ideas with certainty, for Spinoza, is their most fundamental feature: their representational character. We find Spinoza saying precisely this in the *Treatise on the Emendation of the Intellect*

§35: "certainty is nothing but the objective essence itself, i.e. the mode by which we are aware of the formal essence is certainty itself." In speaking of the objective essence of a thing, Spinoza is using a traditional term, used also by Descartes and a host of other philosophers, to refer to the representation of a thing's essence. So Spinoza is saying that certainty is just representation itself.[24] Spinoza's account of certainty in terms of representation alone is also apparent from 2p43s where he says that certainty is understanding [intelligere] itself (G II 124). As we saw, for Spinoza, to represent is to explain or to understand or to make intelligible. So, given this conception of representation, he is saying in 2p43s that certainty is representation itself.

For Spinoza, then, by having a particular representational character, an idea is certain. In order for an idea that one has to be certain, one does not have to take the representational features as given and then ask the question: In virtue of what is an idea with these representational features certain (if it is certain)? No, his point is that the idea is certain by virtue of its representational features alone. Spinoza sums it up in remarkably similar fashion early and late in his career:

> truth requires no sign, but it suffices, in order to remove all doubt, to have the objective essences of things, or, what is the same, ideas.
>
> (TdIE §36)

> What can there be which is clearer and more certain than a true idea, to serve as a standard of truth? As the light makes both itself and the darkness plain, so truth is the standard both of itself and of the false.
>
> (2p43s)

In these passages, Spinoza clearly removes the primitive separation, removes the daylight, between representational character and epistemic status that is the hallmark of skepticism. Thus, just as he holds that ideas are inherently active, inherently affirmed, and inherently conscious, he also holds that ideas are inherently certain. In this case as in the others, Spinoza accounts for an important feature of the mind in terms of representation alone.

Once again, we have the twofold use of the PSR. Spinoza demands an account of—an explanation of—certainty and epistemic status in general. Certainty cannot be a free-floating, inexplicable feature of mental states. And the account he gives is of certainty as representation itself and thus as finding something intelligible in thought, i.e. as explaining a thing. Certainty is therefore explained in terms of explanation itself.

Of course, as in the other cases, to say that ideas are all inherently certain is not to say that they are all perfectly certain. For Spinoza, certainty comes in degrees, and so, as we have seen, do confusion and adequacy. The degree of certainty we are able to achieve is a function of the power of our mind and the degree to which the mind can do many things on its own. We are obviously quite weak in many ways, but the point remains: we are on the scoreboard when it comes to power. We thus enjoy some degree of certainty; we have some grasp—however confused—of the way the world is. We are not—as the skeptic would have it—completely cut off from knowledge of the world.[25]

Spinoza's strategy—of, in effect, investigating how much anti-skeptical weight the PSR can carry—is intriguing and promising. Whether this strategy can ultimately work would, of course, require further exploration. There are immediate challenges to Spinoza's position: first, this response to the skeptic is only as good as Spinoza's support for the PSR. We will have to wait until the end of this book to see how Spinoza might justify the PSR. A more specific worry is the following: even if the PSR is granted, it is still not clear just how representation, which, for Spinoza, guarantees certainty, can actually do this job. Because the certainty of an idea requires that it be true, the representational features of an idea must then somehow guarantee the truth of the idea. But how can mere representation pull off this remarkable task? The answer to this question—needed to complete Spinoza's case against skepticism—will have to wait until Chapter 7 where we explore Spinoza's account of existence and, hence, truth. But even before resolving these questions, we can see that Spinoza's anti-skeptical strategy testifies to the scope and systematic power of his rationalism and his use of the notion of representation.

SUMMARY

Spinoza's naturalism and rationalism are nowhere more evident and more relevant to contemporary philosophy than in his philosophy of mind. All there is to thought is the having of ideas, representations of certain things. Thus, in laying down requirements on what it is to have an idea or representation of an object, Spinoza is articulating the essence of the mental. Spinoza's strictures on representation turn on the enigmatic but crucial axiom: "The knowledge of an effect depends upon, and involves, the knowledge of its cause" (1ax4). Spinoza says here that to represent a thing is to represent its causes. This understanding of representation derives from his understanding of the essence of a thing as its having certain causes, and from his denial of any explanatory connections between the attributes. (In Chapter 7, we will see a different justification of this axiom.) The axiom is the primary support for Spinoza's mind-body identity thesis which, like his claim of the identity of the thinking substance and the extended substance, stems from his commitment to the Principle of the Identity of Indiscernibles and the PSR. For Spinoza, my mind is simply an idea in God's intellect; in particular it is God's idea of my body. Because each detail in extension is paralleled by and represented by an idea, it follows that my mind represents all the states of my body and that, likewise, each extended thing is represented by (and identical to) an idea in God's mind, an idea that is the mind of that thing. Spinoza thus embraces panpsychism, the thesis that all things are mental. He can mitigate some of the counterintuitive consequences of this view by attributing ever diminishing degrees of consciousness and mentality to less powerful beings. Spinoza's account of mental power constitutes a sharp critique of Descartes's theory of belief or judgment. For Spinoza, as for Descartes, judgment is simply a function of mental power or assent brought to bear on a certain idea. But whereas for Descartes, this mental power comes from a separate non-representational mental state (a volition), for Spinoza, assent is internal to an idea: each idea is, by its nature, powerful to some degree and so commands a degree of assent. This refusal to bifurcate mental states, as Descartes does, into passive, representational ideas and active, non-representational volitions reflects Spinoza's naturalism and his rejection of inexplicable disparities. Here the PSR is at work. The PSR similarly guides his response to radical skepticism. The radical skeptic draws a sharp line between the representational character of ideas (their clarity and distinctness, in Descartes's terms) and their epistemic status, i.e. their amounting to genuine certainty or knowledge. Thus the skeptic sees himself as showing that our clear and distinct ideas, our ideas that are representationally most in order, do not amount to knowledge. Spinoza rejects this sharp separation implicit in skepticism between the representational character of ideas and their epistemic status. This separation is, for Spinoza, an inexplicable bifurcation every bit as objectionable as the sharp Cartesian separations between mind and body, between will and intellect, and between consciousness and representation.

FURTHER READING

Edwin Curley (1975) "Descartes, Spinoza, and the Ethics of Belief." (Classic account of Spinoza's rejection of Descartes's theory of judgment.)

Donald Davidson (1980) "Mental Events." (Highly influential statement of the view that mental events are identical to physical events despite the fact that, as in Spinoza, certain explanatory connections between the mental and the physical are ruled out.)

Michael Della Rocca (1996a) *Representation and the Mind-Body Problem in Spinoza*. (Extended discussion of the requirements on representation of an object and of Spinoza's reasons for embracing mind–body identity.)

————. (2003b) "The Power of an Idea: Spinoza's Critique of Pure Will." (Spinoza's representational theory of the mind together with a defense of the view that for Spinoza all ideas are beliefs.)

————. (2007) "Spinoza and the Metaphysics of Scepticism." (Spinoza's anti-skepticism as stemming from the PSR.)

Willis Doney (1975) "Spinoza on Philosophical Skepticism." (Useful overview of Spinoza on skepticism.)

G. H. R. Parkinson (1954) Spinoza's Theory of Knowledge. (Good account of all aspects of Spinoza's epistemology.)

Daisie Radner (1971) "Spinoza's Theory of Ideas." (Classic paper on Spinoza's theory of representational content.)

Alison Simmons (2001) "Changing the Cartesian Mind: Leibniz on Sensation, Representation and Consciousness." (Excellent account of Leibniz's representational theory of mind.)

Michael Tye (1997) *Ten Problems of Consciousness*. (Contemporary version of the representational theory of mind.)

Margaret Wilson (1999) "Objects, Ideas, and 'Minds': Comments on Spinoza's Theory of Mind." (Trenchant and important criticisms of Spinoza's philosophy of mind.)

Four

Striving and self-preservation

Near the beginning of Part III of the *Ethics*, Spinoza introduces a notion that guides him throughout the rest of that work and that also structures his thought in his political writings. This is the notion of the universal striving for self-preservation, or as Spinoza puts it in 3p6: "Each thing, insofar as it is in itself, strives to persevere in its being." In this and the next two chapters, this principle will structure our thought just as it structures Spinoza's: we will investigate the meaning of and argument for this claim as well as the multifarious uses to which Spinoza puts it. We will find that with 3p6 Spinoza takes a notion that Descartes and Hobbes employ, deepens it, and extends it in ways that his predecessors never dreamed of.

1. CONATUS

Although there are important advance indications of this principle in Spinoza's theory of physical individuals in Part II, indications that I will return to in due course, this thesis seemingly emerges without the help of anything prior to Part III of the *Ethics*. 3p6 seems to depend only on the two preceding propositions in Part III. Let's begin, then, our elucidation of 3p6 by turning to these earlier propositions.

3p4 is the claim: "No thing can be destroyed except through an external cause." This proposition is not demonstrated by appeal to previous definitions, axioms, or propositions: in 3p4d, Spinoza explicitly sees it as a self-evident truth.[1] But, of course, nothing really emerges from nowhere in Spinoza, and it is a pretty safe bet that when such a fundamental claim as 3p4 is introduced with little or no argumentation, the PSR must be lurking not far behind. Indeed, as we will see, 3p4 is, perhaps the simplest and most powerful expression of Spinoza's rationalism.

Why should 3p4 be true? After all, there seem to be all too many obvious counterexamples, cases in which things bring about their own destruction without the help of external causes. Thus, to take a couple of examples that Spinoza himself considers: a person who commits suicide seems to be the cause of his or her own destruction. Less sadly, consider a burning candle that eventually will go out of existence seemingly on its own.[2] Finally, consider a case not discussed by Spinoza: a time bomb which in the fullness of time will destroy itself (and other things too). Aren't these obvious cases in which, contra 3p4, a thing destroys itself?

To handle these cases, we must get clearer on the meaning of 3p4, and we can, as usual, begin to do this by looking closely at the demonstration. After asserting that 3p4 is self-evident, Spinoza nonetheless goes on to offer a potentially helpful argument:

> The definition of any thing affirms, and does not deny, the thing's essence, or it posits the thing's essence, and does not take it away. So while we attend only to the thing itself, and not to external causes, we shall not be able to find anything in it which can destroy it.

In the first sentence, Spinoza makes the familiar point that the definition of a thing affirms its essence, a point he elaborates by saying that the definition does not take the essence away. What exactly this elaboration comes to is not yet clear. But the emphasis on essence in the first sentence suggests that when Spinoza says in the second sentence "while we attend only to the thing itself," he is speaking particularly about the *essence* of the thing. Thus the point seems to be that if we focus on the essence of the thing and not on the things external to the essence, we shall not be able to find anything which can destroy the thing.

Recall the point made a number of times already that, for Spinoza (as well as other philosophers), there are properties of a thing that are explained by its essence alone and properties that are explained by other things as well as by its essence. Thus, to take a Cartesian example, the essence of a body explains why it has some shape or is capable of motion. But its having a specific shape or its moving in a particular way will be due, not only to its essence, but also and crucially to the things with which the body interacts. Spinoza's point in 3p4d is that the destruction of a thing is one of the features that never follows from the essence alone. Factors beyond the essence must be brought in to explain the destruction of a thing.

The power of Spinoza's claim can be better appreciated when we recall that, for Spinoza, the essence of a thing is to have certain causes. So Spinoza says here that, taking into account only the essence of a thing and thus taking into account only the causes of the thing, we must posit the existence of the thing. If the causes of the thing are in place, then trivially the existence of the thing follows. Thus, looking only at the essence of the thing, we can find nothing that would prevent the thing from existing. If—from this restricted point of view—the thing nonetheless did not exist, that would have to be a brute fact. So, focusing on the essence of a thing alone, one would have to view the non-existence of a thing as an unexplained fact. The explanation for the non-existence of a thing must, therefore, come from something beyond the thing's essence. In this way, we can see the PSR as driving 3p4.

I will deal with an important challenge to 3p4 so understood in a moment, but already we can see how this focus on the essence of a thing can help us deal with the troubling counterexamples. It's important to draw a distinction between the essence of a thing and what may be called the total state of a thing. The essence of a thing just consists, as we have seen, of those properties of a thing that explain what the thing is. For Spinoza, these properties are ultimately, as we have seen, the properties of having such-and-such causes. Of course, not all the properties of a thing follow from its essence alone, as I have emphasized. Thus, the property of wearing the same blue shirt that I wore while watching The Godfather, Part II for the seventeenth time is a property due in part to things other than my essence; in particular, it is due to the state of my wardrobe on that fateful day. The totality of my properties at a given time is my total state which is, of course, much broader than the properties that my essence comprises.

We can also see that those of my properties that do not follow from my essence alone—that are, in a sense, external to my essence—also follow from things external to me. To see this, consider that a property of me that does not follow from my essence alone and is thus not fully explained by my essence must nonetheless be fully explained by something. This is a boilerplate use of the PSR. But what could this something be? If something external to me is a partial explanation of this property of mine, then we've achieved the result that the property is in part due to causes external to me.

Is there any way to avoid the conclusion that the property must be explained by something external to me? Well, other than my essence and things external to me, the only possible source of this property of mine would be some other property of mine that does not follow from my essence alone. But to appeal to such a property only pushes the problem one step back, and we are quickly off on an infinite regression of properties of mine that do not derive from my essence alone. Ultimately, to explain the entire series of properties of mine that do not derive from my essence alone, we would need to appeal to things external to me. We cannot appeal to my essence because then the properties in this series would follow from my essence after all. So, in the end, all my properties which are not due to my essence alone must be due to things external to me.

Let's return to the example of the time bomb. It has the property of being destroyed at a certain point. Arguably this property follows from its total state the moment before. Given this total state—including the ticking away of whatever mechanism leads to the destruction—its destruction follows. In this sense, the time bomb destroys itself. But nonetheless the time bomb's destruction is not brought about by its essence alone: the destruction is brought about, ultimately, because the time bomb was set. Someone or something external to the time bomb had, it seems, to flick a switch or start the mechanism or whatever. And this initiation of the process—by something external to the time bomb—is not the result of the essence of the time bomb. One could conceive, for example, that this time bomb was not set. So the time bomb's destruction follows not from its essence alone, but rather from its total state which comprises facts that go beyond its essence and extend to things other than the time bomb itself. In this sense, even the time bomb is destroyed, and must be destroyed, by external things.

The other counterexamples can be handled in a similar way. The burning candle destroys itself, but only and ultimately because of some fact beyond the essence of the candle and ultimately something beyond the candle itself, e.g. the fact that someone lit the candle.

Spinoza handles the case of suicide in precisely this way. He acknowledges that a person can destroy himself, but also requires that in all such cases the destruction does not follow "from the necessity of his own nature" which, for Spinoza, is the same as the necessity of one's essence. Rather, for Spinoza, "those who do such things are compelled by external causes" (4p20s). Spinoza then cites various cases in which, due to some externally caused duress, one is led to kill oneself.

Spinoza's 3p4 amounts to the claim that the essence of a thing never suffices for its destruction. So interpreted, 3p4 may avoid certain obvious counterexamples, but might it still not be challenged in the following way? Perhaps there is a thing whose essence is such that the thing, upon coming into existence, continues to exist but does so for precisely fifteen minutes and then at that point ceases to exist—not due to external factors but due to the essence alone. On this scenario, given that the causes of a thing are in place, i.e. given the essence of the thing, the thing—by virtue of its essence alone—continues to exist for precisely fifteen minutes and then—again due to its essence—goes out of existence. This would be like the time bomb case but, instead of the destructive mechanism having to be initiated by some outside object, in this case the destructive process is, as it were, initiated by the essence of the thing. I can't think of a plausible concrete example along these lines, but it's not clear that such a case—what might be called the case of the essential time bomb—is inconceivable, and so Spinoza would need to rule it out in order to preserve 3p4. But how would he do so?

Spinoza does not explicitly consider this kind of case, but there are several points he could invoke to rule it out. I'll mention just one. The essential time bomb must during the fifteen minutes be impervious to destruction. If something else, call it "A," could destroy it, then if the essential time bomb does persist for those fifteen minutes, its persistence will be due not just to its essence, but to whatever prevented A from being able to exercise its power to destroy the essential time bomb. So for this counterexample to work, there cannot be anything that could destroy the essential time bomb during its 15 minutes of fame. But, for Spinoza, this would be absurd. Certainly, for Spinoza, there could be another finite thing with more power. Spinoza says as much in the lone axiom of Part IV:

> There is no singular thing in nature than which there is not another more powerful and stronger. Whatever one is given, there is another more powerful by which the first can be destroyed.

Although this claim is an axiom, we can see it as grounded in the PSR. Each finite thing has a certain limited degree of power (1p36). For a thing with a certain degree of power, it seems that there is no bar to there being a finite thing with a greater degree of power. The lack of such a more powerful thing would seem, for Spinoza, to be a brute fact. Thus, a presupposition of this purported counterexample—namely that the essential time bomb is, for a time, impervious to any other finite thing—is one that would be rejected by Spinoza on rationalist grounds.

But, one might object, perhaps I have set the standards for being an essential time bomb too high. The essential time bomb, one might say, need not be indestructible before its 15 minutes of fame are up. The point of the counterexample is not that the essential time bomb cannot be destroyed early, but that when the fifteen minutes have elapsed, the essence of the thing by itself brings about the destruction of the thing, if it has not already been destroyed by some more powerful external cause. In such a case, the thing's essence, if the thing is lucky enough to have survived to this point, suffices for its destruction, and this would seem to be contrary to 3p4.

Spinoza, however, would reject the legitimacy of this case for the same reason that he would reject the previous one. Because by 4ax there can always be something more powerful than a given thing, it follows that just as a thing is always subject to destruction by other, more powerful things, so too a thing that is hell-bent on destroying itself can always be prevented from doing so by the appropriate, more powerful external causes. And just as the PSR underwrites the claim that there can always be an external destroyer, the PSR would also underwrite the claim that there can always be an external sustainer. So if the allegedly essential time bomb does go out of existence at the fifteen-minute mark, this would be due not to its essence alone, but rather to the thing's essence *and* the absence of such an external sustainer.

So, in the end, I think we must see 3p4 as a claim with considerable intuitive appeal. It remains to be seen, however, whether this claim, so defended, can have any substantive metaphysical implications, as Spinoza claims. To see whether it does, we must turn to the aftermath of 3p4.

In 3p5, Spinoza says:

> Things are of a contrary nature, that is, cannot be in the same
> subject, insofar as one can destroy the other.

Here (as well as in 3p6) Spinoza is concerned to rule out a thing's
having something "in it" which can destroy it. In 3p5d, he tries to
preclude this by invoking 3p4. But can 3p4 perform this task? To
justify 3p4, we needed to distinguish between the essence of a
thing and its total state, and I granted that the total state of a thing
can lead to its destruction (even if the essence by itself cannot).
Isn't the total state of a thing in that thing? After all, as we saw in
Chapter 2, for Spinoza, to be in a thing is somehow to inhere in
the thing, and doesn't the total state of a thing inhere in that thing
and thus isn't it in that thing? But then how can Spinoza say, as he
wants to in 3p5, that nothing in a thing can destroy it?

To resolve this problem, we need to see that for Spinoza being in
a thing can be a matter of degree. Yes, the total state of a thing
can lead to its destruction, and, in a way, the total state is in the
thing. But it need not be fully in the thing. To the extent that that
total state is due to outside causes (i.e. causes other than those
involved in the essence itself), then that state is not in the object
but in the outside causes. As I noted in Chapter 2, because of the
equivalence of the in-relation and the causal relation, whenever and
to the extent that an object is acted on by outside causes, it is not
fully in itself, but must be partly in those other things. So Spinoza's
point in 3p5 is that to the extent that or, as he puts it, insofar as
something can destroy another thing, the two cannot be in the
same thing.[3]

Finally let's turn to 3p6, the central proposition in Spinoza's
psychology, ethics, and political philosophy. In this proposition,
Spinoza introduces a new notion, that of striving, which—even
if we grant everything in 3p4 and 3p5—seems extremely problematic.
Spinoza says:

Each thing, insofar as it is in itself, strives to persevere in its being.

Before seeing whether 3p6 is true, we must understand its meaning. And, in particular, we need to specify what Spinoza means by strives (*conatur*) and what he means by saying that a thing strives *insofar as it is in itself* (*quantum in se est*).

Let's turn first to the meaning of "strives." I believe that Spinoza's notion of striving derives from Descartes's use of the same term, but that Spinoza also transforms this notion in a characteristically more thoroughgoingly rationalist way. In the *Principles*, Descartes's work devoted to outlining the metaphysical principles that govern the extended world, he introduces the notion of striving in his discussion of a certain kind of physical object:

> When I say that the globules of the second element "strive" to move away from the centers around which they revolve, it should not be thought that I am implying that they have some thought from which this striving proceeds. I mean merely that they are positioned and pushed into motion in such a way that they will in fact travel in that direction, unless they are prevented by some other cause.
>
> (*Principles* III 56)

The first thing to note is that Descartes is at pains here to emphasize that the notion of striving is not an intrinsically psychological one. These globules strive, for Descartes, but are, like all physical objects, not mental and so incapable of any striving psychologically understood. Striving is, for Descartes, neutral with regard to thought.

The second point to note is that Descartes speaks here of the striving to remain in the same state, but stresses that this is a striving that a thing has only insofar as it is simple and undivided. As we will see, Spinoza articulates a similar principle but significantly does not restrict it, as Descartes does, to simple and undivided things.

Finally, and most importantly, Descartes's notion of striving is what I call a stripped-down notion of striving.[4] Not only is the notion not specifically psychological, but the fact that a thing strives is nothing more than the truth of a certain hypothetical claim: for a thing to strive to do x is for its current state to be such that if it is not prevented from doing x by external causes, then it will do x. Thus Descartes says that by "strives" he means merely [tantum] that the globules "are positioned and pushed into motion in such a way that they will in fact travel in that direction, unless they are prevented by some other cause." For Descartes, striving consists simply in the truth of such a conditional claim.[5]

Leibniz raises a pertinent objection to this Cartesian stripped-down notion of striving. For Leibniz, this merely hypothetical notion of striving does not do justice to the causal power and genuine force to resist that is present in things that strive. Leibniz puts the point this way in a letter to a follower of Descartes (namely de Volder):

> I admit that each and every thing remains in its state until there is a reason for change; this is a principle of metaphysical necessity. But it is one thing to retain a state until something changes it, which even something intrinsically indifferent to both states does, and quite another thing, much more significant, for a thing not to be indifferent, but to have a force and, as it were, an inclination to retain its state, and so resist changing.
>
> (Leibniz 1989: 172)

Here Leibniz objects to the way that Descartes has stripped down the notion of striving. For Leibniz, striving and the causal power to resist cannot be explained by a mere if–then claim, but must involve something more, a full-blooded causal oomph, as it were. It's not clear that Descartes has the resources to respond satisfactorily. We'll return to this point after laying out Spinoza's equally stripped-down notion of striving.[6]

Spinoza agrees with Descartes that striving is not necessarily psychological and that it is to be defined merely conditionally as Descartes defines it. Spinoza is quite familiar, of course, with the Cartesian account of striving and he captures it accurately in his book on Descartes.[7] Further, in his account of the persistence of bodies in the interlude on bodies after 2p13s, Spinoza clearly employs this notion of striving although without, in that context, employing the term "strives." (More on the persistence of bodies shortly.)

For Spinoza, then, what a thing strives to do is what its current state will lead it to do unless it is prevented by external causes. But if this is the account of striving, then how could Spinoza say, as he appears to in 3p6, that each thing strives to preserve itself? As we have seen, for Spinoza, the total state of a thing can lead to the thing's destruction and so, on this account of striving, it seems that there can be striving for destruction after all. How is this consistent with 3p6?

Here is where the puzzling phrase in 3p6 "insofar as it is in itself" becomes crucial. Although, as we've seen, a thing may strive for its destruction insofar as its total state is concerned, it cannot strive for self-destruction insofar as its essence is concerned, i.e. insofar as one considers only the causes through which it is conceived, i.e. insofar as it is in itself.[8] To the extent that a thing is in itself and thus independent of causes that do not figure in its essence, it will persist. This is, in effect, Spinoza's point in 3p4. So, given the stripped-down notion of striving that Spinoza shares with Descartes, each thing, insofar as it is in itself, strives to persist. In this way, 3p6 follows from 3p4, just as Spinoza indicates in 3p6d.

In light of the way Spinoza thus links striving, self-preservation, and essence, we can gain some insight into Spinoza's account of the persistence of extended objects. The general claim about bodies, of course, is that each body, insofar as it is in itself, i.e. insofar as its essence is concerned, strives to persist. For what Spinoza calls the simplest bodies, this amounts to the claim that these bodies, insofar as they are in themselves, strive to remain in motion, if they are moving, and strive to remain at rest, if they are at rest. This follows because Spinoza defines the simplest bodies as those "which are distinguished from one another only by motion and rest, speed and slowness" (2ax2″). So, for these bodies whose *essence* is their state of motion or rest, preserving this state is, as it were, a matter of life and death, and thus these bodies will tend to persevere in this state insofar as they are in themselves.[9]

Although more complex bodies have some tendency to remain in motion or at rest, the way in which their essence figures into their striving involves more than simply the preservation of the state of moving or being at rest. Consider Spinoza's definition of complex individual bodies:

> When a number of bodies, whether of the same or of different size, are so constrained by other bodies that they lie upon one another, or if they so move, whether with the same degree or different degrees of speed, so as to communicate their motions to each other in a certain fixed manner, we shall say that those bodies are united with one another and that they all together compose one body or individual, which is distinguished from the others by this union of bodies.
>
> (Def. after 2ax2″)

The point here is that a complex body is individuated by—its essence consists in—the way its parts are related to one another. In 2le4, Spinoza calls this relation the *nature* of this body and, of course, nature, for Spinoza, is equivalent to essence.[10] But not just any relation among the parts will suffice for the existence of a complex individual. Rather, the parts must be related to one another in a certain fixed [*certa quadam*] manner. Consider a living organism such as a human body. This body comprises many smaller parts, and what makes the body as a whole an individual is that these parts (the heart, the kidney, and, yes, the pancreas) interact with and are responsive to one another in such a way as to maintain some kind of equilibrium. Even complex but apparently non-living bodies, such as the pan, have parts which maintain certain relations to one another:[11] for example, if one moves one part of the pan, then the other parts have a very strong tendency to follow. These parts, as Spinoza interestingly puts it, are constrained so that they lie upon one another. This overall relation among parts that a complex body has some tendency to preserve is what Spinoza calls its ratio of motion and rest (e.g. 2le5).[12] He doesn't characterize the relation further than that and the account is left at a very general level, but nonetheless the picture is quite compelling. Here is one way to see why it is.

Consider two different collections of bodies—first, the collection of bodies that make up my body and, second, the collection of bodies that consists of my pancreas, your pancreas and Emma Thompson's right thumb. The former collection (obviously) constitutes a genuine complex individual and, it seems, the latter does not. Spinoza would agree, and his reason would be that, while the members of the former collection interact with one another in order to preserve relations that hold among them, the members of the latter collection have little or no tendency to be responsive to one another in such a way. The relations between my pancreas and yours vary all the time and very little that my pancreas does can be said to have the result that the relation between my pancreas and yours remains constant. By contrast, the changes in my heart are part of what helps to keep its relations to my pancreas and the other parts of my body more or less constant.

One of the nicer features of Spinoza's account of individuation is that it allows complex individuals to gain and lose parts over time and still to maintain their identity. As long as the new parts retain the same kind of relation to the remaining parts, the individual persists. Thus, happily, Spinoza can account for phenomena such as growth, decay, digestion and excretion (see 2le4–2le7). Precisely because the relations that are preserved through these changes constitute the essence of one's body, that body, insofar as it is in itself, *strives* to preserve these relations. By contrast, the collection of the two pancreases and Emma Thompson's thumb does not manifest such striving.

Of course, for Spinoza, analogous claims hold for minds whose striving, as we shall soon see, is to be understood in the same way as bodily striving. But, before turning to minds in particular, I'd like to return to Leibniz's powerful criticism of the general stripped-down account of striving—a criticism he directs at Descartes, but that might be thought to apply with equal justice to Spinoza. I will argue that the resources of Spinoza's more thoroughgoing rationalism may provide him with an answer to Leibniz that is not available to Descartes. Recall Leibniz's worry: The mere fact that a thing is such that it will do F unless prevented by external causes does not show that this thing actually strives against or resists such external causes. To use Garber's example, the mere fact that a child will keep playing with her doll unless her father gets her to do something else does not mean that, when the time comes, she will resist doing something else. On the contrary, she might go on to the new activity willingly. Similarly, the fact that a moving body will, unless external bodies intervene, keep moving does not by itself entail that when it comes into contact with those external bodies, it will resist them, it will exert some causal power against them. Leibniz thinks that bodies actively resist change in this way, and he seems to be right. Just feel the pressure against your hand as you try to stop the motion of a billiard ball. The point, for Leibniz, is that Descartes's merely conditional notion of striving cannot account for this seemingly obvious fact.

The challenge then is to show how, on a merely conditional account of striving, there can be an exercise of force, of causal power, even in a case where the striving is unsuccessful. To see how Spinoza can meet this challenge, let's return to Spinoza's account of causation in general. As we saw in Chapter 2, for Spinoza, causation consists in a conceptual dependence of one thing on another. The motion of the rock causes the window to break and this is true, for Spinoza, simply because the concept of the window's breaking depends on and can be derived from the concept of the rock's motion (together, of course, with the concepts of a number of other things). This account of causation as conceptual dependence is, as we saw, part and parcel of Spinoza's rationalism and is merely one of the many twofold uses of the PSR that we have encountered.

In light of this account, can we find any causal, i.e. conceptual, connection between, say, the rock's motion and another state of affairs in a case of unsuccessful striving? It seems we can. Let's take a case in which a rock strikes a window and yet the window doesn't break (perhaps because it is reinforced with steel). In such a case, the rock stops moving, but it resists doing so, it resists the window, as it were. But what causal power is, on Spinoza's terms, exercised by the rock? Notice first that in this case we cannot derive the concept of the window's breaking from the concept of the rock's motion. This is simply because, in this case, there is no breaking of the window. However, there is here a conceptual connection between the rock's motion and the rock's continuing to move unless other things prevent it, or between the rock's motion and the rock's breaking the window unless other things prevent it. This is a conceptual connection between the rock's motion and what may be called a conditional state of affairs, but it is a conceptual connection nonetheless. And if, as Spinoza holds, causation just is conceptual connection then we have in this case of unsuccessful striving a genuine causal connection between the rock's moving and, not the window's breaking, but the state of affairs whereby the window will break unless something prevents the rock from breaking it. It is because Spinoza reduces causal connections to conceptual connections that his stripped-down, merely conditional notion of striving can allow for cases in which there is genuine causal power at work even in a case of unsuccessful striving. Thus, on Spinoza's terms, we can see the rock as exercising causal power even in the unsuccessful case, and thus we can see how Spinoza might be able to answer Leibniz's objection.

Of course, one may reject this response because one rejects the equivalence of causal and conceptual relations on which this response depends.[13] But this is a separate debate which, as we saw in Chapter 2, Spinoza would seek to bring to an end by invoking the PSR in its twofold use: causation must be explained, but it will remain a mystery unless it amounts to some form of conceptual or explanatory connection.

We can see in this way that this response to Leibniz is not one that Descartes is in a position to give. This is because Descartes rejects the equation of causation and conceptual dependence. For Descartes, as we have seen, there can be causal connections without any conceptual connection. (This occurs, for example, in the case of mind-body causal relations, for Descartes.) Also, Descartes shows no sign of accepting Spinoza's thesis that there are no conceptual dependencies without causal dependencies. This is, of course, merely another manifestation of the way in which Spinoza is a more thoroughgoing rationalist than Descartes.

A further rationalist feature in Spinoza's account of striving is the similarity between us and God. As I have stressed, a crucial aspect of Spinoza's rationalism is his naturalism, his refusal to see different things as playing by different rules because then the relation between the different things would be inexplicable. This refusal extends, I believe, to the case of divine-human relations. For Spinoza, God is not different from us (or from other finite things) in kind, only in degree and particularly only in degree of power. This emerges nicely from Spinoza's emphasizing in 3p6 that, just as God is in itself, we too are in ourselves if only to some degree. In other words, we possess to some extent a defining characteristic of God: we are conceptually independent of other things to some extent at least.

The notion of striving reveals another similarity between us and God: our striving is not different in kind from what might be called

God's striving. The same kind of conditional claims hold for God as well as for us. Just as we will preserve ourselves unless other things interfere, so too God will preserve himself unless other things interfere. The only difference is that with regard to God there are no other things and so his striving for self-preservation is necessarily unimpeded. Of course, the term "strive" may seem inappropriate when speaking of God because it might suggest some kind of struggle against another which, of course, God is not subject to. But this is a mere terminological point. The crucial metaphysical point remains: the truth of the kinds of conceptually grounded conditional claims that constitutes striving and indeed causation for finite things is in place for God as well.

Finally, not only is Spinoza's notion of striving in accordance with his naturalism, his account also evinces the twofold use of the PSR. For Spinoza, the striving of a thing must be made intelligible, and it is made intelligible in terms of the thing's ability to cause changes unless it is prevented from doing so by other things. In other words, the explanation of striving is in terms of a thing's ability to be the explanation of changes. Striving is explained in terms of explanation itself.

2. DESIRE, JOY, AND SADNESS

Spinoza's account of emotions and our affective life is wholly and ingeniously based on his stripped-down account of striving. To see how, recall first that for Spinoza "striving" is not an inherently psychological term: bodies as well as minds can be said to strive and, indeed, given Spinoza's parallelism of causal chains, whenever a human mind strives, the human body parallel to that mind also strives, and vice versa. Thus we can speak of the striving of the human mind in particular or the striving of the single entity that is the human mind and the human body, i.e., as Spinoza would say, of the man or human being, without specifying that the striving is of the mind or body exclusively. Spinoza calls the striving of the mind *will* and he calls the striving of the human being—of the mind and body together—*appetite*. (Spinoza doesn't have a further term for the striving of the human body in particular.) Desire, for Spinoza, is just "appetite together with consciousness of the appetite" (3p9s).

However, there's not a lot riding on this apparent distinction between appetite in general and desire in particular. This is in part because, as we have seen, all mental states, for Spinoza, are conscious to some degree, thus all appetites would be accompanied by some form of consciousness and would thus count as desires for Spinoza. Although Spinoza does not make this point about degrees of consciousness in this context, he does explicitly downplay the distinction between desire and appetite later in Part III when he offers his definitions of the affects. There—in the first of these definitions—he says, "I really recognize no difference between human appetite and desire" and he goes on to stipulate that "by the word *desire*, I understand any of a man's strivings, impulses, appetites, and volitions."

Spinoza defines desire here in terms of a *man's* striving, but, of course, given Spinoza's naturalism, his point applies more generally. *All* individuals strive to do things and thus all individuals *desire* things. We can, for Spinoza, meaningfully speak of the pan's desires as well as of our own. Indeed, since my pancreas strives—and its striving is part, in effect, of my striving—my pancreas also can be said to have desires. The point applies even, I would say, to God. At the end of the previous section, I noted that God can be said with some propriety to strive. To that extent God can also be said to have desires. Despite the implicit universality of Spinoza's account of desire, I will continue to focus—as Spinoza does—on human desires and human psychology in particular.

There is one crucial respect in which human striving and desire may seem to have no echo in the striving and desire of simpler individuals. In speaking of a human being in particular, Spinoza stresses that we strive not only to persist but also to increase what he calls our power of acting. First, let me say a bit about power of acting before turning to the problems this feature of our striving raises.

Spinoza specifies that for something to act is for it to be the adequate or complete cause of some effect. A thing is acted on or is passive to the extent to which it is only a partial cause of some effect (3def2). Of course, a thing can be the complete cause of a certain effect to a greater or lesser degree. Recall the example from the previous chapter of my varying degrees of ability to lift the pan or my greater or lesser independence of external causes in the production of a certain effect. These varying degrees of ability are, for Spinoza, varying degrees of power of acting.

On the basis of his claim that we strive, insofar as we are in ourselves, to persevere in being, Spinoza says that we also strive to increase our power of acting. He makes this claim about the human mind in particular in 3p12. There he says that, if having certain ideas will increase the mind's power of acting, then the mind will strive to have those ideas.[14] Given the parallelism, a similar claim would apply to the human body and its strivings.

Two puzzles confront us here. First, in the crucial part of his demonstration of 3p12, the claim that we strive to increase our power of acting, Spinoza relies on 3p6 which concerns the striving for self-preservation. But it is far from clear how, even if we grant that we do to some extent strive for self-preservation, it follows that we also and thereby strive to increase our power of acting, our ability to be the complete cause of certain effects. Perhaps striving for self-preservation requires that we maintain some degree of power of acting with regard to certain effects, but why should it follow that the striving for self-preservation requires us to increase our power of acting?

What is also far from clear is the extent to which Spinoza sees this claim about striving to increase power as applying, not just to human beings, but also to simpler objects such as the pan. In the *Ethics*, Spinoza discusses this claim only for the case of human beings, and, while in the *Short Treatise* there is some indication that he sees this claim as having more general import (see KV I, chap. 5, G I 40), there is no sign of this in the *Ethics*. If the claim about striving to increase power is, however, restricted to human beings, then how is that compatible with Spinoza's naturalism which leads him to espouse his truly universal claims about striving?

We will make progress on both of these puzzles much later in the chapter after we have explained some of Spinoza's views on anticipation. The crucial ideas will be (1) that, because we can anticipate future threats to our well-being, it is in our interest to increase our power now and not just to do the bare minimum to stay in existence, and (2) that simpler objects such as the pan which are not capable of anticipation to the degree that we are do not, for that reason, strive to increase their power. To reach these conclusions will require some philosophical stage-setting concerning Spinoza's two other basic kinds of affects in addition to desire. These are joy and sadness.

Spinoza defines joy as "a man's passage from a lesser to a greater perfection" and sadness as "a man's passage from a greater to a lesser perfection" (3da2–3). By perfection here, Spinoza means power of acting (3da3exp, 4 pref). So joy and sadness are simply the passage to a greater or lesser power of acting, a greater or lesser ability to bring about certain effects. Given Spinoza's parallelism, whenever the body increases in perfection and power, the mind does so as well, and so joy and sadness are equally mental and physical phenomena. However, in speaking of joy and sadness, Spinoza often concentrates on the mental aspect of these affects— as, for example, when he introduces these terms in 3p11s.

This account of joy and sadness is a reflection of Spinoza's naturalism. The notions of increase and decrease in power apply not just to human beings, but to individuals in general, and so less complex individuals such as the pan can also be said to undergo joy and sadness. Here too everything plays by the same rules. However, for understandable reasons, at least one individual—namely God— may not be able to experience joy or sadness. And this is because God—as a maximally powerful being—is incapable of moving to a greater or lesser power of acting (5p17).

Nonetheless, Spinoza does say that God loves himself with an infinite intellectual love (5p35). Because, for Spinoza, as we shall see, love is a kind of joy, it is initially unclear why Spinoza attributes this love to God. I think Spinoza's point here is that there is a kind of joy or self-satisfaction that one has simply from contemplating one's power of acting, whether or not one has made a transition from a lesser power of acting. This kind of joy—self-satisfaction—can be had not only by God, but also by finite things, including human beings.[15] So there is no violation of naturalism here, merely a harmless broadening of Spinoza's account of joy to include enjoyment of power even without transition from a lesser degree of power.

Spinoza's treatment of the mental aspects of each of the three basic affects—desire, joy, and sadness—is fundamentally representational in a way which we have come to see as characteristic of Spinoza's rationalism. Let's start with joy. When the body passes to a greater degree of perfection, what is the mind doing? Given parallelism, the mind must, of course, likewise pass to a greater degree of perfection. But what does the shift at the mental level involve? Recall that the mind is the idea of the body and that the mind thus *represents* each bodily state. So prior to the change, the mind represented a certain bodily state and, after the change, the mind came to represent a more perfect and more powerful bodily state. This passage to a new idea of a more powerful bodily state is, given parallelism, a passage to a more powerful mental state. So, in making the transition which is constitutive of joy, the mind simply moves from one representation to another. That's all. Similarly, sadness is simply the mind's transition from one representation to another. Desire, on the part of the mind, is simply the mind's tendency to go from one representation to another. Of course, the tendency may not always be successful—desires can be frustrated—but this tendency is a tendency to have certain ideas. And, insofar as we are in ourselves, the mind's desire is simply the tendency to come to have an idea of a more powerful bodily state, an idea that itself is a more powerful mental state. As Spinoza says in 3p12: "The mind, insofar as it can, strives to imagine those things that increase or aid the body's power of acting."

In the case of all these affects, there is no feeling involved over and above these representations and the transitions between them. This runs counter to the view of the person in the street which I outlined in the previous chapter. On this more or less common-sense view, there is more to affects such as joy, desire, and love than mere representations or ideas. To feel joy is not simply to represent a certain state of affairs, but to come to have, perhaps on the basis of such representations, a different kind of mental state, a non-representational state, a kind of mental buzz that is distinctive of a feeling of joy. But Spinoza will have none of this. For him, representation is all there is to joy as well as to sadness and desire and, indeed all the other affects, for, as we will see presently, Spinoza constructs all the other affects out of these three. The representational nature of the affects is fully on display in Spinoza's general definition of the affects at the end of Part III of the Ethics:

An affect which is called a passion of the mind is a confused idea, by which the mind affirms of its body, or of some part of it, a greater or lesser force of existing than before, which, when it is given, determines the mind to think of this rather than that.

An affect is just an idea, an affirmation. Here Spinoza defines passions and so he speaks of confused ideas which are ideas caused from outside the mind and, as such, are passive. Active affects would be various unconfused or adequate ideas.

This thoroughgoing representationality of the affects is, like Spinoza's representational account of consciousness, part and parcel of his naturalism and rationalism. This view is naturalistic in that it reflects Spinoza's requirement that there are no fundamentally different kinds of things at work in the mind, each operating according to different principles. This naturalistic insistence on no disparity of states within the mind is at bottom also a manifestation of rationalism, for the connection between such apparently disparate states would, for Spinoza, be inexplicable.

This representational account of the affects is also more deeply rationalist in the following way. For Spinoza, affects must be able to be explained, we must be able to say what they are. We must not treat them as primitive, as the person on the street would be inclined to do. The explanation of the affects that Spinoza gives is in terms of representation and the (often unsuccessful) striving to have certain representations. As we have seen, representation is, for Spinoza, nothing but mental explanation, explaining something in thought. And this striving is, as we saw in the previous section, simply a matter of the causal and conceptual connections between one state and another. So affects are explained in terms of representation and striving, each of which is in turn explained in terms of the notion of explanation itself. Here again we see the twofold use of the PSR: a crucial phenomenon is to be explained or made intelligible in terms of the notion of explanation or intelligibility itself.

But there is yet another rationalistic and naturalistic feature of this account of the affects. For Spinoza, as we have seen, all human desire is to some extent—i.e. to the extent to which we are in ourselves—directed at our self-preservation and at increasing our power of acting. Given the definitions of joy and sadness, this amounts to the view that in all we do we always to some extent desire not only our continuation in existence but also our own joy or happiness. Thus, for Spinoza, there can be no desire that is totally divorced from a concern with our self-interest. In particular, there can be no desire to do something simply because it is the right thing to do, irrespective of any connection the action may have to our own joy or preservation. To think that there could be such a desire and action independent of our self-interest would be, for Spinoza, to introduce a motivational source within the mind that is radically different from more egoistic motivations and, for this reason, these purported desires would violate Spinoza's naturalism and his rationalism. I will develop this line of thought in the next chapter when I outline Spinoza's egoistic moral psychology.

3. LOVE, HATE AND ALL THAT

Let's turn to Spinoza's construction of the rest of our affective life on the austere basis of desire, joy, and sadness. As we will see, Spinoza is able to tell a surprisingly rich and plausible story once he brings in certain rationalist-inspired principles governing the connection between mental states.

Love and hate, for Spinoza, are an opposed pair of affects that follow directly from joy and sadness. Love is simply "joy with the accompanying idea of an external cause" and (unsurprisingly) hate is "sadness with the accompanying idea of an external cause" (3p13s). All forms of love fall under this rubric: thus parental love, love of friends, romantic love, sexual attraction, love of inanimate objects, love of certain pursuits all have a common core in joy seen as caused by a particular object. Here, as in the case of the more basic affects discussed in the previous section, these affects are fully representational. There is no feeling of love, no burning affection over and above the representation of an object as the cause of an increase in power. Furthermore, this increase, as we saw, is on the mental level nothing but a transition from one idea, one representation, to another, and the causal relation between the object and the increase is, again on the mental level, nothing but a certain conceptual relation between ideas.

The affects of love and hate naturally give rise to certain other affects, including certain desires. Because of the joy and sadness at the core of love and hate, and because joy and sadness are the objects of our striving, Spinoza says:

> [O]ne who loves necessarily strives to have present and preserve the thing he loves; and, on the other hand, one who hates strives to remove and destroy the things he hates.
>
> (3p13s)

Spinoza seems to have a good point here: we strive to distance ourselves from things we hate and to get closer to things we love. This striving is only a tendency, of course, so it is compatible with our not in fact getting closer to or further from the things we love or hate.

Further, because the continued presence of the loved one makes us happy, according to Spinoza, we strive to bring about whatever helps the loved one, whatever increases its power of acting, i.e. whatever gives it joy. And if an object benefits the loved one, it also thereby benefits us. So we love this other object too (3p21–22). Spinoza calls this kind of love *favor*. For the same reason, we hate an object that harms a loved one—Spinoza calls this *indignation* (3p22s).

Similarly, if we hate an object, we desire that it have less power of acting, that it undergo sadness, and we may actually strive to bring on this sadness in the one we hate. Such striving is, for Spinoza, *anger* (3p40s2). If the desire for the unhappiness of the hated one is satisfied we will, of course, be happy. Correlatively, we will be saddened by the joy of the hated one. Spinoza calls this phenomenon *envy* which he defines as "hate, insofar as it is considered to dispose a man that he is glad at another's ill fortune and saddened by his good fortune" (3p24s). The case of envy just described is one in which we feel joy or sadness at the sadness or joy of one we antecedently hate. But, as we will see presently, Spinoza articulates a mechanism by which we can experience envy directed at someone toward whom we antecedently have no affect.

Love can turn to hate and Spinoza describes the mechanism of this process with such detail as to make one suspect that he is writing from his own experience. For Spinoza, I strive that the one I love loves me in return. The process is as follows: I strive to make the one I love happy, i.e. I strive to be a cause of the loved one's happiness. Because, for Spinoza, love is joy accompanied by the idea of an external cause, Spinoza concludes that I therefore strive that the one I love loves me in return. This doesn't quite follow, however, because even if I strive to be the cause of the loved one's happiness, it doesn't follow that I strive that the loved one *recognizes* that I am the cause of his or her happiness. Such recognition is, of course, required for the loved one to feel love toward me.

However, it seems that we can easily reach the desired conclusion on Spinoza's own terms. For Spinoza, I desire not only to keep the loved one in existence and happy, I also desire, as he puts it, to have the loved one present simply because the presence of the loved one increases my own power of acting, makes me happy. If the loved one loves me in return, the loved one will strive to be in my presence and so will make me happy. Thus I naturally strive that the loved one loves me in return.

If I find, however, that the loved one withdraws his or her affections from me and transfers them to another, then, as one might say, all hell breaks loose. Thus because the love for me is taken away, I undergo a decrease in power, a decrease in happiness. This new sadness is brought on by the one I love and so I will come to hate the loved one as well as love him or her. At the same time, I will also come to hate the new object of the loved one's affections whom I will also regard as a cause of my newfound sadness, and I will envy this rival's success and happiness (3p35).

Spinoza, of course, describes here the phenomenon of jealousy. Although he recognizes it to be a general phenomenon, Spinoza— in a passage that is simultaneously unsettling and, in some ways, strikingly insightful—sees this jealousy as manifested primarily in love toward a woman. Spinoza says that the mingling of love and hate characteristic of jealousy...

> is found, for the most part, in love toward a woman. For he who imagines that a woman he loves prostitutes herself to another not only will be saddened, because his own appetite is restrained, but also will be repelled by her, because he is forced to join the image of the thing he loves to the shameful parts and excretions of the other. To this, finally, is added the fact that she no longer

receives the jealous man with the same countenance as she used
to offer him. From this cause, too, the lover is saddened.

(3p35s)

Spinoza obviously has strong opinions about the power of sexual
emotions. In another striking passage, from the autobiographical
opening section of his *Treatise on the Emendation of the Intellect*, he gives
expression to a similar view:

> as far as sensual pleasure is concerned, the mind is so caught up
> in it, as if at peace in a [true] good, that it is quite prevented from
> thinking of anything else. But after the enjoyment of sensual
> pleasure is past, the greatest sadness follows. If this does not
> completely engross, still it thoroughly confuses and dulls the
> mind.

(§4)[16]

Spinoza is obviously far from letting his austere representational
account of the emotions blind him to their power.

Matters get even more complex and fascinating when Spinoza
explores certain other mechanisms governing the relations between
affects and other ideas. The crucial mechanism here is what may
be called the association of mental states—or since, for Spinoza,
mental states are all ideas, the association of ideas. This is not Spinoza's term, but rather Hume's who, despite many sharp differences from Spinoza, invokes a similar mechanism to similar effect.
For Spinoza, if the mind has two ideas simultaneously or in a
certain order, then when afterwards it has again one of these ideas,
it will—or at least will, other things being equal—have the other
idea. Thus, say that when I first saw an Audrey Hepburn movie
and thus had the idea of Audrey Hepburn, I also saw Billy the bully
who followed me to the theater. Later when I see Billy again—as I
do all too often!—I will again have the idea of Audrey Hepburn, an
idea which has come to be associated in my mind with the idea

of Billy. The point applies to my mental states more generally which are thus, in Spinoza's eyes, not isolated from one another: two mental states that occur together always occur together. As Spinoza says:

> If the human body has been once affected by two or more bodies at the same time, then when the mind subsequently imagines one of them, it will immediately recollect the others also.
>
> (2p18)

Of course, this claim holds only for the most part, and nothing prevents Spinoza from acknowledging that associations which have once been established in the mind can over time be weakened.

But, although experience suggests that something like this principle seems to be operative, what reason does Spinoza give from the resources of his system for accepting this principle? I believe Spinoza is thinking along the following lines. Let's say that my body is affected by distinct objects A and B at the same time and thus that I come to perceive both these objects. While the objects are distinct, the states that each produces in my body—given that they occur at the same time—are not wholly distinct. Consider a rather simple case: Let's say an impression of a coin is made in a block of wax and that an impression of a different coin is superimposed on the first impression. The effects of the two coins on the wax blend into one another, one might say, in such a way that the impression made by one is not entirely distinct from the impression made by the other. Similarly, if two different objects affect my body at the same time, then the effects those bodies have on me—their impressions on my body, as it were—will not be entirely distinct. Thus when my body comes again to be in the bodily state that A originally caused, it will also, in some measure, again be in the state that was originally caused by B. Given Spinoza's parallelism, therefore, when I recall A, come to have again an idea of A, I will also and thereby come to have again the idea of B. Spinoza invokes exactly this point—that the bodily state caused by A is not distinct from the bodily state caused by B—in his demonstration of the doctrine of association in 2p18d.

This doctrine enables Spinoza to explain how some of our most intriguing affects are constituted. Thus consider again that jerk Billy the bully who has caused me considerable pain in the past and whom I therefore hate. Whenever Billy hurt me in the past, I had—unfortunately—a good glimpse of his sweaty upper lip. So the idea of a sweaty upper lip comes to be associated in my mind with the idea of a decrease in power—i.e. with pain. Many years after the traumatic events involving Billy, I find myself acquainted with Johnny who has no particular connection to Billy and who is, in fact, the nicest guy in the world. However Johnny—just like Billy—has a sweaty upper lip and, crucially, I see that he is similar to Billy in this regard. This sets off the following chain of ideas: the idea of Johnny is associated with the idea of a sweaty upper lip which is associated with the idea of Billy which is associated with the idea of a decrease in power which idea is itself pain or sadness. Thus I will again experience pain, but this time—through no fault of his own—the pain is caused by Johnny, and so I will come to hate Johnny even though he is the nicest guy in the world. Spinoza says that, in such a case, Johnny is the accidental cause of sadness (3p15–16). We can also imagine that I love or desire a thing through similarly indirect or accidental means. The phenomenon that Spinoza has in his sights here will, of course, later come to be called transference.

This kind of association between an affect directed at one person and a similar affect directed at similar others helps explain, in Spinoza's eyes, the phenomenon of class-based and other forms of prejudice. Thus Spinoza says:

> If someone has been affected with joy or sadness by someone of
> a class, or nation, different from his own, and this joy or sadness
> is accompanied by the idea of that person as its cause, under the

> universal name of the class or nation, he will love or hate, not
> only that person, but everyone of the same class or nation.
>
> (3p46)

The reasoning here is quite simple: to the extent members of the same class or nation are similar to one another and are perceived to be so, then we will inevitably transfer the affect we have toward one member of such a group to the others in the group

A different principle governing the affects is at work in what Spinoza calls the imitation of affects. Though different from the association of mental states, imitation can be seen as deriving from association, as I will argue. For Spinoza, when I perceive someone similar to me to have a certain affect, I will have a similar affect:

> If we imagine a thing like us, toward which we have had no affect,
> to be affected with some affect, we are thereby affected with a
> like affect.
>
> (3p27)

Something like this certainly seems true to experience: laughter is contagious and an ebullient person's mirth as well as a morose person's depression can spread across a room. Spinoza specifies only that we emulate affects of beings similar to us. This restriction also seems plausible. We have less of a tendency to imitate the affects of creatures very unlike us: the enjoyment a snail takes in its food is not something I am likely to imitate.

How can Spinoza ground these plausible claims about imitation within his system? Spinoza's official proof of 3p27 is hard to make work. In it, Spinoza seems to claim that when we perceive an object to be affected in a certain way, we thereby come to have a similar affect. But why should this be so? It is not the case that by perceiving your red hair—a way in which you are affected— I thereby have a tendency to have red hair.

Nevertheless, Spinoza's doctrine of association can help us to see how the doctrine of imitation is grounded in Spinoza's system. Let's say that Mary comes to feel sad. Seeing that, I come to feel sadness too. I become aware of Mary's sadness by observing her behavior—her crying, moping around, etc. Now in the past when I was sad I may have behaved similarly and I may have been aware of such behavior on my part. Thus my own experience has established an association between an idea of a certain kind of behavior and a feeling of sadness. When I perceive such behavior in Mary, the general principle of the association of mental states determines that I will also experience sadness. In this way, I come to imitate Mary's affect of sadness. We could, in a similar fashion, explain any of the other cases of affect imitation that Spinoza's account is meant to cover. Thus Spinoza's doctrine of association can be called in to secure his doctrine of imitation.

The doctrine of imitation leads to new and insightful claims about the structure of affects. Spinoza accounts for pity as a kind of imitation: thus my sadness in imitation of Mary's sadness is pity (3p22s, 3p27s). There is also an even darker side of imitation, for it can lead to envy and ambition. Let's say I antecedently do not have any negative affect directed at Tommy or positive desire directed at blueberry pie, but when I see that Tommy has greedily grabbed the last slice of the pie, I will—in imitation of Tommy's desire—come to desire the slice too. But since I cannot now have that slice, one of my desires will be frustrated and I will see Tommy as the frustrator. Thus—although I previously did not want the pie and didn't hate and envy Tommy—I now quickly find myself in this situation with a new desire that is frustrated because of Tommy whom I thereby hate and envy. How did things spiral out of control so quickly? Answer: because of the imitation of affects, because of my imitation of Tommy's desire. In this way, we can see, as Spinoza insightfully observes, "from the same property of human nature from which it follows that men are compassionate"—i.e. because of the imitation of affects—"it also follows that the same men are envious and ambitious" (3p32s).

Spinoza accounts for a number of other affects through the doctrine of imitation, including ambition (3p29) and shame (3p30). One of its most important uses occurs in Spinoza's moral philosophy, where it is the basis of Spinoza's important claim that it is in our own interest to aid other people. We will turn to this argument in the following chapter.

Finally, I would like to explore the important ways in which the anticipation of mental states—itself a kind of association and imitation—helps structure our mental life and our affects.

A simple case of anticipation is the following: In the past, I have experienced a succession of objects A, B, and C. I have just experienced A again and am currently experiencing B again and ... and then what? Naturally, because of the association already established, I expect to experience C again. As Spinoza puts it, I have an idea of C as related to a future time and not to the present (3p18s1). Unfortunately, Spinoza's account of what it is to relate something to the present or to the future is very sketchy. I will have a bit to say about this account later.

This notion of anticipation helps Spinoza to define the affects hope and fear. Let's say that in the past C gave rise to considerable sadness in me. Thus, in anticipating C, I will also anticipate sadness, i.e. I will have the idea of a decrease in bodily power and relate that idea to a future time. For Spinoza, this anticipation of sadness itself involves sadness, i.e. the anticipation of pain is itself painful. Why should this be so? Both the initial perception of C and the anticipating of C are constituted in part by an idea of C. In the past, an association was established between the idea of C and pain. Thus, given the doctrine of association, when I anticipate C (and thus have an idea of C), I will likewise feel pain. Similarly, the anticipation of pleasure will itself be pleasurable. This insight leads to Spinoza's account of hope and fear. Hope is simply a kind of joy, in particular, it is "an inconstant joy which has arisen from the image of a future or past thing whose outcome we doubt." Likewise, fear "is an inconstant sadness which has also arisen from the image of a doubtful thing" (3p18s2).

Given that the anticipation of pain is itself painful, we can see how, for Spinoza, future pain can motivate present action. Prima facie, such motivation presents a problem: we can see how present pain can motivate us to stop the pain, but how can merely future pain have the power to motivate? This seems to be psychic action at a distance. Even if we represent the future pain, why should this be enough to motivate an action taken to avert the pain? There seem then to be two radically different kinds of motivated action: first, action in response to present pain, action taken to stop an ongoing decrease in power of acting; and second, action taken in the absence of any relevant pain to avert future pain. The first kind of action seems very easy to explain on Spinozistic terms. The second kind seems rather different and thus threatens to spoil a unified account of motivated action and threatens Spinoza's naturalism.

However, the threat is illusory because, as we have seen, it is not right to say that in the case of anticipation there is presently no relevant pain. There is: it is the pain of anticipation which is the present pain, the present diminution of power, that prompts us to act in order to avert future pain.

The painful anticipation of pain can be seen as a kind of imitation by one's present self of one's future self, or of one's supposed future self. As standard cases of imitation, and as in cases of association generally, the state and its imitation may not be precisely the same. In this case, Spinoza holds that typically the pain of anticipation is less powerful than is the anticipated pain when it comes to be present (4p9 and 4p9s). And thus, for Spinoza, typically and contrary to the adage, it is not the case that the anticipation is worse than the pain.

It is not entirely clear why, on Spinoza's system, the two pains should differ in motivational power. Spinoza's thought seems to be something like the following: When I relate an idea of an object to a future time, I have ideas of present things that somehow exclude the present existence of the object in question. These present things may, unlike the painful anticipated object, give rise to pleasure or at least not give rise to pain. And so this present object may engender affects that offset the painful anticipation of the painful object. But when the anticipated object comes to be present, there are no longer any present objects that can generate affects to offset the pain that the former object causes. These kinds of consideration are, I believe, at work in Spinoza's claim:

> An imagination ... is more intense so long as we imagine nothing which excludes the present existence of the external thing.
> Hence, an affect whose cause we imagine to be with us in the present is more intense or stronger than if we did not imagine it to be with us.
>
> (4p9d)

That the anticipation is typically less powerful than the anticipated pain is crucial to Spinoza's account of irrational action. Irrational actions—actions performed contrary to our own acknowledged better judgment—pose a particular challenge for a rationalist. Let's say that after many episodes of taunting by Billy the bully, I finally haul off and punch him right on that sweaty upper lip of his. And let's say I do this despite realizing—even at the time—that such an action can only do more harm than good for me in the long run. (Such an action may lead to even more painful forms of punishment.) Why then did I do it? What reason can be given for this action which overrides my own best judgment? The action—if it is truly an action of mine—might seem to be a brute fact: I seem to have done this stupid thing for no reason, or at least for no good reason. So irrational action may seem, by its very nature, to violate the PSR.

In this context, it may seem natural to appeal to the strength of emotions—something independent of the strength of reason—as generating my action. The strength of the emotions would seem to derive from some feature of the mind independent of those features that figure into our judgments qua judgments, i.e. independent of the representational content of mental states. This appeal to some non-representational emotional force to explain irrational action is another respect in which the account of irrational action seems to run counter to the rationalism which, as we have seen, puts pressure on one to account for affects in purely representational terms.

How then can Spinoza account for the all-too-common phenomenon of doing something against one's own better judgment? For Spinoza, as we have seen, the pain of anticipation is less strong than the anticipated pain. Further, for Spinoza, the degree of the pain of anticipation is a function of how far off in the future the anticipated pain is (4p10). Thus, if pleasure A is weaker than pain B, but pleasure A is in the near future and pain B in the very distant future, it can happen that the pleasure of anticipating pleasure A will outweigh the pain of anticipating pain B, even though in itself pain B is greater than pleasure A and even if I am aware of this fact. So, because of the temporal disparity of two affects, it can happen that the anticipation of a less strong affect is more able to get us to act than the anticipation of a stronger affect. In this way, while allowing that there can be action against one's own better judgment, Spinoza also insists that such action is not unintelligible: when acting irrationally, we act in response to the stronger present affect but we do so while subject to a distortion in our motivation produced by the temporal disparity between the objects of two rival, anticipated affects.[17] Spinoza appeals to such temporal disparity immediately after claiming that there can be irrational action. (See 4p17s and also 4p60, 4app30.)

The challenge, however, is now for Spinoza to explain how we can avoid these motivational glitches brought on by variations in temporal distance, how we can be less susceptible to irrational action. More generally, Spinoza needs to explain how we can avoid actions that, in the long run, are detrimental to us and contrary to our goal of self-preservation and of increasing our power of acting. Spinoza attempts to meet this challenge in Part V of the Ethics (as we'll see in Chapters 5 and 7).

We are at last in a position to return to the two puzzles raised at the beginning of Section 2. First, how can Spinoza justify the derivation—simply from the claim that we strive to preserve ourselves—that we also strive to increase our power of acting? As I mentioned, Spinoza nowhere justifies this inference, but we can now see that he has the resources to make progress on this problem. Assume that we strive to preserve ourselves and also that we are capable of anticipating future threats to our existence and to our well-being. Of course, the threats are many and diverse and it is in our own interest to accumulate as much power as possible to be able to meet these various threats when they occur. There is, as we might say, no telling which ability, which power, may come in handy, and so our striving to preserve ourselves dictates that we strive to acquire as much power as possible.[18]

This answer to our first puzzle also points the way to a resolution of the second puzzle which concerned whether Spinoza intends his claim that we strive to increase our power of acting to apply also to less complex individuals such as the pan. If we see the claim that we strive to increase our power as depending crucially—as I have just argued—on our ability to anticipate threats to our well-being that are in the future, perhaps in the distant future, then we would not expect that individuals that lack the complexity to anticipate events in the distant future to strive to increase their power of acting. And Spinoza does think that individuals such as the pan do lack the requisite complexity to anticipate (see 2p17c). Thus we would expect that individuals that are very much less complex than we are strive only to preserve themselves and do not strive to increase their power of acting.

Spinoza nowhere takes up these puzzles about increase in power of acting, and so it is hard to be sure whether he would try to solve them in the ways I have just suggested. But these answers are clearly Spinozistic, even if not Spinoza's.

SUMMARY

Spinoza's psychology, his moral philosophy, his political philosophy, and other areas of his system all derive from his claim that no thing destroys itself and, indeed, that each thing tends or strives to stay in existence and to increase its power of acting. Spinoza's preclusion of self-destruction is, more specifically, the claim that the essence of a thing never suffices for its destruction. This claim can be seen as deriving from the PSR. Ordinary, apparent cases of self-destruction (suicide, time bombs, etc.) are actually cases in which outside causes overwhelm a thing and, together with the thing's essence, lead to the thing's destruction. This account of tending or striving is not specifically psychological in character, and thus even tables, chairs, and rocks can be said to strive to persist. Spinoza's account of human affects or emotions derives entirely from his theory of striving. For Spinoza, there are three fundamental affects: desire, joy, and sadness. All others are constructed from these three. Desire is simply a mind's striving for persistence and for increase in power. Joy is the transition of a mind to a greater power, and sadness is the transition to a lesser power. These strivings and these transitions are, in keeping with Spinoza's austerely representational and rationalist account of the mind, all there is to the other less fundamental affects. Through his account of the affects, Spinoza is able to give, within the context of his overarching rationalist system, plausible accounts of various irrational phenomena such as acting against one's better judgment and jealousy and love that turns into hatred.

FURTHER READING

Antonio Damasio (2003) *Looking for Spinoza: Joy, Sorrow, and the Feeling Brain.* (Engaging defense of a Spinozistic approach to the emotions in light of contemporary neuroscience.)

Michael Della Rocca (1996b) "Spinoza's Metaphysical Psychology." (Overview of most aspects of Spinoza's psychology.)

Daniel Garber (1994) "Descartes and Spinoza on Persistence and Conatus." (Spinoza's theory of striving in light of his physics, and some illuminating contrasts with Descartes's notion of striving individuals.)

Don Garrett (2002) "Spinoza's Conatus Argument." (Excellent account of the doctrine of the universal striving for self-preservation.)

Susan James (1997) *Passion and Action: The Emotions in Seventeenth-Century Philosophy.* (Helpful account of Spinoza and his contemporaries.)

Wallace Matson (1969) "Death and Destruction in Spinoza's Ethics." (Classic account of Spinoza's conatus doctrine.)

Jerome Neu (1977) *Emotion, Thought, and Therapy: A Study of Hume and Spinoza and the Relationship of Philosophical Theories of the Emotions to Psychological Theories of Therapy.* (Useful account of Spinoza's connections to Hume and Freud.)

Five

The Ethics of the *Ethics*

Wholly on the basis of his account of human psychology, which is, in turn, based wholly on his metaphysics, Spinoza constructs his moral philosophy. In other words, by examining the metaphysical grounds of our psychology, Spinoza believes he is able to determine what is good for us and what we are morally obligated to do. Further, things in general are to be evaluated simply in terms of what they most fundamentally are, in terms of their natures. Since, as we have seen, our nature and the natures of things in general are shot through with intelligibility, what is good for, and morally required, of each person or thing is a function of that person's or thing's intelligibility.

This perspective on my nature leads to Spinoza's view that it is good and right for me to do whatever is conducive to my happiness, well-being, and power. Thus Spinoza's rationalist emphasis on intelligibility generates an ethical system that is fundamentally egoistic—centered on the interests and power of the self. But, for Spinoza, ethics is not simply a power grab. As we will see in the second half of this chapter, Spinoza attempts in various ways to smooth out the selfish edge of his egoism by incorporating in this system a genuine concern for others and by articulating methods we can employ to become more powerful and less at the mercy of our passions, and thus to help others as well as ourselves.

1. THE GOOD NOTION OF THE GOOD

Initially, it might seem as if the prospects for a robust account of morality in Spinoza are not very good. After all, Spinoza disparages the ordinary use of evaluative distinctions such as good/bad, perfect/ imperfect, distinctions which, he seems to say, have no basis in reality. For Spinoza, we typically evaluate things in terms of the degree to which they are useful or pleasing to us. As he says, people judge that...

> what is most important in each thing is what is most useful to them, and ... rate as most excellent all those things by which they were most pleased.
>
> (1app, G II/81)

And precisely because we desire things because they are pleasing to us, Spinoza sees our ordinary judgments of goodness as based on our desires. As Spinoza says,

> we neither strive for, nor will, neither want, nor desire anything because we judge it to be good; on the contrary, we judge something to be good because we strive for it, will it, want it, and desire it.
>
> (3p9s)

Because our ordinary judgments of goodness stem from our desires, Spinoza goes on to claim, the goodness we seem to find in things is not properly located in the things themselves, but rather in our way of responding to those things. We can see why Spinoza reaches this conclusion by noting that different individuals react differently to the same thing: the same thing may be pleasing to me and not to you. For Spinoza, my evaluative judgment, based as it is on what the object does to or for me, has no more claim to be reflective of any goodness in the object than your contrary evaluative judgment, based as it is on what the object does to or for you. Spinoza makes this point well in the preface to Part IV:

> As far as good and evil are concerned, they also indicate nothing positive in things, considered in themselves, nor are they anything

other than modes of thinking, or notions we form because we
compare things to one another. For one and the same thing can,
at the same time, be good, and bad, and also indifferent. For
example, music is good for one who is melancholy, bad for one
who is mourning, and neither good nor bad to one who is deaf.

(G II 208)

Unsurprisingly, we can see at work here a concern with arbitrariness
and brute facts. To say that my evaluative judgments—and not yours—
are reflective of the goodness in the object itself is to make a wholly
arbitrary claim: why should my interests be, or be conceived to be,
the standard for goodness any more than yours? Nothing about the
object itself points to my interests in particular as setting the standard
here. To the extent that we employ our ordinary evaluative judgments
to generate a ranking of objects as good or bad in themselves, we
are positing a brute fact—that a certain thing is good because it is
pleasing *to me*. And of course, positing a brute fact is illegitimate,
for Spinoza. We can see then the PSR as behind Spinoza's dismissive treatment of our ordinary use of evaluative terms.

Another way to see the connection between this dismissive
treatment and the PSR is by recalling Spinoza's tirade against purposiveness in nature. For Spinoza, we tend to see all that happens
as happening for our sake, and when we see or think we see that
some things are not beneficial to us, we believe that nature has
failed (4pref, G 206, 208). And when we see that some things are
beneficial to us, we believe that nature has succeeded, it has done
well. Our evaluations of things in nature are really evaluations of
things as successful or unsuccessful realizations of nature's goal of
aiding us. Spinoza draws this connection between purposiveness in
nature and our evaluative judgments in a passage from the appendix to Part I of the *Ethics*:

After men persuaded themselves that everything which happens,
happens on their account, they had to judge that what is most

important in each thing is what is most useful to them, and to rate as most excellent all those things by which they were most pleased.

(G II 81)

As we saw at the end of Chapter 2, to see nature as having goals directed at us in particular and not at other things, is to appeal to a brute fact: there's no good reason why we should be singled out in this way. Here again we can see that Spinoza's rationalism requires that he reject our ordinary evaluative judgments.

The worry that ordinary evaluative judgments are infected with arbitrariness applies not just to the evaluations of things in terms of my interests in particular or in terms of your interests in particular, but even to evaluations that appeal to certain apparently less arbitrary standards. To see why, let's focus for the moment on the evaluation of a particular action—my helping Mother Theresa across the street. Such an action may be good relative to Mother Theresa's interests, and it may be bad relative to the interests of Mother Theresa's sworn enemies, but again all such verdicts are arbitrary and do not point to anything good or bad about the action in itself. However, perhaps we can evaluate that action more neutrally, not in terms of my interests, or Mother Theresa's, etc., but in terms of the interests of persons in general. We might say that if (and only if) helping Mother Theresa leads to a greater overall amount of happiness or pleasure (or whatever) in the world, if the benefit to Mother Theresa and others outweighs the disadvantages to Mother Theresa's enemies, then that action is good. This standard of the goodness of an action—tied to the overall happiness that results from the action—is precisely the kind of standard of goodness that utilitarian moral theories appeal to, and it does seem appealingly non-arbitrary: in determining the good, we must take each person's interests into account equally.

However, I believe that Spinoza would see this apparently less objectionable standard as arbitrary for the same kind of reason that me-focused or you-focused standards were seen as arbitrary. The goodness of the action is, in this case as in the others, not a function of the thing to be evaluated—the action—in itself; rather it is still a function of the action in relation to the interests of certain individuals, here the interests of each person. But, Spinoza would ask, why should *overall* well-being or happiness be the standard of goodness, instead of, for example, the standard whereby actions are evaluated relative to the interests of all fans of the Beatles, or all Albanians, or all living beings including non-persons? The problem is that nothing about the action itself points to any of these standards, including the most inclusive standards, rather than any of the other standards. Each of these standards is arbitrary. In this way we can see that one of Spinoza's objections to utilitarianism would be the arbitrary conception of the goodness of an action on which it depends. (Spinoza would similarly object to the utilitarian conception of the right, as we'll see shortly.) For Spinoza, what we need to do in order to arrive at a viable conception of the goodness of actions and things generally is to find a standard of goodness that derives from the very nature of the thing to be evaluated. Only such a standard—if one could be found— would not be arbitrary and would be in keeping with Spinoza's rationalism.

Spinoza is certainly eager to find such a non-arbitrary standard so that he can redeem the notion of the good. This eagerness fits in with a pattern we have observed on a number of occasions. Thus consider, for example, Spinoza's treatment of our ordinary notions of consciousness, epistemic standards, and causation which, for him, also violate rationalist principles of explicability. As we have seen, for Spinoza, we tend to see consciousness and epistemic standards as hovering inexplicably over mere representation; we tend to see causation as a brute power not grounded in any explicable conceptual connection, etc. Despite their suspect pedigrees, Spinoza does not give up on the notions of consciousness, epistemic standards, and causation; instead he redeems them by showing how they amount to, in different ways, nothing but the notion of intelligibility. Similarly, Spinoza seeks to redeem the notion of goodness; he wants to have a legitimate way to say that things, people, and actions are good in themselves, not merely in relation to this or that arbitrary standard.[1] Without that kind of legitimate standard, the *Ethics* and, indeed, ethics itself would be impossible. Spinoza makes precisely this point—about the need to find some legitimate standard—in the preface to Part IV of the *Ethics* immediately after lamenting the arbitrariness of ordinary judgments of good and evil:

> But though this is so, still we must retain these words. For because we desire to form an idea of man, as a model of human nature which we may look to, it will be useful to retain these same words with the meaning I have indicated.
>
> (G II 208)

So Spinoza must look for a non-arbitrary standard in the very thing to be evaluated. What does he find there? Let's begin again with the goodness or badness of a particular action. Later we will turn, on this basis, to the evaluation of things in general. Consider again my wonderful action of helping Mother Theresa across the street: what is the nature of this action? It is, for Spinoza, fundamentally a striving to enhance my power. As we saw, for Spinoza, all my actions are strivings to increase my power. Of course, to some extent, an action of mine may be a striving to decrease my power (consider the case of suicide, for example) but insofar as I am in myself, my action is a striving to increase my power. An action that is not in some measure a striving to increase my power could not intelligibly be seen as an action of mine.

Obviously, this striving to increase my power can have a greater or lesser degree of success. My attempt to help Mother Theresa may, for example, result in my being praised, which can, in obvious ways, lead to my greater happiness and power. This would be one way in which the striving that constitutes the action would be successful. Alternatively, my action may lead some jealous friend of Mother Theresa to punch me in the nose. In this case, the striving would, in this respect, not be successful, for my action, it turns out, results only in a decrease in my power.

Here, then, Spinoza would say, is at last a non-arbitrary standard by which to evaluate actions: an action is positively evaluated to the extent to which the striving that constitutes the action is successful, and it is negatively evaluated otherwise. In other words, an agent's actions are good to the extent that they increase that agent's power and they are bad to the extent that they decrease that agent's power. Thus Spinoza says in 3p39s: "By good here I understand every kind of joy, and whatever leads to it." Recall that joy is simply the increase to a greater power of acting. So Spinoza's implication here is that my actions are good to the extent to which they increase my power. This standard is not arbitrarily imposed on the action; rather it stems from the very nature of an action as a striving to increase one's power. Similarly the agent himself—and, indeed, things in general—are good to the extent to which they strive successfully. Spinoza makes this claim in terms of *perfection* in the appendix to Part I of the *Ethics*: "the perfection of things is to be judged solely from their nature and power" (G II 83). Notice that here Spinoza crucially sees the correct evaluative standard as deriving from the very nature of the things evaluated. Similarly, I believe, Spinoza would say that, if we are to avoid arbitrary evaluative judgments, the *goodness* of things must be judged solely from their nature and power (and not from any response those things may prompt in us or in other things). Indeed, I believe that the emphasis on power in both the definition of "good" in 3p39s and this passage from the appendix to Part I indicate that perfection and goodness are coextensive: a thing is perfect to the extent to which it is good and vice versa.

Finally, the connection between power, essence, and evaluation emerges quite vividly in 4def8:

> By virtue and power I understand the same thing, that is (by 3p7)
> virtue, insofar as it is related to man, is the very essence, or
> nature of man, insofar as he has the power of bringing about
> certain things, which can be understood through the laws of his
> nature alone.

I see no reason not to generalize this definition in order to say that
virtue, insofar as it is related to any thing, is simply the very
essence of that thing. Certainly, Spinoza's gloss on 4def8 in 4p18s
is completely general:

> virtue (by 4def8) is nothing but acting from the laws of one's own
> nature [*ex legibus propriae naturae agere*].

As in the case of perfection, I believe that Spinoza's explicit tying of
both goodness and virtue to power indicates that, for him, a thing
is virtuous to the extent to which it is good, and it is good to the
extent to which it is virtuous.[2]

Thus, for Spinoza, absolutely anything can be evaluated in a non-
arbitrary way. Rocks are good (and perfect and even virtuous) to
the extent to which they are powerful. Our actions are good to the
extent to which they are powerful, i.e. to the extent that they lead
to the successful realization of the striving that constitutes those
actions. I am good to the extent that I am more powerful. Even
God can be evaluated in this way. In the previous chapter, I suggested that, for Spinoza, there is a meaningful sense in which God
can be said to strive, to have a tendency to cause certain things.
Precisely because this tendency meets with no resistance, God's
striving meets with no resistance. God's strivings are all successful,
and thus God is maximally good, perfect, and virtuous.

The familiar relativistic, arbitrary evaluative judgments have their
place against this more objective evaluative background. Thus,
although a scorpion, say, is good—and even non-arbitrarily so—to
the extent to which it is powerful, I will judge the scorpion to be

bad precisely because it can harm me. My perspectival judgment is right as far as it goes, but it is perspectival. As such, it is compatible with a non-perspectival, more objective evaluation of the scorpion in terms of its degree of power. It is this kind of objective evaluation—the kind of evaluation that can be applied to ourselves and our actions—that, for Spinoza, is the only way to redeem ethics itself and to put it on a secure, rationalist footing.

We see here, of course, another twofold use of the PSR. In order to make ethics itself possible, Spinoza seeks to give an account of what goodness consists in; he seeks to *explain* goodness. For Spinoza, the goodness of a thing would be inexplicable and our standards of goodness would be arbitrary unless goodness is a function of the thing's very nature, and thus of the thing's striving to increase its power. The power of a thing is simply its ability to bring about changes in itself or in other things, changes that are thus conceived through and explained in terms of that thing. Thus, for Spinoza, goodness must be explained—that's the first use of the PSR. And—here comes the second use—it must be explained in terms of that thing's ability to be the explanation of changes in things. For Spinoza, goodness can be made intelligible only in terms of intelligibility itself, in much the same way that the many other crucial notions we have examined so far are to be made intelligible. Spinoza's rationalism thus courses through his moral philosophy as much as it does through all other regions of his system.

2. THE RIGHT NOTION OF THE RIGHT

Even with the redemption of the notion of the good, the redemption of ethics itself is not yet complete. An ethical theory must provide not only an account of the good, but also an account of the right, of what we are morally *obligated* to do, what we, morally speaking, *ought* to do. Determining what is good doesn't necessarily settle what one ought to do. Many philosophers have espoused such a divergence and, as we will see, Kantian-style views do precisely this. As it turns out, however, for Spinoza, in keeping with his general rationalist principles and his general rationalist tendency to assimilate apparently disparate notions, the good and the right coincide.

Let's consider again a particular action of mine. Thus, fresh from helping Mother Theresa across the street, I rush out to buy the latest Paul McCartney CD. Is that an action that I'm morally obligated to perform? If we assume that this action is a moral requirement, then in virtue of what ought I to perform this action? Perhaps, my buying the CD makes McCartney happy and, for that reason, I ought to buy it. But, by the same token, the purchase may make McCartney-haters sad, and so perhaps it is not the case that I should make the purchase. Indeed, perhaps then I should not buy it. Nothing about the action itself seems to point to one of these "oughts" as opposed to another.

Alternatively, perhaps what I ought to do in this case is not a function at all of the happiness or sadness my action may create. Perhaps the action is morally required to the extent that it promotes the popularization of silly love songs. This standard—which buying McCartney's CD certainly meets—may seem odd, indeed it is odd. But why should this standard be any more objectionable than one of the standards geared to the happiness of some or all individuals? Again, the action itself doesn't seem to point to or suggest any one of these standards, and so, from this point of view, all these standards will seem equally arbitrary and brute.

As in the case of goodness, the only way out—the only way to emerge with a legitimate notion of rightness—is to see what standard is generated by the nature of the action itself. And, as before, the standard that the action's own nature provides is the degree of success of the striving that is the action. Thus we can see that, just as power is the standard of goodness (and perfection and virtue), so too it is the standard of rightness, the standard of what we ought to do. We ought to do something to the extent that it makes us more powerful, just as something is good to the extent that it makes us more powerful. In the case at hand, I ought to buy the

McCartney CD and doing so is good if and only if buying it makes me more powerful. Thus goodness and rightness coincide for Spinoza, and they don't just happen to do so; rather, we must affirm—on pain of accepting a brute fact—that they each derive from the very nature of an action as a striving.

Perhaps because Spinoza does not see rightness as in any way separate from goodness, he has few pronouncements specifically on what we *ought* to do, but he does make clear in key passages that, for him, what we ought to do is, like what is good, a matter of power. Thus Spinoza says that reason

> demands that everyone love himself, seek his own advantage, what is really useful to him, want what will really lead a man to greater perfections, and absolutely, that everyone strive to preserve his own being insofar as he is in himself.
>
> (4p18s, translation modified)

Later in that scholium, Spinoza remarks that we *ought* to want virtue for its own sake. Since, for Spinoza, virtue is power (4def8), he is saying that we ought to want power for its own sake.

Here, in the case of the moral oughts, we have again the characteristic twofold use of the PSR. For Spinoza, rightness is to be explained, and it must, like goodness, be explained in terms of the power of a thing, its ability to serve as the explanation of certain things.

3. KNOWLEDGE AND MORALITY

The use of the notion of intelligibility in the case of evaluative standards of rightness and also of goodness is of a piece, I have stressed, with Spinoza's similar use of this notion in other areas of his philosophy. The analogy between Spinoza's treatment of moral standards and his treatment of epistemic standards is particularly striking and illuminating. As we saw, for Spinoza an idea is evaluated as certain or not in virtue of the idea itself and its nature as representational: the degree of certainty an idea enjoys is simply a function of the clarity with which it represents things. If the epistemic evaluation of an idea were to derive from anything other than its representational nature, its epistemic status would, as we have seen, be a brute fact. Similarly, in the case of goodness, the standard of evaluation must derive from the thing itself. Further, in each of these cases, the thing in question is evaluated simply in terms of intelligibility itself. Certainty is a matter of representation which is, as we saw, just mental intelligibility. Similarly, goodness is a matter of power itself which is just the ability to serve as the explanation of things, to make them intelligible.

But this is not a mere analogy between Spinoza's epistemology and his account of moral notions; his epistemology is also integrated into his moral philosophy. For Spinoza, knowledge is the object of morality. That is, for Spinoza, what is good for us to do and what we ought to do is to acquire knowledge. The crucial link here is via the notion of power and, ultimately of course, explanation. For Spinoza, it is good and right that we seek more and more power, more and more ability to act on our own, relatively independently of external things. As we saw in Chapter 3, for Spinoza our ideas are confused, inadequate and uncertain to the extent that they are caused from outside our mind, i.e. to the extent that they manifest our passivity and not our power. But to the extent that our ideas are caused from within our minds, i.e. to the extent that our ideas are a manifestation of our power, they are unconfused, adequate, and certain. Given that it is good and right for us to increase our power, it follows that—on the mental level—it is good and right for us to increase our knowledge (4p26–27). We ought—morally speaking—to acquire a greater number of adequate ideas or, at least, ideas with a greater degree of adequacy. Knowledge, for Spinoza, is the greatest good and the object of the highest obligation precisely because knowledge is power.

The knowledge that will invest our minds with the greatest power is the knowledge of that thing with the most fundamental explanatory connections to other things. By mirroring in our minds the source of things, our minds become less dependent on external causes in coming to cognize things. Thus the mind becomes more active. For this reason, we should strive to understand the most fundamental source of things so that we may more actively understand things in general. Of course, this fundamental source is none other than God, and for this reason Spinoza says: "Knowledge of God is the mind's greatest good; its greatest virtue is to know God."[3] Spinoza gives expression to similar thoughts in TdIE when he says:

> The most perfect method will be the one that shows how the mind is to be directed according to the standard of the given idea of the most perfect being.
>
> (§39)

He then exhorts us to...

> Bring all of [the mind's] ideas forth from that idea which represents the source and origin of the whole of nature, so that that idea is also the source of the other ideas.
>
> (§42)

4. FREEDOM AND MORALITY

Spinoza correlates the notion of freedom with the notions of goodness, rightness, adequacy of ideas, adequacy of causation, and power. In this section, I will explore some of the ways Spinoza's account of freedom drives his moral philosophy.

For Spinoza, freedom is simply the absence of external determination together with—since given the PSR everything must be determined—the presence of internal determination. Freedom is thus a thing's ability to act, to bring about changes on its own. Thus Spinoza says near the beginning of the *Ethics*:

> That thing is called free which exists from the necessity of its nature alone, and is determined to act by itself alone. But a thing

is called necessary, or rather compelled, which is determined by
another to exist and to produce an effect in a certain and
determinate manner.

(1def7)

Because, as we have seen, a thing's *power* is its ability to cause things on
its own, freedom is simply power. Thus in striving for more power—
as is good and right—and thus in striving to have more knowledge,
we are striving to become more free. This connection between power,
freedom, and knowledge is succinctly summed up in the full title
of Part V: "Of the Power of the Intellect, or of Human Freedom."

Because, for Spinoza, our power comes in degrees and is,
obviously, limited (4ax, 4p4), it follows that our freedom comes in
degrees and is limited as well. Spinoza acknowledges that freedom
comes in degrees at, for example, 4p73d: "a man who is guided by
reason desires, in order to live *more freely*, to keep the common laws
of the state" (my emphasis). And he claims that freedom is limited
and subject to degrees at TP, ch. 2, §8:

it is not in every man's power always to use reason and be at
the highest pitch [*summo ... fastigio*] of human freedom, but yet
he always endeavors, insofar as he is in himself, to preserve his
own being.

(translation altered)

Spinoza puts our freedom on the same scale as God's in this passage from the previous section of TP:

a man can certainly not be called free on the grounds that he is
able not to exist, or that he is able not to use his reason; he can
be called free only insofar as he has power to exist and to act in
accordance with the laws of human nature. So the more free we
consider a man to be, the less we can say that he is able not to
use his reason and to choose evil before good; and so God, who

> exists, understands, and acts with absolute freedom, also exists, understands, and acts necessarily, that is, from the necessity of his own nature.

Here again we can see Spinoza's naturalism at work: finite things and God share the same kinds of features, are explained in the same kind of way, and differ from each other only in the degree of limitation to which they are subject.

Because of the inevitable limitation of our freedom, we can see that Spinoza employs the notion of the "free man" at the end of Part IV of the *Ethics* as an idealization. As Spinoza says, a free man would be a person "who lives according to the dictate of reason alone" (4p67d) and thus has only adequate ideas (4p68d), and is perfectly active. Spinoza sees such an individual as—to use his phrase from the preface to Part IV—a model to which we may look in shaping our actions. (See also TdIE §13.) Like all individuals, such a person's actions would be prompted by his desires, but unlike other, more passive individuals, the free man's desires are not externally determined, and so they are fully active and thus fully rational and free. Of course, given our inevitable passivity, the free man is strictly impossible, as Spinoza indicates in 4p68s, and only God can be fully free. Nonetheless, we can achieve a greater and greater degree of freedom and thus become more and more like the model of the absolutely free person.

Because freedom comes in degrees and because the goodness and rightness of our actions is a function of their freedom, it follows that, for Spinoza, whenever an action is wrong and bad, the action is correspondingly less free. We less freely perform actions that are negatively evaluated and we more freely perform good and right actions. Indeed, one can see that, to the extent that an action is bad and wrong, it is less fully mine and more fully the action of external things. For Spinoza, one might say that only free actions are fully our own. I will return to this theme in Chapter 7 when we take up Spinoza's account of the nature of existence.

Just as freedom comes in degrees for Spinoza, so too does moral responsibility. Thus, for example, not only are we less free in performing bad and wrong actions, but we are also, for Spinoza, less responsible for those actions. This take on moral responsibility emerges in Spinoza's account of praise and blame. Often Spinoza dismisses these notions as depending on a mistaken belief. We praise or blame persons because we mistakenly think that these persons freely perform certain actions. As Spinoza says, "because [people] think themselves free, these notions have arisen: praise and blame, sin and merit" (1app, G II 81, translation altered).[4] However, given that praise and blame are tied to freedom, it follows that Spinoza is committed to the more nuanced view that praise and blame are appropriate to the extent that the action in question is freely performed. Thus praise and blame are not to be thrown out entirely. This more subtle position is implicit in 3p48. There Spinoza says that the affects of love and hate toward an individual are *diminished* to the extent that we recognize that the individual was not the sole cause of a helpful or harmful action. Thus love and hate come in degrees that depend on the degree to which an agent is seen as free. The affects of praise and blame— themselves responses to helpful and harmful actions (3p29s)—can therefore also come in degrees that depend on the degree to which an agent is seen as free. This suggests that such affects would be appropriate and, indeed, rational to the extent to which an agent actually is free and that, therefore, an agent is genuinely responsible for her actions to that degree.

This diminishment of the affects of love and hate, praise and blame, is the basis of one of the key ways in which Spinoza says we may free ourselves from the power of harmful affects. By coming to see that stupid Billy from Chapter 4 as determined in his bullying ways, the presupposition of freedom on which my negative affects of blame and hate were erected is undermined. To that extent, those negative affects slip away. But why, one might ask, isn't the negative affect now simply transferred from Billy to the whole deterministic series of causes, leading perhaps back to God, a series which I now see as causing the harmful effects? In this way, the affects of blame and hate would be shifted, but would still remain as strong as before. Spinoza responds to this difficulty by pointing out that my realization of the determination of Billy's actions is my way of having a more adequate idea of those actions and thus of the passions they caused in me. To the extent that I now enjoy this broader view, I am more active and so happier. The negative affects of blame and hate give way, at least to some extent, to the active joys of understanding. (There is a similar line of argument in 5p18 for the claim that no one can hate God.) Spinoza seems to think that the passive affects of blame and hate can be *eliminated* in this way (5p3). However, it's not clear why this would be true, especially given that Billy has in fact harmed me, decreased my power of acting. Nevertheless, the harm may be compensated for to some degree by the benefits of understanding, and this may be enough for Spinoza to show that we can gain some measure of control over our passive affects. Whether or not this is an effective strategy for overcoming the affects, Spinoza can be seen as expressing a genuine and Freudian insight: passions may lose some of their power to harm us when we have a clearer understanding of how we came to have them and to be in their power. For Spinoza, then, the ability to see things in their causal network, the ability to explain things, is our ticket out of bondage. Knowledge, for Spinoza, and in particular knowledge of explanatory connections is power, and, since power is good, explanation itself is a force for good in the world.

Let's return to the notion of degrees of freedom and responsibility. What bearing does this notion have on Spinoza's account of punishment and reward? It might seem that, because finite agents are not absolutely free or responsible, punishment for harmful actions or reward for beneficial ones is therefore never justified. But this is not so for Spinoza. Punishment and reward, like all other actions, can be justified only by virtue of the way in which these actions would enhance the power of the agents who perform them. The degree of freedom of the punished or rewarded agent is not relevant to the justification of the punishment or reward. Thus for Spinoza punishment or reward, even of unfree agents, can be rational and good and right. As Spinoza says, with characteristic pith:

> If only those were fit to be punished whom we feign to sin only from freedom, why do men try to exterminate poisonous snakes?
>
> (CM II, chap. 8, G I 265)

Spinoza also says that...

> a judge who condemns a guilty man to death—not from hate or anger, and the like, but only from a love of the general welfare— is guided only by reason.
>
> (4p63cs, see also KV II 18, §5, Letter 58 (end), Letter 78)

In these passages, punishment is dictated by the interests of the punisher. Notice, however, that the interests are somehow general: the punisher acts on behalf, not only of himself, but also of a broader community. How is it possible to act on behalf of others in Spinoza's egoistic system? This is the topic of the next section.

5. HELPING OTHERS

Strongly egoistic moral theories are inevitably seen as harsh and heartless, exhorting individuals to trample on the interests of others in a headlong rush to satisfy their own desires. Although Spinoza is certainly an egoist, it is equally certain that the prevailing caricature of egoism does not apply to him. Spinoza's egoism embodies a robust concern for the well-being of others. Indeed, his rationalism itself dictates that it is rational to promote the interests of others. For Spinoza, acting on behalf of others—like any other action—would be unintelligible if such action did not follow from our own nature, a nature which is the striving to enhance our power of acting and to make more things conceivable through, explained by, our nature. Here is another twofold use of the PSR: acting on behalf of others must be explained, and it is to be explained in terms of our endeavor to make other things explainable in terms of ourselves. But this result shows only that if there is action on behalf of others, such action must follow from our nature as striving to increase our power of acting. But we have yet to see how action on behalf of others can flow from our nature, and so we have yet to see how Spinoza removes the harsh edge from his egoism.

The crucial claim here is 4p37:

> The good which everyone who seeks virtue wants for himself, he also desires for other men.

If a rational person seeks only his own benefit, why should he care whether others get the beneficial things he seeks for himself? Because the foundation of virtue is—as Spinoza stresses—the endeavor to preserve oneself—why should a rational and virtuous person take any interest in whether others also succeed in attaining virtue, also succeed in becoming more powerful? A virtue based on power, as virtue is for Spinoza, would seem to leave no room for concern for others.

But this Spinoza denies, and he has two separate arguments for doing so. The first argument begins with the claim that people who are rational, who seek their own interest and who, therefore, tend to have greater power are most useful to other people. As Spinoza says, "There is no singular thing in nature which is more useful to man than a man who lives according to the guidance of reason" (4p35c1). Given this claim, it is clear that a rational person—a person bent on his own self-interest and power—has an interest in other people becoming and being rational, in their having the kind of good that virtue entails and that the rational person himself seeks.

But why does Spinoza think that rational individuals are beneficial to people in general? Spinoza's answer in 4p35c1 is that:

what is most useful to man is what most agrees with his own
nature ... that is (as is known through itself) man.

By "nature", Spinoza means essence (4def8) and thus his claim
here that two people can agree in nature may be puzzling given
Spinoza's commitment—outlined in Chapter 3—to the uniqueness
of essences. But there I also stressed that Spinoza speaks of essences
at different levels of generality. At the most specific level, essences
are unique and not shared. But there are also general essences—
such as the essence of human beings—which can be shared by
more than one individual. The notion of more and less general
essences is helpful also because it enables us to see how two things
can agree in essence to greater or lesser degrees. Two human
beings will agree in nature more than, say, one human being and
one bat, etc. The notion of degrees of agreement in nature will be
important in what follows.

Spinoza implies in 4p35c1 that things that are *most* useful to me
are things that *most agree* with my nature. This suggests the general
view that things are useful to me to the extent to which they agree
with my nature. Why should this be so? I think we can go some way
in illuminating Spinoza's answer to this question, although some
deep difficulties will nonetheless remain. Recall that, for Spinoza,
acting solely on the basis of one's nature—doing only those things
that follow from one's nature—constitutes being powerful and is
thus beneficial to one. Acting on the basis of your nature is beneficial to you and, similarly, acting on the basis of my nature is
beneficial to me. To the extent that you and I agree in nature, we
have the same nature, your nature is my nature. And to that extent,
acting on the basis of your nature is acting on the basis of my
nature. Since acting on the basis of my nature benefits me, acting on
the basis of your nature—which just is to some extent, as we have
just seen, acting on the basis of my nature—benefits me. In other
words, given the commonality between our natures, acting on the
basis of your nature not only benefits you, but it also benefits me.

So we can see that, for Spinoza, whether your action benefits me is a function of two separate matters that are matters of degree: the extent to which you and I agree in nature and the extent to which you are rational, the extent to which you act on the basis of your nature. The more it is true both that you and I agree in nature *and* that you are rational, the more your actions also benefit me.

The flip side of this harmonious picture is, of course, that to the extent that (given the overlap in nature) you are passive, less powerful, less rational, to that extent your actions, your pursuits may clash with mine and so we may not be useful to one another and may even be harmful to one another. Since you and I are inevitably passive to some degree—since we inevitably act in a way that is not exclusively determined by our natures, you and I will have some tendency to clash. As Spinoza says,

> Insofar as men are subject to passions, they cannot be said to agree in nature.
>
> (4p32)

> Insofar as men are torn by affects which are passions, they can be contrary to one another.
>
> (4p34)

However, the more we act out of our own nature, the more we benefit one another:

> When each man most seeks his own advantage for himself, then men are most useful to one another.
>
> (4p35c2)

Notice also that, given that you are active, your actions benefit me to the extent to which you and I agree in nature. If you are a particularly active and rational ant, your virtuous actions will do little to benefit me because there is so little in common between your nature and mine. But if you are a particularly rational human being, then, given that I am—let me be bold!—a human being, your action will thereby benefit me.

It follows from Spinoza's view, as I have presented it, that given that you and I agree in nature, the more you and I both become rational and act on the basis of that nature, the less there is to distinguish us. As Spinoza might put it, the fewer passions there are to tear us asunder, the smaller the basis on which we can be distinguished. At the ideal point, you and I would act solely from our shared nature and would thus become indistinguishable. Given the identity of indiscernibles—the principle according to which things that can't be distinguished are identical—you and I will thus be a single person. Of course, neither you nor I can act fully rationally, and, for the same reason, the free man is also an impossible ideal. But this impossible ideal presents for us the character our aspirations should take. As Spinoza says,

> Man, I say, can wish for nothing more helpful to the preservation of his being than that all should so agree in all things that the minds and bodies of all would compose, as it were, one mind and one body.
>
> (4p18s)

This is the kind of unity that only God enjoys fully, but that you and I can partake of to some degree.

Thus we can see why, for Spinoza, I have an interest in benefiting my fellow human beings by making them more rational: their increased rationality, by itself, benefits me as well as all other human beings. This interest in benefiting others is not the standard way in which to incorporate concern for others into an egoistic ethical system. A typical Hobbesian's, say, basis for generating such concern for others lies in the argument that if I help others then those others will be more likely—out of their self-interest—to seek to help me in return. One hand washes the other, in effect. But

Spinoza's egoistic concern for others does not rely in this way on the increased good will of others toward me. Instead, Spinoza argues that my helping the others become more rational will benefit me even without those others coming to have an increased desire to help me in particular and to return the favor to me in particular. For Spinoza, the ones I help will benefit me simply by being more rational, simply by acting on the basis of their nature. Because they share their nature with me, their rational actions will *automatically* benefit me too even if they are not aware of me in particular. Doubtless, of course, when I do benefit others by making them more rational, these others will often be cognizant that I have aided them, and the others will therefore have an increased desire to help me in return. Spinoza's psychology of love accounts for this phenomenon very well. But the important and distinctive point here is that one need not appeal to such increased goodwill directed at me in particular to generate an egoistic reason to help others by making them more rational.

Though intriguing, Spinoza's argument is deeply problematic. As it stands, the argument seems to have the implication that any rational person, insofar as she is rational, automatically benefits each other person, no matter how distant in space and time. Thus, a rational human being on the other side of the world—a person with whom I have no direct contact—benefits me by her rational actions. Similarly, a person in the distant past—long since dead, a person unknown to me—benefits me now. These are very implausible implications, but Spinoza may nonetheless be willing to accept them.

One might see Spinoza's reasoning here as calling attention to the lack of a sharp boundary between different finite individuals. For Spinoza, as we have seen, there cannot be two distinct things that are exactly qualitatively alike. This is just Spinoza's commitment to the Principle of the Identity of Indiscernibles. Identity, therefore, is to be understood as exact qualitative similarity. Because similarity obviously comes in degrees and because, for Spinoza, there is nothing more to identity than qualitative similarity, it follows that identity also comes in degrees, or at least that two things can approximate being identical—i.e. can be similar—to a greater or lesser degree. While two distinct things cannot be strictly identical, they can be more or less similar and so, for Spinoza, more or less identical. Given this notion of degrees of identity, understood as degrees of similarity, we can begin to make sense of the claim that by helping myself—i.e. by being rational—I am, to a greater or lesser degree, helping those who are, to a greater or lesser degree, identical to me, i.e. those who are to a greater or lesser degree similar to me, i.e. those who are to a greater or lesser degree rational. Nonetheless, Spinoza's apparent commitment to the view that rational persons automatically benefit other rational persons no matter how remote is still very implausible.

Spinoza's second mechanism for generating a rational concern for others is the imitation of affects. As we saw in Chapter 4, Spinoza plausibly holds that we tend to imitate the affects we observe in others when we perceive those others to be similar to ourselves. Thus, if we perceive others to desire to be more rational, more active, more powerful, we will tend to emulate that desire and also seek to be more powerful. Since becoming more powerful is beneficial, imitating the desire of others to be more powerful is also beneficial to me. For this reason, I have a reason to benefit others by inculcating in them the desire to be more rational. This reason for helping others is, like the previous one, more direct than the standard egoistic basis for concern for others. Here Spinoza says that I should help others not so much because they will thus be inclined to help me in return. Rather, I should help them because I can then simply observe their newfound or newly strengthened desire for the good, a desire which I will thus imitate. Spinoza argues this way in the alternative demonstration of 4p37.

This argument, however, is less sweeping than the first which presupposes that rational others as such benefit me. The second requires that rational others *whose desire for good I observe* benefit me.

The second argument, unlike the first, requires that I observe the others in order for the benefit to me to kick in.

5. LIES AND DEGREES OF FREEDOM

Spinoza's incorporation of a concern for others into his egoistic system is welcome. He may, however, go too far in this direction when he argues that "A free man always acts honestly, not deceptively" (4p72; see also 4p18s). The "always" is problematic, for does Spinoza really want to say that reason dictates that we should *never* deceive others, not even in the most dire situations, for example not even to save your own life or someone else's when Billy the bully, now grown up and more lethal, knocks on your door with murderous intent? This is precisely the question that Spinoza himself raises and unequivocally answers in 4p72s:

> Suppose someone now asks: What if a man could save himself from the present danger of death by treachery? Would not the principle of preserving his own being recommend, without qualification, that he be treacherous?
>
> The reply to this is the same. If reason should recommend that, it would recommend it to all men. And so reason would recommend, without qualification, that men should make agreements to join forces and to have common laws only by deception—that is, that really they should have no common laws. This is absurd.

It's clear from this scholium that Spinoza sees the ban against lies as flowing from the interest that each person has in the existence of common law and a civil society. This interest in a common society arises from what Spinoza sees as our interest in enhancing those respects in which we agree with, share properties with, one another. (This is clear from Spinoza's reliance on 4p31c in 4p72d.) In the previous section, we saw reason to doubt the usefulness of such similarity, but Spinoza's reasons for this prohibition on lying are not my direct concern here. Rather, I'm interested in two problems: one internal to Spinoza's system and one external. Internal problem: How is the prohibition on lying even to save one's life compatible with Spinoza's fundamentally egoistic ethical system? It's all well and good to say that in many circumstances it's in someone's interest not to lie because it's in one's interest to help maintain a well-working community, but how could it be in one's interest to help maintain a well-working community if by doing so—by not lying—one will not be around to enjoy the benefits of such a community?

One could try to alleviate this internal problem by pointing out that it doesn't matter if one dies by following what Spinoza sees as the dictates of reason because, for Spinoza, there is some kind of eternal life for the mind. So it may be that one is not harmed in dying (5p38s) and thus telling the truth—even if it means losing one's life—may not be ruled out, even on egoistic terms. However, although Spinoza does hold that, in some sense, the mind is eternal—as we'll see in Chapter 7—he does not invoke his views on the eternality of the mind in order to render his argument about lying consistent with his egoism. Thus I, too, will not invoke these views in order to respond to the internal problem which still remains.

The external problem is this: Doesn't it just seem wrong—intuitively wrong—to insist that one is obligated not to lie, even to save one's life? One does not have to be a card-carrying utilitarian to think that, in some extreme circumstances, lying is the only human and the only right thing to do. Kant, who more famously espouses a ban on all lying, faces this difficulty too. I'll have more to say shortly about Kant's connection to Spinoza here.

Is there, then, any way to make Spinoza's strictures against lying seem not only more plausible but also compatible with his egoism? On both counts, degrees of freedom come to the rescue. Spinoza's prohibition on lying specifically concerns the free man. Recall that the free man is merely an idealization: human beings, as finite modes, are subject to causation from without and so cannot be absolutely free. A _completely_ free human being—an impossible being—therefore would never find himself in a situation in which he needs to lie in order to save his life: being subject to a gunman's threat or other such unpleasant situations which may prompt one to lie are ways of being passive that a free person is not subject to. But we more-or-less passive beings do face such situations and so from time to time we may need to lie in order to save our lives. So it is compatible with 4p72, which requires that the free man not lie, that we passive beings may sometimes need to lie in order to save our lives and thus—given Spinoza's egoism—may sometimes even be obligated to lie (as Spinoza explicitly acknowledges in TTP, chap. 16, p. 240, G III 192). And Spinoza's point is that in such a situation, although one may, and even must, lie, the obligation to do so does not arise insofar as we are free and active, but precisely insofar as we are not free.[5]

The strictures against lying do, though, apply to us in some way too. For Spinoza, as we have seen, the rightness and wrongness of an action is a function of the power of the agent and the agent's freedom. And since power and freedom are matters of degree, so too is rightness and wrongness. Thus the obligation not to lie—the wrongness of lying—comes in degrees: for maximally free individuals, the obligation not to lie is absolute. For individuals with lesser degrees of freedom, the obligation not to lie is tempered. Individuals with less power are under less of an obligation not to lie. Individuals with more power are under more of an obligation not to lie. This view, intuitively, has much to recommend it. Not only is there no absolute obligation for human beings not to lie— even in order to save their own lives—but individuals with more power (more freedom) are under more stringent obligations than individuals with less power, less freedom. This view is completely compatible with Spinoza's egoism: each individual—no matter how weak or strong—should do what's in her interest. Thus Spinoza does have the resources to address both the internal and the external problems he faces here.

Seeing how the PSR underlies Spinoza's flexibility with regard to the prohibition on lying will enable us to draw some illuminating parallels to Kant. For Spinoza, we are not absolutely obligated not to lie because we are not absolutely free. And, of course, that we are not absolutely free is, for Spinoza, a result of the PSR: were we—finite beings—absolutely free, then our behavior would not be determined in any way from outside us and thus there would be no way to explain the relations that hold between us and other finite things, there would be no way to explain why these things all exist together and why there are no others. Thus free finite individuals would bring the taint of brute facts with them. The PSR dictates that finite individuals can, at most, have a degree of freedom and so, to that degree only, are they subject to the requirement not to lie. In this way, not only does the PSR lead to Spinoza's account of rightness, as we have seen, but it also helps to generate a realistic flexibility in Spinoza's account of what is morally required.

Kant would agree with Spinoza that we must see something like the PSR as generating the notion of rightness. For Kant, as for Spinoza, rightness would be unintelligible—a brute fact—if it did not have its source in our very natures. This demand is, I believe, behind Kant's search at the beginning of the *Grounding for the Metaphysics of Morals* for something good without qualification. Kant's concern with avoiding unintelligibility is admirable, from Spinoza's point of view. But Kant does not employ the PSR in order to make moral requirements more flexible, and so Spinoza's way out of the no-lying-even-to-save-your-life objection is not available to Kant. Kant and Spinoza agree that, insofar as an agent is free, she is obligated not to lie. (As Spinoza does in 4p72s, Kant appeals to the view that reason would somehow undermine itself if it sanctioned lies.) However, unlike Spinoza, Kant regards finite agents as at least capable of absolute freedom, as capable of acting in a way that is determined only by themselves. So, for Kant, because we are capable of acting with absolute freedom, our obligation not to lie is absolute. Thus Kant is committed to biting the bullet: no lying to Billy the bully knocking at your door.[6]

This lack of flexibility would be very unappealing to Spinoza and it would be so fundamentally because the Kantian scene with free and independent finite agents would be teeming with brute facts, violations of the PSR. That is how Kant wants his scene to be, of course: although he has some sympathy for the PSR, he doesn't think that the PSR is unrestricted in its application. This commitment to only a restricted PSR structures much of his metaphysics. This difference between Spinoza and Kant with regard to the PSR grounds—perhaps surprisingly—the difference between them with regard to the obligation not to lie. From Spinoza's point of view, Kant's failure—as Descartes's—lies in his only half-hearted allegiance to the PSR.

SUMMARY

Spinoza's major work is called the *Ethics* and, in many ways, his philosophy is devoted to explaining how we ought to live our lives. Spinoza seeks to make the notions of moral goodness and rightness naturalistically respectable, and he does so by showing how moral norms can be founded on the metaphysics of striving, or conatus. For Spinoza, ordinary evaluative judgments are simply a reflection of our desires and have no bearing on what is objectively good or right in the object or action evaluated. The only legitimate ground for moral evaluation of a thing is the way in which the thing meets or fails to meet the standards set by its own striving for persistence and power. Thus a thing or person or action is morally good, right, and virtuous to the extent to which it is powerful. Any other source of moral evaluation beyond the object's own nature as striving for self-preservation and power would be inexplicable, without a real purchase on the object to be evaluated, and would thus be ruled out by Spinoza's PSR. Thus Spinoza has a radically egoistic ethics: it is good and right that we increase our power. Because, for Spinoza, understanding and knowledge are coextensive with power (i.e.

ideas are adequate and certain to the extent to which they are not caused from outside the mind), Spinoza's ethics is extremely intellectualistic: it is good and right that we should acquire more knowledge, and indeed the acquisition of knowledge is, fundamentally, all that is good and right. Spinoza plausibly defines freedom and moral responsibility in terms of independence of outside causes, and so it is also good and right that we should be more free and more morally responsible. Given Spinoza's determinism, we cannot be absolutely free or absolutely morally responsible or absolutely good and virtuous, but we can achieve greater degrees of freedom, responsibility, etc. Spinoza also seeks to make his egoistic moral philosophy less harsh by showing how the more rational one is, the more one does and should seek to help others. He grounds this rational concern for others both in problematic aspects of his doctrine of essence and in his penetrating insights into the psychological mechanisms by which we imitate the affects of others who are similar to us. Spinoza's tempering of his egoism may go too far when he says that a free man should never lie, not even to save his own life. But the tension in Spinoza's system can be resolved if one recognizes that, for Spinoza, the obligation not to lie comes in degrees proportional to one's degree of freedom and power. This flexibility provided by degrees of freedom derives ultimately from Spinoza's PSR: to say that finite individuals could be absolutely free and not merely free to a certain degree would be to introduce brute facts into one's philosophical system. Spinoza, of course, does not allow such brute facts, but arguably Kant does. This difference is perhaps the fundamental difference between their ethical systems.

FURTHER READING

Edwin Curley (1973) "Spinoza's Moral Theory." (Good overview.)

Michael Della Rocca (2004) "Egoism and the Imitation of Affects in Spinoza." (Consideration of two different arguments Spinoza offers for the rationality of helping others.)

Don Garrett (1990) "'A Free Man Always Acts Honestly, Not Deceptively': Freedom and the Good in Spinoza's *Ethics*." (Insightful way of understanding Spinoza's strictures against lying.)

———. (1996) "Spinoza's Ethical Theory." (Good survey of the key terms Spinoza employs in his moral philosophy.)

Six

The State, Religion, and Scripture

1. RIGHTS AND POWER

Political philosophy examines the way in which people should be governed and the way in which a state should be structured. A guiding question of political philosophy, so understood, is: What are my rights? What actions do I have a right to perform and what actions do I not have a right to perform? By determining the extent and scope of one's rights, one determines the nature of our obligations to one another, obligations that, in many cases, the state exists in order to enforce. Spinoza's answer to the guiding question is deceptively simple: I have a right to do whatever is in my power. And the same goes for you and for all other human beings too. Indeed, the same goes for any individual whatsoever, whether table, chair, dog, pancreas or pan: each of these has a right to do whatever is in its power. Spinoza says:

> [E]ach individual thing has the sovereign right to do all that it can do; i.e. the right of the individual is coextensive with its determinate power.
> (TTP, p. 173, G III 189; in this chapter, unless otherwise noted, all page references will be to the TTP)

Or, as Spinoza says even more succinctly in the *Political Treatise*, "right is defined by power alone" (chap. 7, §16, p. 84; see also TP, chap. 2, §4, p. 38). This doctrine applies also to the individual that is the state, the individual which comes into existence, as we will soon see, in order to secure the safety and freedom of finite individuals such as you and me. In explicitly extending the notion of right to individuals in general, Spinoza's naturalism is at work: the rights of human beings are not new additions to the furniture of the universe. Here again, the kinds of notions needed to understand human beings are applicable to things in general.

In order to understand Spinoza's claim that right is power and to appreciate its deeply rationalist character, we need to articulate an important qualification that Spinoza makes most directly in the context of discussing the rights of the state (and of the sovereign who wields the power of the state). The right of the sovereign is what is in its power *in the long run*. If some course of action is within a sovereign's power to perform now, but threatens to lead eventually to the downfall of the state, then, Spinoza says, the sovereign doesn't really have the power to perform that action and so doesn't have the right to do it. Spinoza makes this point in connection with the actions of particularly oppressive states. First, Spinoza says that sovereigns can act oppressively and that they have the power to do so:

> It is true that sovereigns can by their right treat as enemies all who do not absolutely agree with them on all matters, but the point at issue is not what is their right, but what is useful. I grant that by this right they can govern in the most oppressive way and execute citizens on the most trivial reasons, but all will deny that they can do so while preserving the judgment of sound reason.
>
> (p. 223, G III 240)

Spinoza immediately adds his important qualification:

> Indeed, since they cannot so act without endangering the whole fabric of the state, we can even deny that they have the absolute power to do these and similar things, and consequently that they do not have the absolute right to do so. For we have

> demonstrated that the right of sovereigns is determined by
> their power.
>
> (p. 223, G III 240, translation altered)

Thus, for Spinoza, a sovereign doesn't have the right to do what is ultimately not in the state's interest, what does not preserve or enhance its power. Similarly, Spinoza would also say—more positively—that a sovereign has the right to do whatever maintains or enhances the state's power in the long run.

Given Spinoza's naturalism about rights, a similar point applies to human beings and to individuals more generally: we have a right to do whatever will, in the long run, maintain or increase our power. And so, for Spinoza, right is defined in terms of power alone, but more specifically, in terms of power in the long run.

With this qualification in mind, we can see that, for Spinoza, the notion of an individual's right just is the notion of what is right for an individual to do. As we saw in the previous chapter, for Spinoza, it's right for one to do whatever increases one's power. Because, as we have just seen, an individual has a right to do whatever increases its power, it follows that an individual has a right to do whatever it is right for the individual to do, and an individual, strictly, doesn't have a right to do anything that is not right for that individual to do. The notion of our rights and the notion of what is right for us to do are coextensive, for Spinoza. One might have thought, contra Spinoza, that these notions can diverge. In particular, it might plausibly be thought that certain actions one has a right to perform are nonetheless not right for one to do. For example, arguably, one might have the right to refuse to give time or money to the more needy, but one may not be right in so refusing. Spinoza is simply denying this intuitive position, and, in this denial, he is motivated by his rationalism: one cannot, for Spinoza, make sense of the notion of a right that one has unless one unpacks this notion as the notion of what it is right for one to do. Further, the notion of what it is right for one to do is, as we have seen in the previous chapter, just the notion of what it is good for one to do, and this in turn is just the notion of what increases or maintains one's power. For Spinoza, as we have seen, one's power just is the power to make things intelligible in terms of oneself. It follows that one's right just is one's ability to make things intelligible in terms of oneself. Here we have a characteristic two-fold use of the PSR. For Spinoza, we must find the notion of a right intelligible. That is the first use of the PSR. A right can, for Spinoza, be intelligible only in terms of the notion of intelligibility itself. This is the second use of the PSR. Rights, like so many other central features of Spinoza's philosophical system, are to be explained in terms of explanation itself.

Here is another way to see Spinoza's rationalism as generating his account of rights. As we've seen, for Spinoza, the power of a thing is its essence or nature. By tying one's rights to one's power, Spinoza sees one's rights as simply a function of one's essence. If my rights did not stem from my very essence, then what would make them my rights, what would tie them to me? The connection between my rights and me would be ultimately arbitrary—a brute fact—unless the connection stems from my very nature. In the previous chapter, we saw that any notion of what is good for me or what I ought to do that is not generated by my very nature would be arbitrary and could have no intelligible purchase on me. Why should this external standard be endorsed rather than another? But a standard that derives from my very nature obviously has a purchase on me. Similarly, the standards determining what I have a right to do will be arbitrary and not really mine unless they stem from my own nature.

What does my right to do whatever will increase my power get me? By itself, not a whole lot. Given that each human being has the same right as I do and given the universal striving to increase one's power, there will inevitably be threats, conflicts, and violence that prevent me from realizing my good, my right to increase my power. Just as I have the power and right (at least in the short run) to take whatever I can from you and to kill you, so too you have the same rights against me (p. 174). And, given our striving for self-preservation, you and I will exercise these rights if need be and if given half a chance. In this condition in which each person exercises or attempts to exercise her rights against all others, human life "must necessarily be most wretched" (p. 175). Here—obviously guided by Hobbes—Spinoza gives expression to the bleakness of existence in the so-called state of nature, a condition that Hobbes famously called in the *Leviathan* "solitary, poor, nasty, brutish, and short."[1]

Spinoza also takes a Hobbesian path out of the state of nature. Spinoza, like Hobbes, realizes that in order for people to be brought to cease seeking to exercise their rights against one another, they must somehow "unite in one body" and arrange that

> the unrestricted right to all things naturally possessed by each
> individual should be put into common ownership, and that this
> right should no longer be determined by the strength and appetite
> of the individual, but by the power and will of all together.
>
> (p. 175, G III 191, translation altered)

People must, that is, pledge

> to keep appetite in check insofar as it tends to another's hurt, to
> do to no one what they would not want done to themselves, and
> finally to uphold another's right as they would their own.
>
> (p. 175, G III 191, translation altered)

But given the naturally avaricious and power-seeking ways of human beings, how can such an agreement—an agreement to give up some rights and power—have any meaning? Why would any one person trust others to keep their end of the bargain?

Obviously, a mechanism of enforcement is needed, and the mechanism is implicit already in the nature of what it is for individuals to give up some of their rights. Our rights—our powers—

are to be pooled together and are to be possessed by a sovereign which exercises this greater power. The agreement, in other words, brings into existence a new individual—the state—more powerful than any of us taken singly. That a new individual comes into existence is in keeping with Spinoza's definition of singular things in 2def7, "if a number of individuals so concur in one action that they are all the cause of one effect, I consider them all, to that extent, as one singular thing." Because the members of the state act together in making the agreement and abiding by it, we form, to that extent, one thing, more powerful than any one of us. As a more powerful individual, the state will have the power to enforce the agreement among the individual human beings and the sovereign will do this by specifying and exacting punishments for breaking the agreement "to uphold another's right as [one's] own" (p. 175, G III 191). It is this threat of punishment that gives the pledge, the agreement, its meaning. As Spinoza says, "nobody is going to keep any promises whatsoever, except through fear of a greater evil or hope of a greater good" (p. 176, G III 192; see also p. 180, G III 196). Once we have entered into this agreement, which is backed by the power of the state, human beings can work together to counter the threat to their safety from the environment and from other states. Also they can now work together to enhance their own well-being (pp. 62–63, G III 73). By contrast, Spinoza adds—with an echo of Hobbes's famous line about the brutishness of the state of nature—"those who live in a barbarous way with no civilizing influences lead wretched and almost brutish existence" (p. 116, G III 73; Hobbes's Latin is *bruta*, Spinoza's, *brutalem*).

Precisely because in the state of nature each individual has the right to do anything to anybody, there is no such thing as wronging anybody in the state of nature; there is no such thing as injustice. Spinoza explains:

> A wrong occurs when a citizen or subject is forced to suffer some injury at the hands of another, contrary to his civil right, i.e.

> contrary to the edict of the sovereign power. For a wrong cannot
> be conceived except in a civil condition.
>
> (p. 179, G III 196, translation altered)

The formation of the state with its sovereign power brings into existence the possibility of injustice. Thus, justice and injustice are, for Spinoza, human creations, in the same way that, as we will see in the next section, religion and sin are.

Although one has entered into an agreement with one's fellow citizens, one may legitimately break that agreement if one can and if it is in one's interests to do so. Of course, it is in one's interest to break such an agreement only if the mechanism of enforcement and of the punishment of pledge-breakers is not working properly. If the agreement cannot be enforced, then one's earlier pledge carries no force and one may legitimately go against one's earlier promise. Thus, under certain circumstances, I have the right to break a promise and to lie, and, as we saw in the previous chapter, it is right for me to do so. As Spinoza says, in a passage I cited in the previous chapter:

> [S]uppose that a robber forces me to promise to give him my
> goods at his pleasure. Now since, as I have already shown, my
> natural right is determined by my power alone, it is quite clear
> that if I can free myself from this robber by deceit, promising him
> whatever he wants, I have the natural right to do so, that is, to
> pretend to agree to whatever he wants.
>
> (p. 176, G III 192)

Spinoza thus reaches the general conclusion, "no agreement can have any force unless by reason of its usefulness, and if the usefulness is taken away, the agreement is at the same time removed and stands invalid" (p. 176, G III 192, translation altered; see also TP chap. 2, §12). When I go against an earlier promise to Jenny, I am treating her unjustly only if there is a way for the agreement between us to be enforced. Absent such a means of enforcement, no promise has been genuinely broken and there can be no injustice.[2]

The state which comes into existence through this agreement among individuals is itself an individual and, as such, has power. Like all other individuals, the state strives to maintain and to increase its power and—again like all other individuals—it has the right to do so and it is right for the state to do so. How can the state maintain and enhance its power? Because the state's existence depends simply on the agreement among its citizens and because the agreement depends on the willingness of the citizens to abide by it, one way—and perhaps the only way—to destroy the state is to make its citizens unwilling to abide by their agreement. This unwillingness can occur either through the extreme repressiveness of the state—i.e. by the state's allowing its citizens too little freedom—or by the state's being too lax—its allowing its citizens too much freedom. Consider the too-repressive state first. The more restrictions a state places on our freedom, the less reason do we have to abide by the agreement whose purpose, after all, was to secure our power and freedom. And the less reason to abide by the agreement, the more reason do citizens have to act against the power of the state and to seek to undermine the state. Spinoza articulates with real psychological insight the way in which this phenomenon can arise:

> [H]uman nature will not submit to unlimited repression, and, as Seneca says in his tragedy, rule that depends on violence has never long continued, moderate rule endures. For as long as men act only from fear, they are doing what they are most opposed to doing, taking no account of the usefulness and the necessity of the actions to be done, concerned only not to incur capital or other punishment. Indeed, they inevitably rejoice at misfortune or injury to their ruler even when this involves their own considerable misfortune, and they wish every ill on him, and bring this about when they can.
>
> (p. 63, G III 74)

If a repressive state were to be undermined in this way, the state would not, strictly speaking, destroy itself. For Spinoza, nothing—as we saw in Chapter 3—can destroy itself. Rather, such a state would come to be destroyed through the actions of individuals that are, to some extent, independent of the state, individuals that are not integrated into the state precisely because the state represses these individuals so severely that they are no longer willing to abide by the state-forming agreement.

If a state, by contrast, does not restrain its citizens enough, it is also thereby threatened. As Spinoza says, "no society can subsist without government and coercion, and consequently without laws to control and restrain men's lusts and their unbridled urges" (p. 63, G III 73–74).

The trick, then, for a successful state is to strike the proper balance between being too repressive and not repressive enough. Some of Spinoza's most revolutionary and also some of his most troubling views emerge when he attempts to strike this balance. Before we see how he does so, however, I would like to call attention to a general feature of the ideal state, as Spinoza conceives it, a feature that exhibits the intricacy and elegance of Spinoza's political philosophy.

The most powerful state is, as we've just seen, not the most repressive state or the least repressive state. Those states will more or less quickly be destroyed. Rather the most powerful state is the one that accords its citizens the most freedom as is compatible with the existence of the state itself. Thus a truly powerful state enhances the power of its citizens. Similarly, a truly powerful citizen enhances the power of the state. This is because the more powerful a citizen is, the more rational and free she is. The more rational a citizen is, the more she will appreciate that it's in her interest to strengthen the bonds between citizens that make for their willingness to abide by the agreement that constitutes the state. Further, the more rational a citizen is, the more she will appreciate that the most effective way for a state to be threatened is for its citizens not to be free and powerful. Thus the rational citizen will strive to enhance her own power partly in order to enhance the power of the state. This enhancement in turn enhances the power of the citizen. And this enhancement in turn enhances the power of the state, and so on. Thus a wise and powerful state will seek to make its citizens as powerful as possible. And a wise and powerful citizen will seek to make her state as powerful as possible. The activity of free individuals and the activity of a free state harmonize and reverberate in an ever-increasing fashion.

Return now to the proper balance between constraints that need to be placed upon individuals for the sake of the state and freedoms that need to be allowed to individuals. Spinoza quite remarkably and boldly allows a great deal of scope for freedom of thought and speech, but, as we will see, he also draws—and problematically so—a sharp line between speech and other forms of action, and countenances sweeping restrictions on the latter even while granting almost complete freedom of the former.

Let's begin with Spinoza's commitment to freedom of thought. For Spinoza, as we saw in Chapter 3, simply by having certain ideas, we see that certain things are so and we thus have certain beliefs or judgments. A belief, as we saw, is nothing over and above the representation itself. So simply by having a mind—i.e. by representing things—we have certain beliefs. As we saw, the account of belief in terms of representation is an instance of the twofold use of the PSR in Spinoza. Because of this tight connection—indeed identity—between representation and judgment, nothing can interfere with one's belief as long as one has a certain representation. Spinoza puts the point vividly:

> [N]o one can surrender his faculty of judgment; for what rewards or threats can induce a man to believe that the whole is not greater than its parts, or that God does not exist, or that the body, which he sees to be finite is an infinite being, in

short to believe something that is contrary to what he perceives
or thinks?

(TP chap. 3 §8, p. 51)

For this reason, the state simply cannot control one's faculty of
judgment, of assenting to what one represents:

[N]o one is able to transfer to another his natural right or faculty
to reason freely and to form his own judgment on any matters
whatsoever, nor can he be compelled to do so.

(p. 222, G III 239)

Even though one's thoughts cannot be controlled directly, Spinoza
is well aware that one's thoughts may be controlled indirectly, and
he is troubled by this constraint on freedom. Through education or
indoctrination, certain desires and beliefs can be inculcated in
individuals. Thus simply by ordering me to believe that Billy the
bully is well-intentioned, the state cannot make me change my
assessment of Billy in this drastic way. However, through what can
only be called brainwashing, the state has the power indirectly to
manipulate my beliefs and lead me to think well of Billy. We'll see
shortly how Spinoza is also committed to the view that any control
by the state over one's actions also brings with it control of some
kind over one's thoughts.

Since the state does have this power, the state has the right—at
least in the short run—to manipulate beliefs:

[A]lthough command cannot be exercised over minds in the
same way as over tongues, yet minds are to some degree under
the control of the sovereign power, who has many means of
inducing the great majority to believe, love, hate, etc. whatever
he wills. Thus, although it is not by direct command of the
sovereign power that these results are produced, yet
experience abundantly testifies they often proceed from the

authoritative nature of his power and from his guidance, that is, from his right.

(p. 186, G III 202)

However, although the attempts to manipulate belief indirectly are not as futile as attempts at direct manipulation, nonetheless indirect manipulation is never, Spinoza believes, completely successful.

I admit that judgment can be influenced in numerous ways. ... But in spite of all that ingenuity has been able to devise in this field, it has never attained such success that men did not find that the individual citizen has his own ideas in plenty, and that opinions vary as much as tastes.

(p. 222, G III 239)

Spinoza doesn't explain why this should be so, but it's easy to see what is driving him. As we have seen, people will always have the power to assent to their representations. Our representations, in many cases, are caused by features of the world that the sovereign does not control and so, to that extent, our judgment or beliefs are not under the sovereign's control. Thus, for Spinoza, the sovereign "will never succeed in preventing men from exercising their own particular judgment on any matters whatsoever" (pp. 222–23, G III 240). Strictly, the sovereign does not have the power or the right completely to repress thought either directly or indirectly. Indeed, if the state does attempt to repress thought indirectly, it will be such a threat to the freedom of its subjects that it "cannot so act without endangering the whole fabric of the state" (p. 223, G III 240). Freedom of thought is thus in the interest of the state itself.

Further, it is in the state's interest to protect, not only freedom of thought, but also freedom of speech—i.e. freedom to express one's thought publicly. For Spinoza, because the state cannot successfully control its citizens' thought:

> utter failure will attend any attempt in a commonwealth to force
> men to speak only as prescribed by the sovereign despite their
> different and opposing opinions.
>
> (p. 223, G III 240)

This is because human nature is, for Spinoza, such that we have
great difficulty in keeping our thoughts to ourselves.

> Not even men well versed in affairs can keep silent, not to say the
> lower classes. It is the common failing of men to confide what
> they think to others, even when secrecy is needed.
>
> (p. 223, G III 240)

Spinoza does not elaborate on why reticence should be so difficult
for us, but the usual suspects in Spinoza's gallery of affects can be
invoked here: pride, love, thirst for power, etc. For Spinoza, any
attempt to infringe on the citizens' right to express their thoughts
will be—and will be seen as—a grave incursion on freedom that
threatens the very existence of the state. Even if freedom of speech
is (in the short run) eliminated,

> it will certainly never come to pass that men will think only what
> they are bidden to think. It would thus inevitably follow that in
> their daily lives men would be thinking one thing and saying
> another, with the result that good faith, of first importance in the
> state, would be undermined and the disgusting arts of
> sychophancy and treachery would be encouraged.
>
> (p. 226, G III 243)

With this remark, Spinoza likely has in mind the converso experience in Portugal and Spain: Jews who maintained their Judaism
despite their seeming conversion to Christianity would dissemble
in precisely the way Spinoza describes here. This passage indicates
that, for Spinoza, denying freedom of speech would loosen the

bonds of trust that hold the state together. Further, because freedom of speech is such an important component of freedom in
general, any restriction of freedom of speech will be strenuously
resisted by citizens who entered into the state-forming agreement
in order to secure their freedom.

> The greater the effort to deprive them of freedom of speech, the more
> obstinately do they resist: not indeed the greedy, the flatterers
> and other poor-spirited souls ... , but those to whom a good
> upbringing, purity of character and virtue have made more free.
> Men in general are so constituted that their resentment is most
> aroused when beliefs which they think to be true are treated as
> criminal, and when that which motivates their pious conduct to God
> and man is accounted as wickedness. In consequence, they are
> emboldened to denounce the laws and go to all lengths to oppose
> the magistrate, considering it not a disgrace but honorable to stir
> up sedition and to resort to any outrageous action in this cause.
>
> (pp. 226, G III 243–44, translation altered)

For Spinoza, the insidious thing about restrictions on speech is that
they lead persons of integrity and good upbringing to rise up
against the state and to stir up sedition. For this reason, it is defi-
nitely in the state's interest to foster freedom of speech. Ultimately,
then, the state has no right to restrict speech.

The reason freedom of speech must be granted, for Spinoza, is
that otherwise citizens would be led to resist the state and to
threaten it, and this would not be in the interests of either the state
or its citizens. Thus Spinoza's defense of freedom of speech presupposes the illegitimacy of certain actions, of resistance to the
state. So Spinoza's defense of freedom of speech goes hand-in-hand
with the rejection of freedom of action more generally. For Spinoza,
the state may legitimately clamp down on action in general—other
than mere speech. The sharp line Spinoza draws between speech
and action is evident in this important passage:

> [W]hile to act against the sovereign's decree is definitely an
> infringement of his right, this is not the case with thinking, judging,
> and consequently with speaking, too, provided one does no more
> than express or communicate one's opinion, defending it through
> rational conviction alone, not through deceit, anger, hatred, or the
> will to effect such changes in the state as he himself decides. For
> example, suppose a man maintains that a certain law is against
> sound reason, and he therefore advocates its repeal. If he at the
> same time submits his opinion to the judgment of the sovereign
> power (which alone is competent to enact and repeal laws), and
> meanwhile does nothing contrary to what is commanded by that
> law, he deserves well of the state, acting as do the best citizens.
> But if on the contrary the purpose of his action is to accuse the
> magistrate of injustice and render him odious to the multitude, or
> if he seditiously seeks to repeal that law against the will of the
> magistrate, he is nothing more than an agitator and a rebel.
>
> (p. 224, G III 241, translation altered)

So although Spinoza understands how persons—even persons of
good character—can be led to act seditiously, he seems to be saying
that such action is never right, that the state is within its rights to
repress such activity and that the citizen must not act contrary to
the decisions of the sovereign, if the citizen wishes to be just and
pious. Doubtless, Spinoza's aversion to anything that might threaten
the stability of a state is grounded in his conviction that over-
throwing a sovereign has never resulted in the institution of a state
that better ensures freedom and often results in a state that is more
repressive. He draws here on examples ranging from ancient Israel
to the Roman empire to seventeenth-century England (pp. 210–
11, G III 227–28). He concludes, "every state must necessarily
preserve its own form, and cannot be changed without incurring
the danger of utter ruin" (p. 211, G III 228).

Spinoza devoted considerable attention in the *Political Treatise* to the
various forms of government, which he divided into monarchy,

aristocracy, and democracy. He believed that each of these forms of government could be so organized as to strike a good balance between the freedom of citizens and the power of the state, and his proposals for the structure of such governments are, in the case of monarchy and aristocracy, detailed and historically well-informed. (Unfortunately the discussion of democracy is fragmentary, for the *Political Treatise* was left unfinished at Spinoza's death.) In the TTP, though not as clearly in the TP, Spinoza favors democracy—which he defined as "a united body of men which corporately possesses sovereign right over everything within its power" (p. 177, G III 193). Spinoza argues that the democratic state seems to be

> the most natural form of state, approaching most closely to that freedom which nature grants to every man. For in a democratic state nobody transfers his natural right to another so completely that thereafter he is not to be consulted; he transfers it to the majority of the entire community of which he is part. In this way all men remain equal, as they were before in the state of nature.
>
> (p. 179, G III 195)

Here, of course, is another place where Spinoza departs from Hobbes, who clearly preferred monarchy to democracy.

Nonetheless, in his licensing of absolute state control over the actions of its subjects, Spinoza seems—despite his preference for democracy—to be as authoritarian as Hobbes, and so the question arises: Is Spinoza justified in restricting freedom of action in this way? Actually this question can be split into two separate challenges to Spinoza's position. The first challenge is the following: Spinoza seems to be all-too-willing to condone large-scale restrictions on the activities of citizens. He even goes so far as to say that no wrong can be done to subjects by sovereign powers (pp. 179–80). But if this is so, Spinoza seems to cut himself off from the ability to criticize— on moral grounds—the actions of repressive states. Curley expresses this worry well in discussing the Roman conquest of Britain:

> If we cannot make sense of the idea that people have a natural
> right to such things [their lives, their property, and their honor]
> then we seem to be handicapped in the criticism we want to
> make of the Roman conduct (or of a tyrant's treatment of his
> own people).
>
> (Curley 1996: 335)

But is this correct? Is it right to say that there are actions by the
state that are not only wrong but that Spinoza cannot condemn as
wrong? Recall that many forms of repression by the state are so
threatening to the freedom of subjects that they undermine the
agreement that holds the state together and so ultimately backfire.
Because they ultimately backfire, such repressive actions are wrong
in the long run, and Spinoza says so and condemns them as such.

Nonetheless, Curley's worry is still in play for, although Spinoza
says that these actions are wrong in the long run, they may nonetheless be right in the short run and we would therefore not be
able to condemn these actions as wrong simpliciter. The most we
could do is condemn them as wrong only insofar as they ultimately
threaten the destruction of the state. Don't we want and need a
more robust way to criticize repressive actions? Again, Curley
makes this point well:

> Perhaps tyrannical governments do inevitably destroy themselves.
> If the power of autocratic rulers is as fragile as Spinoza seems to
> think, this would seem likely. The question I have is whether such
> a dispassionate view of tyranny is acceptable. A tyrant can do a
> great deal of harm even if his tyranny lasts only a short time. ...
> Does viewing things *sub specie aeternitatis* require us to accept
> the success of such governments so long as they are able to
> maintain their power? If so, does being a good Spinozist not
> require a level of detachment from individual human suffering
> which is either superhuman or subhuman?
>
> (Curley 1996: 334)

However, Spinoza would not accept this criticism. He would see Curley and us as hankering after a notion of wrongness, a way of condemning actions that is, in the end, unintelligible. In virtue of what would such repressive actions be wrong, independently of whether they lead to the destruction of the state in the long run? For Spinoza, as we have seen, the rightness or wrongness of an action must have its source in the nature of the action itself and in the nature of the agent itself (in this case, the nature of the state). Any other source of rightness or wrongness would be too extraneous to the action and the agent to have a genuine purchase on them; any other source of the rightness or wrongness of the action could only arbitrarily be connected with the action. Thus, to veer beyond the nature of the agent and action in order to reach an evaluation of the action would be to demand something unintelligible, a brute fact. This demand, of course, would be completely contrary to the character of Spinoza's moral philosophy and his rationalism in general.

The second challenge to Spinoza's apparent endorsement of the state's restrictions on the actions of its citizens arises in the following way. Let's grant that the only way legitimately to criticize the actions of a state is to point to their negative effects on the state itself. Still one may wonder if Spinoza is right that the restrictions on the actions of its citizens *are* best for the state in the long run. This worry is especially pertinent for Spinoza in light of the fact that he emphatically defends citizens' freedom of thought and speech as good and right, not only for the citizens themselves but also for the state. If freedom of speech and thought is to be praised, why not freedom of action in general? As we noted, Spinoza seems to draw a sharp line between thought and speech, on the one hand, and actions that are not speech, on the other. This line now seems unmotivated and—dare I say it?—arbitrary. If restrictions on thought and speech threaten to make the people unwilling to abide by the agreement that instituted and sustains the state, it certainly seems as if there might be other restrictions—restrictions on certain kinds of actions—that would equally well render people unwilling in this way. This is not to say that anything goes—that there should be no state restrictions on action. Rather, the point is that it is not clear, on Spinoza's own terms, that he has a principled basis for drawing the line where he does.

This worry becomes even more acute when we recall other relevant aspects of Spinoza's system. For Spinoza, as we saw in Chapter 3, each thought is itself an action (2def3), and, given his panpsychism, each action is identical to a thought. So, it's not clear that, in Spinoza's system, a state (or any individual) can restrain action without also and thereby restricting thought.

Here's another way to reach this conclusion: By forbidding certain kinds of actions, the state also restricts—renders less powerful—certain thoughts that would, other things being equal, result in the forbidden actions. Thus, if my action is restricted, then my thought that it would be good to act in a certain way cannot have its intended effect. For this reason, that thought is less powerful; that is, the thought is more subject to outside causes—in this case, the state and its enforcing authorities—than it otherwise would have been. Because my thought that a certain action is good is thus less powerful and more dependent on outside causes, it is more inadequate—in Spinoza's sense of "inadequate"—than it would otherwise be. Thus, in restricting action in this way, the state is also and thereby rendering certain ideas more inadequate, more confused; and so the state, by restricting actions, is in the business of restricting thought after all. Thus, if Spinoza is averse to restrictions on thought, he should be averse to restrictions on action as well. In other words, on his own terms, Spinoza seems to have no good reason to draw the sharp line he does between thought and speech, on the one hand, and action in general, on the other.

It may be that Spinoza is aware of this difficulty, that he realized that he is committed to a less restrictive view of state power, but that he felt he couldn't be so bold as to advocate publicly limits on the legitimacy of the state's restrictions on actions. Perhaps he thought it was bold enough that he publicly favored freedom of speech and thought—already a radical move—and felt that he could not wisely advocate even greater freedom for citizens. After all, his motto was *caute*—"carefully." This reading does have a certain plausibility (and is in the spirit of Strauss's discussion of Spinoza in "How to Study Spinoza's *Theologico-Political Treatise*"). But it is, as far as I can see, rather speculative. Certainly one could wish that Spinoza did realize that he was committed to there being no sharp line between thought and action of the kind that he would need in order to legitimate repressive state actions, but I see no direct evidence that Spinoza did come to this realization.

2. RELIGION AND THE STATE

In this section, we take up what Spinoza sees as three fundamental features of the relation between religion and the state. (i) Religion comes into existence only through the state and, once it exists, always depends on the state. For this reason, religion and religious law should remain subservient to the sovereign. (ii) Nonetheless, religion—in states that are not ideally strong and for reasons stemming from fundamental features of human psychology—often is not as subservient to the state as it should be and can thus be a threat to the state. (iii) Nonetheless again, religion is capable of being extremely useful to the state in the state's goal of fostering the freedom of its citizens—as long as the energies of religion are directed in appropriate ways. I will elaborate these three points in turn.

(i) As we saw, prior to the existence of the state, there can be neither justice nor injustice. Because in the state of nature there is no agreement with others, there can be no violation of agreements and there is no scope for treating others unjustly, for wronging them. Without wrong, for Spinoza, there can be no sin and so neither does sin exist in the state of nature. More generally, there can be no religious laws in the state of nature, no divine commands, unless perhaps the command to preserve oneself. For Spinoza,

> justice and, in sum, all the precepts of true reason, including
> charity toward one's neighbor, acquire the force of law and
> command only from the right of the state, that is, ... only from the
> decree of those who possess the right to command. And since ...
> God's kingdom consists simply in the rule of justice and charity,
> or true religion, it follows ... that God has no kingdom over men
> save through the medium of those who hold the sovereignty.
>
> (p. 213, G III 230)

That Spinoza sees God as having authority over human beings only through the medium of the authority of "temporal rulers" (p. 212, G III 228) is completely in keeping with Spinoza's metaphysics. As we saw in Chapter 2, neither God nor his laws—the infinite modes—can cause finite modes directly. For something finite to come into existence, it must be caused by some other finite thing, as well as by God and the laws of nature. God cannot single out a finite mode and directly cause it, without the help of other finite modes. Such activity on the part of God would generate brute facts. This concern with arbitrary divine activity was behind Spinoza's critique of final causation, as I argued in Chapter 2. The same line of thought is at work here in Spinoza's treatment of the origins of religion. God cannot impose religious laws directly on human beings. Rather, divine laws apply to human beings only via another finite individual—the sovereign—just as God's activity in general has a bearing on finite things only via the activity of other finite things.

Thus, for Spinoza, "divine law is entirely dependent on the decrees of rulers" (p. 215, G III 232). For this reason, no religious authority should attempt to impose religious laws on his or her own independently of the sovereign. If religious authorities aspire to make religious law independent of the sovereign, then precisely because the very existence and, indeed, the continued existence of religious laws depend on the authority of the state, these religious authorities will threaten to undermine the proper metaphysical basis of the religious laws. Such aspired-to independence of divine laws is thus not good for religion and religious laws and is, as we shall see in more detail presently, not good for the state itself. For Spinoza, therefore, the state must have complete authority over religion.

(ii) This domination of religion by the state is, for Spinoza, the ideal, but as in the case of other Spinozistic ideals, he recognizes that it is not always, or even ever, completely realized. Despite the fact that religion can come into existence only in a state, human psychology dictates that religious authorities will inevitably seek to rival the power of the state and will thus threaten its security.

For Spinoza (as for Hobbes), fear and uncertainty are common and natural features of human existence. Like any other finite and relatively powerless beings, we face many threats to our security. Because of the urgency of our need, we desperately seek ways to become more secure, more powerful. Indeed, because of our extreme hopes and fears, we are on the lookout for anything that— by our lights—is a sign of good or bad things to come. In this way, our hopes and fears lead to superstition and, in particular, to superstitious religious beliefs. In the preface to the TTP, Spinoza describes well the process leading to superstition:

> [I]n adversity [human beings] know not where to turn, begging for advice from any quarter; and there is no counsel so foolish, absurd or vain which they will not follow. Then even the most trivial of causes are enough to raise their hopes or dash them to the ground. For if, while possessed by fear, they see something happen that calls to mind something good or bad in the past, they believe that this portends a happy or unhappy issue, and they therefore call it a lucky or unlucky omen, even though it may fail them a hundred times. Then again, if they are struck with wonder at some unusual phenomenon, they believe this to be a portent signifying the anger of the gods or of a supreme deity, and they therefore regard it as a pious duty to avert the evil by sacrifice and vows, susceptible as they are to superstition.
>
> (p. 1, G III 5)

In this process, reason is quite likely to be abandoned precisely because "it cannot reveal a sure way to the vanities [human beings] covet" (p. 1, G III 5) and we, in our desperation, are looking for the quick fix, the instant release from insecurity. So, Spinoza says, we call human wisdom vain,

> while the delusions of the imagination, dreams, and other childish absurdities are taken to be the oracles of God. Indeed, they think that God, spurning the wise, has written his decrees not in man's mind, but in the entrails of beasts, or that by divine inspiration and instigation these decrees are foretold by fools, madmen, or birds. To such madness are men driven by their fears.
>
> (pp. 1–2, G III 5)

Because superstition is not rational, it follows that superstition,

> like all other instances of hallucination and frenzy, is bound to assume very varied and unstable forms, and that ... it is sustained only by hope, hatred, anger and deceit. For it arises not from reason but from emotion and emotion of the most powerful kind. So men's readiness to fall victim to any kind of superstition makes it correspondingly difficult to persuade them to adhere to one and the same kind.
>
> (p. 2, G III 6)

For Spinoza, human psychology is such that we strive to make others like the things we like and hate the things we hate (*Ethics* 3p31c and s). Spinoza takes this to follow from his doctrine of the imitation of affects. If we see that someone loves a thing, we will also tend to love it and so to experience the joy that constitutes love. If we already love a thing, then—in order to experience more joy in connection with that thing—we will have some tendency to make others love it too so that we can imitate their joy in the thing. (Just think of my friend's desire that I like the movies that she likes.) Similarly, striving that others hate what we already hate will have the result of strengthening our own hatred of that thing and our own desire to be rid of that thing. Since we do strive to be rid of the thing we hate, we will also have some tendency to increase that desire which will increase the chances of eliminating the hated thing. In general, for Spinoza, the imitation of affects makes it the case that "each of us, by his nature, wants others to live according to his temperament" (3p31s). Spinoza calls this phenomenon "ambition."

Because of ambition, those who adhere to one set of super-stitious religious beliefs will endeavor to make others share these beliefs. Thus the phenomenon of coercive religious beliefs makes its debut. Spinoza says in chapter 7 of the TTP:

> nearly all men parade their own ideas as God's word, their chief aim being to compel others to think as they do, while using religion as a pretext.
>
> (p. 86, G III 97)

In this way, religious authorities arise whose main concern is to uphold the irrational beliefs they have come to adopt out of their fear and uncertainty and to make others see matters the same way. Thus we can see why Spinoza says:

> ambition and iniquity have reached such a pitch that religion takes the form not so much of obedience to the teachings of the Holy Spirit as of defending what men have invented.
>
> (p. 86, G III 97)

Because of the hatred—born of fear—that religion sows, because of the coercion religion gives rise to, religion can, for Spinoza, be inimical to human beings' freedom of thought and action and, for this reason, religion is also a threat to the state itself, which cannot survive if its citizens are not sufficiently free.

> My accusation against [leaders of different religious sects] is this,
> that they refuse to grant to others [what they themselves enjoy].
> All those who do not share their opinions, however righteous and
> truly virtuous the dissenters may be, they persecute as God's
> enemies, while those who follow their lead, however dissolute
> they may be, they cherish as God's elect. Surely nothing more
> damnable than this, and more fraught with danger to the state,
> can be devised.
>
> (p. 158, G III 173)

Indeed, the religious authorities who may arise—if they are not
under the control of the sovereign—will inevitably be a threat to
the sovereign:

> everyone knows how much importance the people attach to the
> right and authority over religion, and how they all revere every
> single word of him who possesses that authority, so that one
> might even go so far as to say that he to whom this authority
> belongs has the most effective control over minds. Therefore
> anyone who seeks to deprive the sovereign of this authority is
> attempting to divide the sovereignty; and as a result, as happened
> long ago in the case of the kings and priests of the Hebrews,
> there will inevitably arise strife and dissensions that can never be
> allayed. Indeed, he who seeks to deprive the sovereign of this
> authority is paving the way to his own ascendancy.
>
> (p. 218, G III 235)

So in a well-functioning state the religious authorities must somehow be kept in check.

(iii) But, as I indicated, despite the danger inherent in religion,
Spinoza believes that a strong sovereign can put it to good use. For
Spinoza, people are subject to passive affects—like fear and ambition—and, as such, are, of course, less than fully free, less than
fully rational. Precisely because they are not fully rational, people

cannot appreciate and make use of purely rational means in order to achieve a greater degree of freedom and rationality. Similarly, a sovereign who seeks to make its citizens more free, more rational—as all strong and free sovereigns seek to do—will employ the less-than-fully rational beliefs of the citizens in order to lead them to greater freedom, greater rationality. If religion can be put to good use in this way, it will enhance the power of the state and the freedom of its citizens. But again—in light of the dangers of religion—how can this feat be pulled off?

To answer this question, Spinoza points out that, although superstitious religious belief is not fully rational, it can play a role in encouraging useful behavior. The behavior Spinoza has in mind here is *obedience* to God, obedience understood as following the commandment to love one's neighbor as oneself. Conveying this message—that one should love one's neighbor as oneself—is for Spinoza "the chief aim of scripture in its entirety" (p. 159, G III 174). If religion can inculcate the importance of obedience in this sense, then the positive effects for human freedom would be enormous. As we saw, for Spinoza, reason dictates that in order to help themselves, that is, to love themselves, people should help, love one another. Indeed, for Spinoza, reason shows that helping another is, to some extent, helping oneself and vice versa. Thus if religion—even a superstitious religion—can inculcate obedience, religion will be leading people to act in a way that is in keeping with the dictates of reason. And thus, since acting as reason dictates is acting freely, people who follow religion in this way would also be increasing their freedom. Of course, those obedient for this reason would not be completely free—after all, in following a religion, which is based not on knowledge but on imagination, the adherents of this religion would be acted on from outside and would thus be passive to some degree. Nonetheless, since acting on behalf of others as well as oneself *does* increase one's freedom and rationality, this religious commitment would have the good effect of generating this desirable increase. This increase in freedom on the part of individual human beings is not only desirable for the individuals themselves, but is also desirable for the state. This is because, as we saw, there is nothing more beneficial to the state than free and rational human beings, just as there is nothing more beneficial to human beings than free and rational human beings.

How can religion instill obedience in this relatively non-rational, but still advantageous way? Much of the power of religion derives from narratives that contain the message that one should love one's neighbor and that are presented in a way designed to fire the imagination, in a way that will make that overarching message of scripture more vivid and effective (p. 79, G III 90). To help excite this wonder, scriptural narratives often include descriptions of miraculous events. It's clear that Spinoza himself denies the existence of miracles. If one understands by "miracles" events that contravene the laws of nature (p. 74, G III 85), then strictly, for Spinoza, there can be no miracles and all miracle-involving narratives must be false in this regard. This rejection of miracles follows simply from Spinoza's naturalism and overarching determinism, which requires that all events be fully determined and law-governed.

The belief that miracles afford proof of God's existence offends against the PSR in at least two ways. First, this belief involves the acceptance of deviations from the natural order, i.e. brute facts. Second, to consider miracles as "evidence of God's existence" presupposes that there are...

> two powers quite distinct from each other, the power of God and the power of nature, though the latter is determined in a definite way by God.
>
> (p. 71, G III 81)

This bifurcation between two radically distinct powers which are nonetheless connected to one another opens up an explanatory gap: If the powers are truly distinct, then in virtue of what do

God's powers determine the power of nature? Such a bifurcation would render unintelligible any connection between the two powers; the relation between them would be as illegitimate as, for example, the relation between mind and body on the Cartesian view. So those who place credence in miracles as demonstrating the existence of God not only accept inexplicable events but also presuppose the kind of bifurcation in reality that Spinoza's naturalism and rationalism are designed to impugn.

Spinoza concludes, therefore, that if we are going to allow for miracles, we must see them not as really contravening the laws of nature but rather as events that surpass human understanding, as events that we cannot explain, but that are intelligible for at least some intellect. Spinoza says:

> So from these considerations—that nothing happens in nature that does not follow from her laws, that her laws cover everything that is conceived even by the divine intellect, and that nature observes a fixed and immutable order—it follows most clearly that the word miracle can be understood only with respect to men's beliefs, and means simply an event whose natural cause we—or at any rate the writer or narrator of the miracle—cannot explain by comparison with any other normal event.
>
> (p. 73, G III 83–84)

Scaled down in this naturalistic way, miracles cannot afford proof of God's existence. For Spinoza, effects are known through their causes—this is the import of Spinoza's master axiom 1ax4. But to the extent that we do not understand the causes of an event, we do not fully understand that event itself. How then, Spinoza asks, can an event that we only imperfectly understand provide us with certain knowledge of its cause, namely God?

> From such an event, and from anything at all that surpasses our understanding, we can understand nothing. For whatever we

> clearly and distinctly understand must become known to us
> either through itself or through some other thing that is clearly
> and distinctly understood through itself. Therefore from a
> miracle, or an event that surpasses our understanding, we can
> understand neither God's essence nor his existence nor anything
> whatsoever of God or nature.
>
> (p. 75, G III 85)

Thus scriptural accounts of miracles cannot be taken as true descriptions of violations of the order of nature, nor can they provide a rational basis for belief in the existence of God. Still, those accounts are useful because they "appeal strongly to the imagination and evoke men's wonder" (p. 75, G III 85) and, as such, can play a role in fostering not only belief in the existence of God but also the desire to obey God.

Such obedience, as I indicated, can be extremely useful to the state and its citizens. The state thus should do all it can—for its own sake and for the sake of its citizens—to inculcate such obedience to God. The best way to do this, i.e. to inculcate obedience in a way that provides the least occasion for the contention religion can often give rise to, is for the state to exercise its control over religion by defining...

> piety and religious observance as consisting only in works, that is,
> simply in the exercise of charity and just dealing, and to allow
> individual free judgment in all other matters.
>
> (p. 209, G III 226)

For Spinoza, the state should dictate that, as long as one acts justly, one is pious and faithful. One's beliefs are to be irrelevant to the evaluation of a citizen as religious or not. Rather, one's deeds are all that matters. Spinoza here once again invokes a sharper distinction between belief and deeds than his naturalism may be able to tolerate consistently. We can see, though, that for Spinoza a well-functioning state should exhibit wide scope, not only for freedom of thought and speech in general, but also for freedom of religious belief and religious practice. However, religious practice can and should be constrained by the state when such practice interferes with justice understood as loving one's neighbor. Of course, the sovereign can crack down on religious belief and practice even when these have no bearing on one's dealings with one's neighbors. But such curtailment or attempted curtailment of religious belief and practice can only lead to resentment and, as such, is a threat to the state itself. Thus, for Spinoza, ultimately the state does not have the right—or, indeed, the power—to crack down on religion in this way.

Because, for Spinoza, faith can be understood simply in terms of acting justly, he regards faith as compatible with the utmost freedom of thought or, as he sometimes puts it, the freedom to philosophize. The aim of faith, for Spinoza, is nothing other than obedience and piety, while "the aim of philosophy is nothing beyond truth" (p. 164, G III 179, translation altered). Obedience and truth do not necessarily coincide: as we saw, one can be obedient—one can act justly—while having radically false beliefs about God and the natural order. Because faith and philosophy are orthogonal in this way,

> faith allows to every man the utmost freedom to philosophize, and he may hold whatever opinions he pleases on any subjects whatsoever without imputation of evil. It condemns as heretics and schismatics only those who teach such beliefs as promote obstinacy, hatred, strife, and anger, while it regards as the faithful only those who promote justice and charity to the best of their intellectual powers and capacity.
>
> (p. 164, G III 179–80)

(This freedom to philosophize extends to the interpretation of scripture, as we'll see in the next section.) Of course, some religious authorities—as Spinoza knew only too well—would disagree and would seek to thwart certain philosophical beliefs as incompatible with genuine faith, but Spinoza's point is that this restriction of freedom to philosophize should not occur and in a well-functioning state does not occur.

It may seem that, for Spinoza, faith and philosophy occupy completely separate realms. Indeed, Spinoza says that knowledge by revelation—the province of faith—and natural knowledge—the province of philosophy—have "nothing in common" and are "completely distinct" (p. 6, G III 10). However, even on Spinoza's own terms, there is not so sharp a bifurcation between faith and philosophy. Yes, philosophy aims at truth, and faith at obedience. But a philosopher by seeking truth is also seeking obedience. For recall that obedience is simply loving one's neighbor as oneself, and, as Spinoza argues, a philosopher guided by reason reaches precisely the conclusion that one should love one's neighbor as oneself. So, for the philosopher to seek the truth is, in the end, an endeavor aimed at obedience. And while, the non-philosopher who seeks obedience does not aspire to the grasp of truth that the philosopher seeks, nonetheless, the non-philosopher who becomes more obedient thereby becomes more rational and thus reaches—as much as he can—the truth. So the obedience of the non-philosopher is not so divorced from the truth of the philosopher; rather these two endeavors are continuous and it does not seem right for Spinoza to characterize them as having nothing in common. As with Spinoza's distinction between freedom of thought and freedom of action that may be too sharp even by his own lights, Spinoza may also draw too sharp a line between faith and philosophy.

3. SCRIPTURE

As we have seen throughout this chapter, for Spinoza, religion can often be a threat to freedom and thus to the state itself. A major source of this threat is the special status that religious leaders accord to scripture as the word of God and as thus entitled to a special authority, an authority that may come into conflict with the authority of the sovereign. Because of this threat to freedom, Spinoza thinks it extremely important to investigate the real status of scripture: in what sense it is true, in what sense it is the word of God, in what sense it is entitled to authority. Unsurprisingly—given his spatio-temporal location—Spinoza's treatment of scripture focuses on the Old and New Testaments. Also unsurprisingly, Spinoza seeks to debunk many of the claims made on behalf of scripture. For Spinoza, scripture must be treated like any other collection of writings directed at a specific audience at a specific time. This no-special-status attitude toward scripture is simply a reflection of Spinoza's naturalism. At the same time—and perhaps more surprisingly—Spinoza also firmly believes that there is a genuine and wholly naturalistic sense in which scripture is divine and the word of God. Spinoza thus—here as elsewhere—attempts to naturalize the divine.

Before we can understand what authority scripture is entitled to, Spinoza believes we must learn how to interpret scripture, to understand what it means. Spinoza says:

> In order to escape from this scene of confusion, to free our minds from the prejudices of theologians and to avoid the hasty acceptance of human fabrications as divine teachings, we must discuss the true method of scriptural interpretation and examine it in depth.
>
> (p. 87, G III 98)

Spinoza's proposed method of interpretation is simple: we should use only scripture to interpret scripture. He says that:

> the universal rule for the interpretation of scripture [is] to ascribe no teaching to scripture that is not clearly established from studying it closely.
>
> (p. 88, G III 99)

He explains this method by drawing an analogy to the study of nature:

> I hold that the method of interpreting scripture is no different from the method of interpreting nature, and is in fact in complete accord with it. For the method of interpreting nature consists essentially in composing a detailed study of nature from which, as being the source of our assured data, we can deduce the definitions of the things of nature. Now in exactly the same way the task of scriptural interpretation requires us to make straightforward study of scripture, and from this, as the source of our fixed data and principles, to deduce by logical inference the meaning of the authors of scripture. In this way—that is, by allowing no other principles or data for the interpretation of scripture and study of its contents except those that can be gathered from scripture itself and from a historical study of scripture—steady progress can be made without any danger of error, and one can deal with matters that surpass our understanding with no less confidence than those matters which are known to us by the natural light of reason.
>
> (p. 87, G III 98)

What we are not to bring to the table in our interpretation of scripture are any prior opinions, i.e. prejudices, we may have about the truthfulness or moral value or beauty of scripture. Strauss makes this point well:

> The knowledge of nature must be derived solely from data supplied by nature herself, and not at all from considerations of what is fitting, beautiful, perfect or reasonable. In the same way, knowledge of the Bible must be derived solely from data supplied by the Bible itself, and not at all from considerations of what is reasonable.
>
> (Strauss 1988: 144)

This method of using only scripture itself to understand scripture makes perfect sense in light of Spinoza's rationalism. Let's say that we use some standard—external to scripture itself—for interpreting scripture. Assume we adopt this standard: scripture means whatever my friend Mario says it means. This standard of evaluation certainly seems wholly arbitrary: why should the meaning of scripture be tied to whatever Mario, in particular, pronounces, instead of, for example, me or you or Emma Thompson? Unless there is something about scripture itself that points to Mario as its interpreter, the proposal must seem arbitrary and illegitimate. Even standards that are less apparently arbitrary, such as, for example, standards according to which scripture means whatever certain religious authorities say it means or whatever is most consonant with science and philosophy, etc., will also be inadequate unless scripture itself points to certain authorities rather than others. Unless scripture itself points to one way of interpreting it, any proposed way will seem groundless. Absent such a basis in the text itself for reading the text this way, to hold that any such extraneous standard for interpretation is legitimate is to hold that a certain fact holds not in virtue of anything. In other words, to adopt an extraneous standard for interpretation is to be committed to a brute fact. In this way, we can see how Spinoza's rationalism dictates that scripture must be interpreted using only scripture itself.

We can also see that this proposed method of interpretation is very much in line with, for example, Spinoza's view that the standard of goodness by which an action is to be evaluated must derive from the action itself. Just as goodness must be evaluated from within, so too scripture must be interpreted from within.

Spinoza has a relatively broad understanding of how scripture itself can be used to interpret scripture. In the long passage recently quoted, it becomes clear that the relevant internal evidence available for interpreting scripture includes facts gleaned from "a historical study of scripture." Spinoza spells out his methodology more fully on the following page. First, he says that the study of scripture:

should inform us of the nature and properties of the language in which the Bible was written and which authors were accustomed to speak.

(p. 88, G III 99–100)

The TTP includes instances of such linguistic analysis and, of course, Spinoza's unfinished Hebrew grammar was devoted to such matters.

The second key feature that Spinoza highlights is a rule: Interpret scripture literally—even if the text interpreted literally asserts something obviously false—unless reasons internal to the text warrant a non-literal interpretation. Spinoza offers the example of the biblical claim, "God is fire."[3] Certainly the belief that God is—literally—fire would, for Spinoza, be irrational. But this fact, by itself, does not preclude a literal interpretation. However, a literal interpretation here would conflict with other passages in which "Moses clearly tells us that God has no resemblance to visible things in heaven or on the earth or in the water" (p. 89, G III 101). To remove this conflict, we must seek a metaphorical reading, if possible. Fortunately in this case, there is internal biblical evidence that the word "fire" is used in a non-literal sense to denote anger (Spinoza cites Job 31:12) and so we can interpret "God is fire" as "God is jealous." If one could not on internal, biblical grounds find a metaphorical reading here, then, Spinoza soberly concludes, we would simply have had to regard there as being an irremediable conflict in the texts.

Of course, the metaphorical reading available here—namely that God is jealous—is, for Spinoza, also contrary to reason, but again unless there is evidence of a non-literal understanding of this term, we must interpret the Bible as saying here that God is jealous. The key point is that any divergence from literal meaning has to be based on reasons internal to scripture.

The final key feature is to gather information about the lives of the biblical authors, their intended audience, and the history of the books themselves, including their various versions and how they came to be accepted into the canon (p. 90, G III 101–2).

In general, for Spinoza, we are to bring to bear on the biblical texts all the linguistic and historical knowledge we can, just as we would in interpreting any other text without any preconceptions as to its meaning or truth.

Once we amass all the relevant historical and linguistic information, we can go about the interpretation of scripture. If there are any claims that are asserted explicitly throughout scripture, then there should be no doubt as to scripture's meaning on these points (pp. 90–91, G III 102). As we saw in the previous section, Spinoza says we find such unanimity within the Bible regarding the command to love one's neighbor as oneself. On non-moral, more purely philosophical matters, however, Spinoza says we find that the biblical authors disagree. Spinoza says:

> [T]he prophets differed among themselves in matters of philosophical speculation ... and their narratives conform especially to the prejudices of their particular age. So we are debarred from deducing and explaining the meaning of one prophet from some clearer passages in another, unless it is most plainly established that they were of one and the same mind.
>
> (p. 92; G III 104)

The fact that Spinoza is willing to allow that different biblical authors disagree is a manifestation of his willingness to allow also that what the Bible asserts—particularly with regard to non-moral matters—is simply false. Spinoza obviously does not bring to the biblical text the presupposition that what it asserts is true. Here Spinoza differs sharply from a number of other biblical commentators, including Maimonides, and Spinoza discusses this difference at length in chapter 7 of TTP.

As Spinoza reads him, one of Maimonides' guiding interpretive principles is that nothing in scripture is contrary to reason. Thus, if scripture appears to teach something contrary to reason, if it is seen to go against some philosophical or scientific truth, then it is necessary, in Maimonides' words "to do violence to the Scriptural texts" and to interpret them in a different, less obvious way. For Spinoza, this methodology is an instance of not using only scripture in order to interpret scripture: for Maimonides, to interpret scripture properly, one must invoke something outside scripture, namely science and philosophy. Spinoza finds this approach to the texts "excessive and rash" (p. 102, G III 115) and, in fact, sees it as rendering scripture worthless:

> If that which is absolutely clear can be accounted obscure and incomprehensible or else interpreted at will, it will be vain for us to try to prove anything from Scripture.
>
> (p. 26, G III 35)

Further, for Spinoza, this approach is positively perverse, for it assumes the truth of scripture when the fact that scripture is true should be derived from a close study of it. With Maimonides clearly among those he has in mind, Spinoza says:

> most of them assume as a basic principle for the understanding of scripture and for extracting its true meaning that it is throughout truthful and divine—a conclusion which ought to be the end result of study and strict examination.
>
> (p. 5, G III 9)

We will return to this point at the end of this chapter.

A particularly pernicious aspect, in Spinoza's eyes, of Maimonides' methodology and of any methodology that allows one to reinterpret scriptural passages that are absolutely clear is that it takes the ability to understand scripture out of the hands of ordinary individuals. For Spinoza, as we've seen, the overall moral message of the Bible—to love one's neighbor as oneself—is perfectly comprehensible to all. The other aspects of the biblical text may not be as clear, but apart from the historical and linguistic knowledge that Spinoza emphasizes, these passages do not require any special philosophical or scientific knowledge. As such, these passages were able to be understood by "the common people of the Jews and Gentiles for whom the prophets and apostles once preached and wrote" (p. 101, G III 114). For Maimonides, such passages could never have been properly understood without the additional philosophical and scientific knowledge that he saw the biblical authors as having access to. Thus,

> he clearly deprives the common people of any confidence they
> can have in the meaning of scripture derived simply from
> perusing it.
>
> (p. 102, G III 116)

Because only experts can properly understand the Bible, Maimonides' methodology helps empower ecclesiastical authorities, authorities over the meaning of scripture who, as such, curtail the freedom of individuals to think and believe as they choose in religious matters. Such restrictions of freedom can, for Spinoza, only be harmful.

In articulating his methodology of scriptural interpretation, Spinoza was drawing upon and extending a long history of biblical interpretation. A key component of the authority given to scripture as the word of God was the traditional claim that the first five books of the Bible—the Pentateuch—were written by Moses who, as Popkin puts it, "received the text directly from God."[4] To cast doubt on the claim that Moses authored these books was central to Spinoza's claim that the Bible is not to be regarded as necessarily a true account of events. In questioning Mosaic authorship, Spinoza acknowledged the twelfth-century Jewish biblical commentator, Ibn Ezra, who—like Spinoza—called attention to the fact that the Pentateuch, supposedly written by Moses, contains a description of

Moses' death and of events that took place afterward. Hobbes—not acknowledged by Spinoza on this point—also made trouble for Mosaic authorship in this way.[5]

Around the time Spinoza was writing the TTP, there were other thinkers who also questioned the status of the Bible in even more searching ways than Ibn Ezra. Among these were Isaac La Peyrere (1596–1677), a French Calvinist who clearly influenced Spinoza, and Samuel Fisher (1605–65), an English Quaker who spent some time in Amsterdam in 1657–58 and who almost certainly came to know Spinoza during this period.[6] La Peyrere and Fisher both challenged the accuracy of the biblical text by pointing out that the text went through innumerable variations before taking on its current form. Given that the text may be corrupt, the question of whether the Bible really is the word of God became salient, as it did for Spinoza, as we will soon see.

4. PROPHECY AND THE TRUTH OF THE BIBLE

Once we have determined to the best of our ability what the biblical text *means*, how can we determine whether what it says is *true* and thus whether what it says is divine, the word of God? For Spinoza, the answers to these questions turn on what kind of access to the truth the prophets—the human authors of the Bible—had and what kind of knowledge prophecy embodies.

Spinoza defines prophecy as "sure knowledge of some matter revealed by God to man" (p. 9, G III 15). Spinoza notes that by this standard even natural knowledge—philosophical and scientific knowledge—will count as prophecy "for the knowledge that we acquire by the natural light of reason depends solely on knowledge of God and of his eternal decrees" (p. 9, G III 15). But Spinoza goes on to say:

> since this natural knowledge is common to all men—for it rests
> on foundations common to all men—it is not so highly prized by
> the multitude who are ever eager for what is strange and foreign

to their own nature, despising their natural gifts. Therefore
prophetic knowledge is usually taken to exclude natural
knowledge.

(p. 9, G III 15)

In accordance with this common understanding, Spinoza thus focuses in particular on the prophecy contained in scripture.

For Spinoza, it is characteristic of biblical prophets—with one noteworthy exception, Jesus—that their prophetic knowledge "was revealed either by words, or by appearances, or by a combination of both" (p. 11, G III 17). (Moses was, for Spinoza, the only prophet who received his prophecy from a real voice [p. 11, G III 17; p. 14, G III 21]; none of the other voices prophets heard were, for Spinoza, real.) Because the prophets received their knowledge through words and images—i.e. through causes external to them—their knowledge was not adequate, not fully rational. Rather, their knowledge was imaginative (p. 14, G III 21). Imagination is Spinoza's general term for knowledge acquired through external causes (2p17s). The prophets, therefore, did not have superior powers of reason; at best they had "a more vivid power of imagination." That the knowledge of prophets was not fully rational is evident from the many false beliefs they had about God and other matters. Spinoza lists a number of biblical claims according to which God is said to have properties that are, in fact, incompatible with God's nature—properties such as being seated, being a dove, according the Jews a special status—and claims according to which certain events, such as purported miracles, occur which are incompatible with a naturalistic, rationalist understanding of the world. As we saw, for Spinoza, apparent miracles can be explained in naturalistic terms.

Because the prophets' knowledge came via the imagination, their beliefs did not enjoy the kind of inherent certainty that, as we saw in Chapter 3, only fully rational, fully adequate ideas have. The prophets thus must have achieved the certainty that is partly constitutive of prophecy through some means other than the revelation itself. Spinoza claims, citing a number of texts, that this certainty was secured through signs (p. 22, G III 30–31). Because the content of the revelation itself was not inherently certain, the revelation itself and the signs that supported it had to be adapted to the beliefs and capacities of the prophets (p. 23, G III 32; pp. 32–33, G III 42).

Among the prophets, however, Jesus was exceptional, according to Spinoza. Unlike the other prophets whose access to God was via words and images, Jesus "communed with God mind to mind" (p. 14, G III 21). Spinoza says that, in this respect, no one "has attained such a degree of perfection surpassing all others, except Christ" (p. 14, G III 21). Because, for Spinoza, God directly placed certain ideas in Jesus' mind without the aid of words and images, those ideas were not imaginative, those ideas could only be adequate.

> Christ perceived truly, or understood, what was revealed. For it is when a thing is perceived by pure thought, without words or images, that it is understood.
>
> (p. 54, G III 65)

This special status for Jesus seems extremely puzzling on Spinoza's own terms. Doesn't this kind of special access to God's mind that Jesus enjoyed violate Spinoza's naturalism? After all, Spinoza makes clear that Jesus was a human being (see, e.g., Letter 73). If the capacity for direct communication with God exceeds human capacity, then Spinoza would be—in effect—allowing a miracle, something that contravenes the laws of nature and this, as we have seen, is something contrary to Spinoza's entire rationalist system. Strauss, for one, believed that Spinoza was saying that Jesus did have this supernatural access to God and that Spinoza thus contradicted himself. This was all, according to Strauss, part of Spinoza's strategy of expressing a view that would placate religious authorities (namely that Jesus has a supernatural capacity) while surreptitiously expressing his real view which contradicted the more publicly acceptable views (Strauss 1988: 171). However, as Donagan (1996) points out, Spinoza does not say that Jesus has a super-human access to the truth. Spinoza's view is compatible with the claim that Jesus' access was in keeping with human nature but still exceptional in that no one else had achieved this *degree* of access to God's mind. Perhaps Spinoza would say that Jesus' access differed from that of other prophets in degree, but not in kind. This interpretation renders Spinoza's claims about Jesus compatible with Spinoza's naturalism.

Still, a problem about the status of Jesus remains. The knowledge that Jesus apparently has is adequate. Adequate knowledge, as we have seen, is knowledge that is not caused from outside a given mind. But Jesus' knowledge is (somehow) caused directly by another mind, namely God's mind. How then can this knowledge be adequate? Spinoza's claims about Jesus' knowledge may, after all, contradict a basic principle of his system, just as Strauss would have it.

But the situation here is not so clear, for the problem we are now considering—how can Jesus' ideas which are not caused from within Jesus' mind be adequate?—is an instance of a general problem. This is the problem of finite minds' acquisition of adequate ideas. The ideas that a finite mind acquires—comes to have—seem to be in each case triggered in that mind by something outside it. Strictly, by Spinoza's own standards as laid down in Part II of the *Ethics*, such ideas cannot be adequate; nevertheless, Spinoza does say we finite minds are able to acquire adequate ideas. The problem of Jesus' acquisition of ideas from outside which are nonetheless adequate is just the same general problem writ small. In his comments about Jesus' special status, Spinoza is not necessarily violating his naturalism nor is he adopting a problematic view for hidden political reasons; rather he is simply getting caught up in a problem that crops up for his epistemology generally.

However, there is a different problem for Spinoza raised by his account of Jesus' knowledge—a problem that is straightforward and, I think, not resolvable. Let's say that the adequate knowledge that Spinoza accords Jesus is naturalistically acceptable and humanly possible. However, to say that it is possible that Jesus had this knowledge does not mean that Jesus in fact had this knowledge. If it is humanly and naturalistically possible that Jesus did have this adequate knowledge, then surely it is also humanly and naturalistically possible that—just like all other human beings—he did not have this knowledge. Why does Spinoza take the biblical text at its word here or at what he takes to be its word? Why is Spinoza so confident that what he takes the New Testament to be relating concerning Jesus—that he had an exceptional knowledge of God—is indeed correct? With regard to the other prophets, Spinoza can, perhaps, be sure that they did have extraordinary imaginative access to certain information which they are able to convey dramatically. But why is Spinoza so sure that Jesus had anything more than such an imaginative apprehension of what he taught? Perhaps we can glean from the Bible, as Spinoza does, that it says that Jesus communed with God mind-to-mind. But why should we believe that the Bible is correct on this point? Isn't it just as easy to believe that Jesus' access was thoroughly imaginative too, but that the biblical authors portrayed it otherwise—this being one of the many false beliefs to which the limited understanding of the biblical authors was subject? So I think that there is a genuine problem—on Spinoza's own terms—a problem that is not general, but is specific to the claims about Jesus' status. Here, as in the case of Spinoza's problematically sharp line between thought and action in his treatment of the freedom of citizens, it is tempting to think—à la Strauss—that Spinoza deliberately tones down some of his more radical views and that he doesn't believe that Jesus' knowledge was in any way special. But again such a reading would be speculative.

Return now to the question with which we began this section: in what sense is the Bible the word of God? Given that the Bible is the work of prophets who—with the possible exception that Spinoza allows for Jesus—were largely ignorant and who asserted many falsehoods, how can one say that scripture is the word of God?

Surely, if scripture is to have that status, what it says must at least be true. If, given these falsehoods, Spinoza calls the Bible divine, isn't this at best wishful thinking on his part and incompatible with his strict naturalistic system?

However, Spinoza does see the Bible—or at least certain strands in the Bible—as the word of God, and Spinoza does so in a naturalistically legitimate way. For Spinoza, "A thing is called sacred and divine when its purpose is to foster piety and religion" (p. 146, G III 160). A text, then, is the word of God, if it is designed to foster piety and religion. This is obviously a stripped-down sense of "divine": it allows any number of things and even any number of texts to count as divine. Why, by this standard, we reach the shocking conclusion that even Spinoza's *Ethics* would count as divine! This austere sense of "divine" is in keeping with Spinoza's naturalism because, by this standard, the word of God need not be arbitrarily restricted to a certain text produced at a specific period in human history.

To see what the status of the Bible is according to this standard, we must recall what piety is, for Spinoza. True piety, as we've seen, is loving one's neighbor as oneself. This is precisely how a strong state will define piety in order to promote the freedom of its citizens. As we've also seen, for Spinoza, the overarching and consistent moral message of the Bible is exactly this: to love one's neighbor as oneself. For this reason, then, the Bible contains the word of God:

> It can thus be readily seen in what sense God is to be understood as the author of the Bible: it is not because God willed to confer on men a set number of books, but because of the true religion that is taught therein.
>
> (p. 149, G III 163)

Thus, for Spinoza, we do have evidence that the Bible is divine, and this claim is, for Spinoza, not illegitimately assumed as a presupposition of one approach to the Bible, but is rather "the end result of study and strict examination" (p. 5, G III 9).

We see here another instance of the twofold use of the PSR. First, Spinoza is asking in virtue of what is scripture divine? Here he insists on an explanation for the divine status of the Bible, whereas, as he claims, many just assume that it has this status. This is the first use of the PSR. His answer to this demand is that the Bible is the word of God because it teaches true piety, i.e. it teaches that which is most in accord with reason, that which enables individuals to be most powerful, most able to make things intelligible in terms of themselves. This reliance on the notion of intelligibility in answer to the demand that the divine status of scripture be intelligible is the second use of the PSR in this case.

Spinoza has offered naturalistic accounts of various religious notions, such as the nature of God, the divine word, miracles, and prophecy. Spinoza thus attempts to make religion safe for naturalism and for rationalism. Indeed, religion plays an essential role in this naturalistic system for it is only through religion that people can achieve the freedom of which they are capable, and that the state can thrive. Can Spinoza go to the well one more time and offer a naturalistic account of yet another central religious notion: eternal life? Spinoza does attempt to do so, especially in Part V of the *Ethics*, and this is where many believe that his naturalistic system finally and spectacularly breaks down. We will take up this most difficult question in the next chapter.

SUMMARY

What rights do human beings have and what rights does the state or sovereign which governs human beings have? Spinoza takes up these fundamental questions of political philosophy in his works *Tractatus Theologico-Politicus* and *Tractatus Politicus*. Spinoza's answers to these questions are as fully rationalistic and naturalistic as are his answers to other key questions in moral philosophy that were discussed in Chapter 5. His account is bold and abrupt: an individual has the right to do whatever is in the individual's power, and the state—which Spinoza sees as an individual—has the right to do whatever is in its power. Spinoza importantly qualifies this bold claim by saying that each individual has the right to do what conduces to its power in the long run. Spinoza thus sees rights, just like the moral goods and moral obligations, as stemming from the nature of an individual, a nature characterized fundamentally by the striving for self-preservation and power.

Human beings, realizing that they cannot achieve much on their own, pool their power and agree to work together for the common interest and to refrain from harming one another. This agreement has no force, however, unless it can be enforced, and this is how the state comes into being. The sovereign is given the power to enforce the agreement without which there would be no joint activity and without which individuals would have very little power. The state which thus comes into being through this agreement seeks to preserve itself and enhance its power. Spinoza argues that a state that is too repressive and curtails people's freedom to a great degree will cause people no longer to abide by the state-forming agreement. In this way, extreme repression leads to a movement to undermine the state. Similarly, a state that is too lax cannot guarantee the basic safety of its citizens and is therefore also liable to be overthrown. A healthy state must seek a middle ground. Spinoza argues persuasively that freedom of thought and speech cannot be curtailed without severely threatening the state itself. But, Spinoza also argues, the state can legitimately limit its citizens' freedom of action. Spinoza thus draws a sharp line between speech and action which is problematic in the context of his naturalism.

Spinoza also places limits on religion. For Spinoza, religion comes into existence only with the state and thus should always remain subordinate to the rulers of the state. Religious authorities who seek to have power independently of the sovereign thus threaten the state itself. But if religion is firmly under the control of the sovereign, it can be very useful in enabling people to increase the degree of freedom and rationality that they enjoy. Spinoza argues that, to this end, the state should emphasize that good works are most important of all and orthodoxy of belief is not necessary for piety.

In an effort to restrain the authority often claimed in the name of religion, Spinoza also seeks to establish a new method of interpreting scripture. Scripture is to be approached as any other natural object, and we should not bring to the text any preconceptions about the divine status of the text. Instead, after determining the meaning of the text, we should, Spinoza says, reach a conclusion about its divine nature. Spinoza argues that the overarching message of the Old and New Testatments is to love one's neighbor as oneself and thus, since this message is in conformity with reason, Spinoza concludes that the Old and New Testaments are divine, despite the fact that they contain many falsehoods. These falsehoods are only to be expected, Spinoza says, in texts that were adapted to the ordinary understanding of the biblical authors and their intended audience. The biblical authors or prophets did not have any special rational insight into the nature of God, but they did have a talent for imaginatively conveying the divine message that one should love one's neighbor as oneself. The only exception among the prophets, according to Spinoza, was Jesus, who had a special access to the mind of God. Whether this special status is compatible with Spinoza's naturalistic approach to the biblical texts is a potential problem with his approach to Jesus.

FURTHER READING

Edwin Curley (1990) "Notes on a Neglected Masterpiece (II): The *Theologico-Political Treatise* as a Prolegomenon to the *Ethics*." (Good account of the metaphysical themes in the TTP.)

————. (1996) "Kissinger, Spinoza, and Genghis Khan." (Contains a powerful, intuitive criticism of Spinoza's claim that the state may control freedom of action.)

Alan Donagan (1996) "Spinoza's Theology." (Overview of Spinoza's religious thought.)

Alexandre Matheron (1969). *Individu et Communauté chez Spinoza*. (Classic account of Spinoza's political and moral philosophy in light of his metaphysics of individuals.)

Leo Strauss (1988) "How to Study Spinoza's *Theologico-Political Treatise*." (Influential statement of some of the difficulties in interpreting the TTP.)

Seven

From PSR to Eternity

Eternal life: nice (perhaps), if you can get it. But is there anything you can *do* to get it? It is a fundamental tenet of many forms of Christianity that there is something one can do to achieve eternality, a kind of existence—perhaps separate from the body—in which one reaps rewards (or perhaps punishments) for the kind of life one lived prior to death. The belief in some kind of eternality was not nearly so central to Judaism as it has always been to Christianity; nonetheless, there is a significant strand in the Jewish tradition that accepts the immortality of the soul and that endorses the notion of some kind of post-mortem reward for a virtuous earthly life. As I mentioned in Chapter 1, in seventeenth-century Amsterdam the Jewish community engaged in a turbulent debate about the kind of immortality—if any—that the soul enjoyed. Uriel da Costa's denial of the immortality of the soul was certainly one of the factors that precipitated the bans against him in the 1620s and 1630s. As I also mentioned in Chapter 1, Spinoza's own convictions about immortality may also have been part of what was behind *his* excommunication in 1656.

But does Spinoza deny that we can be immortal? It seems that he does not. Although Spinoza does not often use the term "immortality", he does say that "The human mind cannot be absolutely destroyed with the body, but something of it remains which is eternal" (5p23).[1] Nonetheless, the kind of eternal existence Spinoza envisages for us is rather different from the kind of eternal existence endorsed in traditional accounts. I would like to focus on three rather important differences.

(1) First, on many traditional accounts, our posthumous existence is somehow independent of the body. One of Descartes's primary motivations in arguing for the real distinction of mind and body is precisely to open up the possibility of the existence of the mind when the body no longer exists. However, for Spinoza, although the mind or a part of the mind may exist after the death of the body, his parallelism of modes of thought and modes of extension dictates that there must be something bodily that corresponds to (and is indeed identical to) the part of the mind that exists eternally (see 2p8c).

(2) On many versions of the view that we are capable of eternal existence, the vehicle of this immortality is a soul or thinking substance. Again, this is certainly the case for Descartes. Because thinking substances do not have parts, they cannot be destroyed, at least not by natural means. For Spinoza, however, the human mind is not a substance and, indeed, it has parts (2p15). So it is capable of being de-composed into its parts and hence destroyed. Any eternality of the human mind would have to be compatible with its status as a non-substantial composite of parts. But, again, how can such a mind be eternal?

(3) In my opinion, the most important way in which Spinoza's espousal of the eternality of the mind departs from traditional notions stems directly from his rationalism and follows from his views on the reward for virtue. On most traditional views, this earthly life—taken on its own—is imperfect because, in effect, the scales of justice are not yet properly balanced. In this life, taken on its own, the good, the virtuous, are not properly rewarded and the non-virtuous are not properly punished. It is only with the afterlife that the proper balance is struck and the goings-on in this life can be properly evaluated with regard to justice. We must take the broader perspective that includes the afterlife in order to arrive at a proper assessment of this life. As we've seen in Chapter 5, for Spinoza evaluations of a thing must come from within that thing's very nature; otherwise the assessment of that thing as good or bad, just or unjust, must be

extraneous to that thing and have no genuine purchase on that thing. An evaluation of a thing by some external standard is, for Spinoza as we saw, wholly arbitrary and generates brute facts. This point applies here too: if the justness of this life is not immanent to this life, if—in order for its justness to be secured—some extraneous reward must be tacked on to this life, then brute facts would abound. If the justness of this life is not secured from within this life, then why can't it stem from a pre-birth existence (with appropriate joys and sufferings) instead of a post-mortem existence? Why can't the justness of this life be secured by a non-eternal, yet very happy post-mortem existence instead of by the eternal post-mortem existence that is typically envisaged? The notion of one's needing another kind of life in order to be rewarded for virtue (or, perhaps, punished for evil) is inimical to Spinoza's notion of intrinsic value, to his view that virtue is its own reward and vice its own punishment (5p42). And, as we saw in Chapter 5, such a view is simply a manifestation of Spinoza's naturalism and his aversion to brute facts.

But if Spinoza endorses a strict psycho-physical parallelism, denies that finite minds are or can be indestructible souls, and repudiates the notion of post-mortem settling of the books, then what remains of the traditional notion of eternal existence? At this point, one may begin to wonder whether Spinoza's affirmation of our eternal existence is mere lip-service to a more or less entrenched and powerful dogma.

But such aspersions on Spinoza would be unwarranted. As with his accounts of the good, the right, rights, consciousness, inherence, etc., Spinoza seeks to preserve a legitimate core of the traditional notion and rehabilitate it for his naturalistic purposes. As in the other cases—and again with the help of the twofold use of the PSR—Spinoza seeks to explain the notion of eternal existence as simply a version of intelligibility.

Let me outline the account of eternal existence that he offers and raise some major problems for it, before seeing how Spinoza's rationalism comes to the rescue.

Spinoza defines eternity this way: "By eternity I understand existence itself, insofar as it is conceived to follow necessarily from the definition alone of an eternal thing" (1def8; translation altered). For Spinoza, something exists eternally just in case its existence follows simply from the definition of an eternal thing. Thus God enjoys eternal existence because God's essence follows simply from God's definition or essence or nature (1p11). Although, as we have seen, my existence does not follow from my definition alone (2ax1), nonetheless my existence does follow simply from the definition of God. This is precisely Spinoza's point in 1p16 and its demonstration, and it is the heart of Spinoza's thesis of necessitarianism that we discussed in Chapter 2. Thus, there is a straightforward sense in which I—and all other things—enjoy, for Spinoza, eternal existence. In this light, we can see why Spinoza says, "It is of the nature of reason to perceive things under a certain aspect of eternity" (2p44c2; translation altered). Reason, of course, perceives things truly (2p44d). Thus since reason perceives things as following from the necessity of God's nature and as thus eternal, these things are eternal.

Spinoza makes this point for the human body in particular in 5p22: "[I]n God there is necessarily an idea that expresses this or that human body under an aspect of eternity". God, as omniscient and as fully rational, conceives of my body as following from God's nature considered as extended. Thus God conceives of my body as eternal, and this conception is, of course, correct.

Similarly, God conceives that his grasp of my body—i.e. God conceives that his idea of my body—follows simply from God's nature considered as thinking. Thus God conceives his idea of my body as eternal, and so this idea genuinely is eternal.

Since—as we have seen—my mind is simply God's idea of my body—it follows that my mind is, for Spinoza, eternal. Thus, for Spinoza, the mind enjoys eternal existence; in accordance with parallelism, the eternal existence of the mind is accompanied by the eternal existence of the body. The eternality I enjoy here is distinctively mine—centered as it is on God's idea of a particular body, namely my body, that occupies a distinctive place in the causal network of bodies. Thus the eternal thing that I am is distinct from the eternal thing that you are because your eternality consists in God's eternal idea of a distinct body, your body. Despite its distinctiveness, the eternality that I enjoy does not seem special, and this is so for at least two reasons: (i) this eternality is a kind of eternality that *all* things—not just my mind and my body and your mind and your body, but the dog, the rock and my pancreas— enjoy. (ii) Because this eternality follows necessarily from God's essence, it seems that there is nothing we can do to *achieve* this kind of eternality. We already have it and automatically so (and the dog already has it and automatically so).

However, Spinoza seems to say that we can—perhaps outstripping dogs and rocks—achieve something more: we can make our minds more eternal; we can increase the size of that part of our minds that enjoys eternality. We can do this, Spinoza says, by increasing the number of adequate ideas in our minds:

> The more the mind understands things by the second and third kind of knowledge, the greater the part of it that remains unharmed.
>
> (5p38d)

> Death is less harmful to us, the greater the mind's clear and distinct knowledge.
>
> (5p38s)

Since the second and third kinds of knowledge exhaust the class of adequate ideas for Spinoza (2p40s2), his point is that the greater the number of adequate ideas we have, the more eternal our mind is. So, for Spinoza, the more rational a person is, i.e. the more powerful he is, the more of his mind is eternal and thus the more of his mind remains after the body's death.

This claim is significant because it promises for our mind a kind of eternality that is not trivial, that is not one that we automatically have and that is not one we automatically share with Fido and my pet rock. Instead, this kind of eternality—secured by adequate ideas—is something we can achieve by working to acquire a greater number of adequate ideas. In this way, Spinoza would be preserving an aspect of the traditional view: what kind of eternality we enjoy is a function of what we do in this life. In particular, it's a function of how many adequate ideas we acquire.

The kind of eternality thus achieved would not involve memory of one's past (5p21). This is because, for Spinoza, all memory is a matter of inadequate ideas (2p17s, 2p18s). It might seem then that the eternal existence I enjoy is not one in which I as a person exist.[2] Spinoza—like Locke—seems to see memory as necessary for personal identity over time (4p39s). However, it's not clear to me that the eternal existence enjoyed by me insofar as I have adequate ideas does not bring with it the existence of me as a person. After all, there is, as I mentioned, something distinctive about the eternal existence I have: it is grounded in God's idea of a particular body, my body. This idea is distinct from the eternal idea in God's mind that forms the basis of your eternal mind. It may be that, when Spinoza indicates in 4p39s that memory is required for personal identity, he is speaking only of the identity of persons insofar as they are not rational. The identity of persons insofar as they are rational may not in the same way require memory.

Even if the eternal existence that I enjoy by having a greater number of adequate ideas is personal and distinctively mine, there is still a non-trivial problem of triviality that this account faces. Spinoza seems to say that, although my inadequate ideas are not eternal and that they perish when the body is destroyed, my adequate ideas are eternal. That is why, for Spinoza, it is a significant achievement to acquire a greater number of adequate ideas. However, given Spinoza's account in 1def8 of eternity as existence that follows from the definition alone of an eternal thing, it seems to follow that even my inadequate ideas are eternal. For consider: all of my ideas—both adequate and inadequate—are, as we've seen, simply ideas in God's mind, in God's intellect. These ideas are each states or modes of God. As such, they seem to follow simply from God's definition. Thus all of my ideas seem to follow from God's definition and thus all of my ideas—even my inadequate ideas— seem to be eternal. If this is so, then what is the point of trying to acquire a greater number of adequate ideas in an effort to be more and more eternal? If my inadequate ideas are as eternal as my adequate ideas, then my mind is already completely eternal and there is nothing I can do to make it more eternal. Once again, Spinoza's thesis of the eternality of the mind seems to be rendered trivial. Spinoza needs to draw a distinction between adequate and inadequate ideas with regard to eternality, but he seems to have no basis for doing so.

The problem with this objection stems from the claim in the previous paragraph that even my inadequate ideas are in God's intellect, are states of God. I grant that anything that is truly in God or a state of God is thereby, for Spinoza, eternal. But I deny that, for Spinoza, my inadequate ideas are genuinely states of God, are genuinely in God. If inadequate ideas are not genuinely in God, but adequate ideas are, then we have the makings of an asymmetry that would establish that acquisition of adequate ideas may increase the eternality of the mind in a way that acquisition of inadequate ideas does not.

But again, how can this be? How can it fail to be the case that inadequate ideas are in God? Isn't everything that exists in God? After all, Spinoza says early on in the *Ethics*, "Whatever is is either in itself or in another" (1ax1). This axiom seems to apply to inadequate ideas. And this "other" that inadequate ideas seem to be in is precisely God. Recall Spinoza's completely general claim: "Whatever is is in God" (1p15). How could 1p15 not apply to inadequate ideas? Notice that 1p15 and 1ax1 apply only to *whatever is* [*omnia, quae sunt*]. So, given 1ax1 and 1p15, if inadequate ideas are not in God, that can only be because, somehow, inadequate ideas do not exist, they are not. And, as I will now argue, this is exactly what Spinoza holds.

To see why inadequate ideas somehow do not exist, let's ask a fundamental question that is not often confronted head on: What is it for a thing to exist? What is existence? To this fundamental question, Spinoza has a characteristically deep and bold answer: existence is intelligibility. For a thing to exist is for it to be intelligible, conceivable, explicable. First, I will show that Spinoza holds this view, and then I'll show why he does. The reason—as you will not be surprised to learn—turns on Spinoza's commitment to the PSR.

It will be helpful to begin by examining Spinoza's account of God's existence, because Spinoza's account of existence is more explicit in this case. For Spinoza, God's existence is identical to God's essence. Thus 1p20: "God's existence and his essence are one and the same." So what it is for God to exist is for God to have a certain essence. I want to highlight here a crucial line of thought at work in the demonstration of 1p20. Spinoza says:

> the same attributes of God which (by 1def4) explain God's eternal essence at the same time explain [*explicant*] his eternal existence, that is, that itself which constitutes God's essence at the same time constitutes his existence. So his existence and his essence are one and the same.

I will not go into the precise way in which attributes relate to essence and existence (and the way in which attributes relate to one other), but I would like to extract an important point that shows the PSR at work. Spinoza seems to be saying that, because God's existence and God's essence are explained by precisely the same things (namely God's attributes), it follows that God's essence is identical to God's existence. The general principle at work here seems to be one to the effect that, if there is no difference between the things that *a* and *b* are explained by, then there is no difference between a and b. Or, to put it fancily: any difference between two things (any non-identity) must supervene on some explanatory difference between the two things.

It is not hard to see why Spinoza would hold such a principle: if a and b were distinct despite being explained by precisely the same things, then the non-identity would not be explicable; there would be no answer to the question: What is it in virtue of which a and b are distinct? In the case at hand, Spinoza would say that if God's existence were distinct from God's essence, the non-identity would, given the complete explanatory overlap, be a brute fact. And, of course, Spinoza rejects brute facts. So God's existence and God's essence must be identical.

Given this identity, we may say that, for Spinoza, what it is for God to exist is for God to have a certain essence. But what is it for God to have that essence? Recall that, for Spinoza, the definition of a thing states its essence. So let us look at two of Spinoza's definitions for help in answering this question. God is, of course, defined as a substance and a substance is defined as that which is in itself and is conceived through itself. So the essence of a substance is to be conceived through itself.[3] So God's essence is just the fact that he is conceivable or intelligible through himself and thus God's essence is just his conceivability, i.e. it is God's conceivability, i.e. it is the conceivability of a being that is self-conceived. This is, as we shall see shortly, a unique feature of God's essence: God's essence is his conceivability, but the essence of other things is not their conceivability.

We can conclude that, just as God's existence is God's essence, so too God's existence just is God's conceivability. If God's existence were something else over and above God's conceivability, then there would be a brute fact, there would be no account of God's existence.

Spinoza's view is that what holds for God also holds for other things, i.e. for God's modes. Of course, modes are not self-conceived as God is. Rather, their essence is to be conceived through something else, namely God (see 1def5, the definition of mode). Nonetheless, just as God's existence is God's intelligibility, the fact that God is intelligible, so too the existence of anything else just is the fact that that thing is intelligible. Thus Spinoza says in 1p25s: "God must be called the cause of all things in the same sense in which he is called the cause of himself." God is the cause of himself in the sense that God's essence makes God conceivable or intelligible and this intelligibility is God's existence. If, as Spinoza says in 1p25s, God is the cause of a mode in the same sense in which he is the cause of himself, then Spinoza must mean that God's essence makes the mode intelligible and that this intelligibility is the existence of the mode. So, given that God's existence is his intelligibility, I do not see how God could be the cause of modes in the same sense as he is the cause of himself unless the existence of modes is their intelligibility. Thus, for Spinoza, the mere intelligibility of a thing is the existence of that thing. Other things differ from God only in that God is intelligible through himself and modes are not, but are rather intelligible only through God. Still, in all cases, the existence of a thing is its intelligibility.

This identification is a vintage case of the twofold use of the PSR. Spinoza requires that—just as with causation, inherence, consciousness, goodness, etc.—there be an account of existence, that existence be explained. This demand is an application of the PSR and represents the first use. In saying that existence is explained in terms of conceivability or intelligibility or explicability, Spinoza says, after insisting on a demand for an explanation of existence, that existence is explained in terms of explicability, that is, it is conceived in terms of conceivability. This second use of the notion of conceivability is the second fold in the twofold use of the PSR.

This identification entails that if ever a thing is only partly, not fully, intelligible, then it only partly exists. As yet, we have no reason to believe that Spinoza accepts, for this reason, the exotic view that there are, in some sense, things that only partly exist, but later I will argue that Spinoza does, indeed, accept this view.

The equivalence of existence and intelligibility sheds light on Spinoza's anti-skeptical views and closes a gap that was left open at the end of Chapter 3. Recall that Spinoza holds the remarkable view that certainty—genuine knowledge—of a particular state of affairs consists simply in representing that state of affairs clearly, having a clear idea of it. As Spinoza puts his point:

> Truth requires no sign, but it suffices, in order to remove all doubt, to have the objective essences of things, or, what is the same, ideas.
>
> (TdIE §36)

The question left unresolved was the following. That an idea amounts to knowledge requires, of course, that the idea be true. But how can an idea—a "mere" representation—by itself guarantee that the idea is true, that the state of affairs the idea is about actually exists? Spinoza's answer: to represent a state of affairs is (as we saw in Chapter 3) simply to find that state of affairs intelligible, to grasp that it is intelligible. But, given the equivalence of existence and intelligibility, it follows that to represent a state of affairs is to grasp that it exists, i.e. to know that it exists. Thus the equivalence of existence and intelligibility supports Spinoza's controversial view that representation constitutes knowledge and guarantees truth.

The equivalence of existence and intelligibility also enables us to derive in a new way the view that to represent a thing is to find it intelligible. In Chapter 3, I showed how this view stems from Spinoza's explanatory barrier between the attributes, his conception of the essence of objects, and the PSR. Here is a different derivation of the same claim. Start with the plausible assumption that to represent a thing is to represent its existence.[4] Then consider that, given the equivalence, for Spinoza, between the existence of a thing and its intelligibility, it follows that when we represent a thing, we represent its existence, i.e. we represent its intelligibility, i.e. we represent the way it is explained. Thus Spinoza's rationalist identification of existence and intelligibility leads to his view that to represent a thing is to explain it.

Let's turn now to another fundamental question that will give us insight into the asymmetry between adequate and inadequate ideas: What is it for one thing to be in another, to be a state of another? We took up this question on Spinoza's behalf in Chapter 2 where we saw that, for Spinoza, for *a* to be in *b* is just for *a* to be explained by, be made intelligible in terms of, be conceived through, *b*. As we saw, if inherence were anything over and above conceivability, then there would be a division between dependence relations, a metaphysical bifurcation that would be an affront to Spinoza's rationalism and naturalism. As we saw, this is another twofold use of the PSR. For Spinoza, inherence must be intelligible and it is intelligible in terms of intelligibility itself, just as existence is intelligible in terms of intelligibility itself. So, for Spinoza, existence = intelligibility = inherence. To exist is to be intelligible is to inhere in something.

For Spinoza, as we briefly discussed in Chapter 2, one thing can be partially dependent on, partially intelligible in terms of, another thing. To use the example I invoked then, the chair is intelligible in terms of the carpenter who made it, but—because there are other causes in addition to the carpenter—the chair is only partly intelligible in terms of the carpenter. The chair would be fully intelligible only in terms of its complete cause. Given the equivalence of intelligibility and inherence, it follows that the chair is—surprisingly—partly in the carpenter. In general, as we saw in Chapter 2, an effect is in a cause to the degree that the effect depends on that cause. Inherence, for Spinoza, is not an all-or-nothing affair.

In this light, what should we say our inadequate ideas are fully in? Take an inadequate idea of mine caused by the object of my love, Henrietta. This idea is certainly not completely in itself because the idea is not self-caused. It's not, after all, a substance. So the idea must be at least partly in other things, namely in its causes.

So let's consider some finite cause of the idea. One of these finite causes is simply my mind itself. As Spinoza stresses, each change in a thing is at least partly the result of the nature of the thing in question (2ax1″). So, since effects are in their causes, the idea will be in my mind. But not wholly in my mind, and that's because the idea—qua inadequate—is caused by things external to my mind. In general, states of mine that are partly caused from outside me are not fully in me, are not fully states of mine. The only states that are fully mine are states that are not caused from without, i.e. states in which I am fully active and free. What, then, if it's not fully in me, is the inadequate idea in question fully in? Let's focus on one particular external cause of my idea—let's focus on Henrietta.

Given that ideas are in their causes, as we have seen, the idea must be in Henrietta. But Henrietta is only a partial cause of the idea; as we have seen, I am a partial cause too. So the idea is in Henrietta to some degree as well as in me to some degree. This is fine, but we still have not found what the idea is fully in. After all, the idea is caused from outside both Henrietta and me. Indeed, no matter how far back we go in the chain of finite causes of the idea, we will not arrive at an individual or collection of individuals that the idea is fully in. So we have not succeeded yet in finding what the idea is fully in, and thus we have not succeeded yet in showing how the idea is fully intelligible.

But it seems that success here is not hard to come by. The reason that the idea is not fully in any series of finite causes is that the idea seems to be caused by something infinite—in particular, it seems to be caused by God.[5] Thus the idea seems to be in God and, since the idea is certainly not caused from outside God—after all, nothing is outside God—it seems that the idea is fully in God. Here, at last, we have found it: we have found what makes the idea fully intelligible, what the idea is fully in.

But just when we seem to have achieved this success, we can also see that none of this can be right, that the idea cannot really be in God at all. Why not? Recall that we are dealing with an *inadequate* idea, i.e. a passive and confused idea. However, as we saw, no idea insofar as it is in God can be confused or inadequate. Rather, ideas— insofar as they are in God—are all adequate and unconfused.[6] As we saw, inadequacy and confusion cannot be in God and cannot characterize ideas insofar as God has them because inadequacy and confusion are, for Spinoza, the result of passivity, and God is, of course, in no way passive. The fundamental point then is that, precisely because an inadequate idea is passive, it cannot be in God, i.e. it cannot be made intelligible through God. But, as we saw, an inadequate idea cannot be fully in or fully intelligible in terms of anything that is not God. And so it seems that inadequate ideas are not fully in anything. For Spinoza, nobody and nothing fully has an inadequate idea. And because, as we have seen, for something to be intelligible it must be in something, it follows that inadequate ideas are not fully intelligible.

But how can this be? Spinoza's PSR commits him to the intelligibility of all things. Spinoza is also committed, as we have seen, to the view that all things are in God. How then can inadequate ideas not be fully intelligible and not be fully in God? We'll see how by making Spinoza's conclusion here even more extreme.

Recall Spinoza's equivalence between existence and intelligibility. What it is for a thing to exist is just for it to be intelligible. It follows, as I noted, that if something is not intelligible, then it does not exist *and* it follows that if something is not fully intelligible, then it does not fully exist. Just as Spinoza's rationalism opens up the possibility that being-in or inherence is not an all-or-nothing affair, so too it opens up the possibility that existence itself is not an all-or-nothing affair; it is not a switch that is either on or off. Instead, for Spinoza, there are degrees of existence, and inadequate ideas insofar as they are passive do not fully exist.

Here we can see how Spinoza's claim that inadequate ideas are not fully intelligible is compatible with his commitment to the intelligibility of all things: the commitment to the intelligibility of all things is a commitment to the intelligibility of all things that exist; as Spinoza says in 1ax1, "whatever is is either in itself or in another." This indicates that a thing with only a certain degree of intelligibility or in-ness must also have a correspondingly limited degree of existence. So Spinoza can, compatibly with 1ax1 and 1p15, hold that inadequate ideas, as such, are not fully in God, and this is because inadequate ideas do not fully exist.

I want to turn in a moment to the implications of this result for Spinoza's theory of the eternality of the mind, but before doing so, it will be helpful to articulate another extreme result of Spinoza's views about the limited existence of inadequate ideas. Not only do our inadequate ideas not fully exist, but—insofar as we have such ideas—we ourselves do not fully exist. Recall that, for Spinoza, my mind is just a collection of ideas. This collection consists in part of certain inadequate ideas, ideas that are not fully intelligible and do not fully exist. Thus, insofar as I have ideas that are not fully intelligible and do not fully exist, I myself am not fully intelligible and do not fully exist. To see this, just ask: What am I in? Insofar as I am passive, have inadequate ideas, I am not fully in myself or in any other finite object, nor am I in God who, of course, has no passivity in him. Thus, insofar as I am passive, I am not fully in anything and I am thus not fully intelligible and I do not fully exist.

In saying that my ideas do not fully exist insofar as they are inadequate and passive and that I do not fully exist insofar as I have inadequate ideas, I am not saying that there is no respect in which the state that is my inadequate ideas and I myself are fully intelligible and fully exist. For the state that, insofar as it is in my mind, is an inadequate idea, is also, insofar as it is in God, an action (of God) and an unconfused and adequate idea. This is a manifestation of the mind-relativity of content. Insofar as this state is unconfused, adequate and active, it is fully in God and thus is fully intelligible and fully exists. But insofar as this state is passive, confused and inadequate, it is not fully in God or anything else, and thus it is not fully intelligible and does not fully exist. Similar points apply to my mind itself which, insofar as it consists of passive ideas is not fully in God or anything else and does not fully exist, but which, insofar as it consists of active ideas, i.e. God's active ideas, is fully in God and does fully exist. More generally, things, insofar as they are passive, do not fully exist and, insofar as they are active states, i.e. states of God, do fully exist.

Obviously, many puzzles concerning the notion of degrees of existence remain, and I cannot address all of them here. Let me mention two rather obvious potential difficulties. In saying that inadequate ideas—qua inadequate—do not fully exist, I seem to commit myself to the claim that there are (i.e. there exist) things that do not fully exist. But haven't I therefore contradicted myself? How could things exist that don't fully exist? Isn't saying that something exists equivalent to saying that it fully exists? The answer is simply no. If we are going to take Spinoza's view seriously, we must be more careful when we say that things exist (i.e. we must be more precise in our use of quantifiers, to use the term from logic). We shouldn't say that there exist things that exist to some degree; rather we should more carefully say that there exist to some degree things that exist to some degree.

Second puzzle: I have said that an inadequate idea (in my mind) is identical to an adequate idea (in God's mind). I have also said that the former idea only partly exists and the latter idea fully exists. But how can something that only partly exists be identical to something that fully exists? Doesn't this difference in properties show that the purported identity would violate Leibniz's Law, which requires that identical things share all their properties? I think we can go a long way toward alleviating this problem by noting that, just as there can be degrees of existence, for Spinoza, so too there can be degrees of identity. Thus, perhaps, the inadequate idea in my mind is only partly identical to the adequate idea in God's mind. There is no strict identity here. The logic of partial identity would need to be worked out and, of course, neither Spinoza nor I have done so, but this notion has the potential to provide a resolution of this second puzzle I have raised.

Let's return to the eternality of the mind. We saw that, in order for Spinoza's thesis of eternality to avoid triviality, one must be able to say that adequate ideas are eternal in a way that inadequate ideas are not. We now have the resources to see how this is so for Spinoza. Ideas, insofar as they are inadequate, are not fully in God, that is, they are not fully intelligible in terms of God's nature. By contrast, adequate ideas *are* fully intelligible in terms of God's nature. As we saw, for Spinoza, something is eternal just in case it follows from the definition or nature of an eternal thing. Thus, because ideas—qua adequate—follow simply from God's nature, they are eternal, but because inadequate ideas—those partly existing, partly intelligible, partly inherent things—do not follow simply from the nature of God, they are not eternal. Inadequate ideas can, perhaps, have a degree of eternality, just as they have a degree of existence—after all, eternality for Spinoza just is a kind of existence. And inadequate ideas that approach adequacy more closely have, perhaps, a greater degree of eternality. But inadequate ideas, as such, are not eternal.

What then are we to do? Spinoza's advice now makes sense: we should acquire a greater number of adequate ideas because then we will, literally, more fully exist and be more fully eternal. Indeed, even if we don't acquire ideas that are fully adequate, we can acquire ideas with a greater degree of adequacy and in doing so we will more fully exist; we will be more fully eternal.[7] And herein lies the advantage that we have over dogs and rocks who—precisely because they are less powerful than we are—are less eternal and, indeed, exist to a lesser degree. Thus the advantage that adequate ideas give is far from trivial: our very existence is at stake, and the more completely we have adequate ideas, the greater the degree to which we exist.

In becoming more fully eternal, we thus become more like God. All the ideas that make up my mind are eternal—insofar as they are in God's mind. But not all of the ideas that make up my mind are—insofar as they are mine, insofar as they are in my mind— eternal. What we should strive to do, Spinoza is saying, is to make ideas insofar as they are in my mind more like the way they eternally are insofar as they are in God's mind. In other words, we should—as Spinoza has been saying all along—strive to become more like God, i.e. strive to be more powerful, more eternal. We certainly will not be able to achieve complete independence of external causes, i.e. we will not be able to make all of our ideas—insofar as they are in our mind and not only insofar as they are in God—eternal. But we can at least make our mind more eternal and so less affected by external causes.

Spinoza indicates that there are degrees of eternality that correspond to degrees of inherence in God, in 5p29s:

> We conceive things as actual in two ways: either insofar as we conceive them to exist in relation to a certain time and place, or insofar as we conceive them to be contained in God and to follow from the necessity of the divine nature. But the things we conceive in this second way as true, or real, we conceive under an aspect of eternity.

Spinoza is saying that insofar as (quatenus)—literally, to the extent that—I conceive things as in God, I conceive them as eternal. Here Spinoza expresses his view on the connection between degrees of inherence in God and degrees of eternality.

For Spinoza, our inevitably incomplete quest for eternality is ultimately a quest for existence itself. And here we can see another illuminating contrast with the traditional quest for eternal existence. On at least some traditional views, we have existence in this life and we have it fully; what we are seeking is this already full existence later too. We strive, in effect, to have more of the same later. But, for Spinoza, our quest for eternality is not a quest to have later what we already have now—namely existence. Rather our quest is a quest to increase the amount of existence that we now have. Instead of striving to have more later, as on the traditional view, we are striving to have more now. The quest for eternality is a quest to bring ourselves more fully into existence now; it is not a quest to continue existing later. This aspect of Spinoza's account is simply a reflection of his view of value as immanent. The value of eternal existence doesn't come to us at some later point; rather the value comes to us now in our increased intelligibility, in our increased inherence in God, in our increased existence. For Spinoza, the eternality we seek is immanent in our lives as we enjoy them now.[8]

This immanentist account of eternality is deeply rationalist. It is because, for Spinoza, existence and eternality and inherence are each equivalent to intelligibility itself, that the acquisition of adequate ideas and also ideas with a greater degree of adequacy can constitute a non-trivial quest for eternality. But, as we saw, these equivalences are each the result of the twofold use of the PSR. Thus yet again the PSR controls Spinoza's system.

This key role only makes more urgent the question I have been dodging throughout this book: how can the PSR itself be justified? Without such a justification, Spinoza's system—elegant and fascinating though it may be—may carry no philosophical weight. In the next chapter—as part of my discussion of Spinoza's influence and legacy—I will at long last begin to take up this vital question.

SUMMARY

Spinoza's doctrine of the eternality of the human mind is, perhaps, the most perplexing and the most heavily criticized of all his positions. But considerable sense can be made of Spinoza's views here which can be seen as cohering very well with his overarching rationalism and naturalism. Spinoza defines eternality as "existence itself insofar as it is conceived to follow necessarily from the definition alone of an eternal thing" (1def7). But by this definition it seems that. since all things, including our minds and bodies and including the rock and dog, follow from the definition of God, all things are eternal. This threatens to trivialize the eternality that the human is said to be able to enjoy, for it seems that this eternality is something we automatically have and not something we can achieve. Also problematic is Spinoza's claim that our mind becomes more and more eternal insofar as we acquire more adequate ideas. Since inadequate ideas also seem to follow from the definition of God, it seems that adequacy of ideas has nothing specifically to do with eternality despite what Spinoza says.

We can make progress on these problems by realizing that, for Spinoza, inadequate ideas, as such, are not fully in anything; they do not fully inhere in anything. This is because, for Spinoza, given that causation and inherence are coextensive (as we saw in Chapter 2) and given that inadequate ideas are caused from outside my mind, inadequate ideas are not fully in, do not fully inhere in, any finite thing. Nor can they inhere in God because God's mind contains no inadequacy. It follows that inadequate ideas are not fully in anything and thus are not fully intelligible. Their relative unintelligibility may seem to violate the PSR, which requires that each thing that exists be intelligible. But there is no such violation because Spinoza holds the highly unusual position—dictated by the PSR—that existence itself is intelligibility, and thus things that are not fully intelligible do not fully exist. The conclusion is that our inadequate ideas do not fully exist and we, insofar as we have inadequate ideas, also do not fully exist. The upside is that, by increasing the number of adequate ideas we have and by acquiring ideas with a greater degree of adequacy, we achieve a greater degree of existence. Our ideas can then be seen as more fully in God, more fully intelligible, and thus as more eternal. The quest for eternality is thus not, for Spinoza, a quest for some kind of existence after this one or apart from this one, but rather it is a quest to achieve a greater degree of existence in this very life. In other words, eternality—of a kind and to a degree—is something we can achieve in this life by having ideas with a greater degree of adequacy. Thus eternality is immanent in this life and not something separate from it. Thus, as is characteristic of his naturalism and rationalism, Spinoza rejects any bifurcation between kinds of existence.

FURTHER READING

Jonathan Bennett (1984) *A Study of Spinoza's Ethics*, chap. 8. (Good overview of Spinoza on time. Chapter 15 on the eternality of the mind is extremely uncharitable.)

Michael Della Rocca (2008b) "Rationalism Run Amok: Representation and the Reality of Affects in Spinoza." (On degrees of inherence and the equivalence of existence and intelligibility.)

Harold H. Joachim (1901) *A Study of the Ethics of Spinoza*. (A reading of Spinoza on the eternality of the mind that is, in some respects, in the spirit of the one offered here.)

Wallace Matson (1990) "Body Essence and Mind Eternity in Spinoza." (A fine paper that goes a long way in trying to make Spinoza's doctrine of eternality plausible.)

Steven Nadler (2001) *Spinoza's Heresy.* (A very clear and accessible account of Spinoza's views on the eternality of the mind, with considerable historical background from medieval Jewish philosophy.)

Eight

The Aftermath of Spinoza

There have been many great philosophers. And many of them are great in part because they have inspired other, also great, philosophers to develop systems that are in the spirit of these predecessors. Thus, even today, we have any number of philosophers who construct broadly Aristotelean, or broadly Humean, or broadly Kantian philosophical systems. However, Spinoza has not been influential in quite this way. Few top-notch philosophers today would identify themselves as Spinozists. Spinoza has nonetheless had a deep impact on all subsequent philosophy.[1] How can this be?

Spinoza's philosophy functions as a challenge: almost all philosophers want to avoid his conclusions. The philosophical challenge, however, is to show how his views can be avoided. Often philosophers have developed their entire systems as direct answers to the kind of challenge that Spinoza presents. Sometimes their answers are more or less explicitly directed to Spinoza. This is certainly the case with Leibniz and, I would say, with Hume. (More on this shortly.) More often, the explicit target is a rationalism of the kind that Spinoza embodies so well. In these cases, Spinoza may or may not be in mind as the target, but nonetheless Spinoza is the most thoroughgoing exponent of the view to be defeated.

Spinozism is thus, in many ways, the specter that haunts all subsequent philosophy. His philosophy has a pervasive, albeit often negative, influence.[2] If one of the chief aspirations of philosophers—and of people in general—is not to be ignored, then Spinoza has achieved this prevalent goal as splendidly and as thoroughly as any other philosopher in history. Another chief aspiration of philosophers and non-philosophers alike is the aspiration to be right. Whether Spinoza can be said to have achieved this goal is much less clear, but—as I will argue in the last section of this chapter—there is reason to believe that Spinoza may be right. In order to pave the way for this incipient defense of Spinoza, I want to give an inevitably too-selective and too-broad overview of Spinoza's influence on later philosophers. This overview will help us to appreciate how much in philosophy is riding on the defense of the PSR. I will begin with Leibniz.

1. LEIBNIZ

Spinoza's philosophical views came under sharp—if not always well-informed—criticism during his lifetime and even more so after his death. But it's not as if there were no contemporaries who could appreciate his philosophical motivations. Leibniz certainly was one such philosopher. Born in 1646, he was only 14 years younger than Spinoza. He was also Spinoza's philosophical equal. He met Spinoza in 1676, not long before Spinoza's death.[3] And for the rest of his career, though he publicly denounced Spinoza's views (see, for example, Theodicy §173), Leibniz obviously grappled deeply with Spinoza's thought. One can't help but think that, had Leibniz been more fair-minded in his public assessment of Spinoza, then Spinoza's fate in the seventeenth and eighteenth centuries—and indeed the entire subsequent course of philosophy—would have been radically different.

Leibniz was uniquely well-placed to appreciate Spinoza's philosophy because Leibniz, more than any other philosopher of the time with the exception of course of Spinoza, understood the power of the PSR and made it the centerpiece of his system. Indeed, Leibniz was, in some ways, more up-front in his use of the PSR. He—not Spinoza—used the term "Principle of Sufficient Reason," and Leibniz explicitly made the PSR one of the "two great principles" on which all reasoning is based. The other principle is the Principle of Contradiction, in virtue of which we judge that which involves a contradiction to be false, and that which is opposed or contradictory to the false to be true.

(Leibniz, *Monadology* §31)

Because of Leibniz's commitment to the PSR, we find him agreeing with some of Spinoza's most important positions, though almost always without acknowledging Spinoza. Thus Leibniz, like Spinoza, accepts—on rationalist grounds—determinism, the identity of indiscernibles (again, the term is Leibniz's, not Spinoza's), and the reduction of consciousness and other mental features to representation.

However, Spinoza would regard Leibniz as losing his rationalist nerve, as not prosecuting his commitment to the PSR thoroughly enough. The first sign of a crack in Leibniz's rationalist edifice is the very fact that he has two independent, fundamental principles, instead of just one. That the PSR is separate from the Principle of Contradiction indicates that, for Leibniz, the PSR is not something that it would be contradictory to deny. That is, for Leibniz, there is no contradiction in saying that a thing exists for no reason. But, then, in virtue of what is the PSR true? Spinoza has no problem in answering this question because, for him, the PSR is a conceptual truth: it is part of the concept of a thing that it be explained. This is simply another twofold use of the PSR: what it is to be a thing must be explained, and it is explained in terms of explanation itself. But, for Leibniz, the PSR cannot be in this way a conceptual truth, for then the denial of the PSR would be a contradiction and so the PSR itself would reduce to the Principle of Contradiction, a result Leibniz does not want.

If the PSR is not a conceptual truth, for Leibniz, then how does he ground it? If it is not grounded on the Principle of Contradiction, then it must be grounded in the PSR itself: the PSR is true because if it weren't there would be a brute fact. But this is no more than to say that the PSR is true because otherwise it would be false. For one seeking a grounding of the PSR, this is hardly satisfactory. Perhaps Leibniz could say that the PSR is self-grounding, that, in some way, it makes no sense to seek a ground outside the PSR for the PSR itself, in the same way that, one might argue, it makes no sense to seek a ground for the truth that contradictions cannot be true together. But if the PSR is not a conceptual truth, then how can it be self-grounding? For this reason, Leibniz's lack of an answer to the question concerning the ground of the PSR is a grave disadvantage for his rationalist system in comparison to Spinoza's more consistent rationalism.

Not only is the PSR not well-grounded in Leibniz's system, it is also not applied as consistently as Spinoza applies it. Thus, despite his many rationalist insights, we find Leibniz denying two theses that are at the heart of Spinoza's rationalism and that stem directly from the PSR. That is, we find Leibniz denying necessitarianism and monism. For Leibniz, unlike Spinoza, some truths are genuinely contingent, and for Leibniz, unlike Spinoza, there is a genuine multiplicity of substances, and finite things are not mere modifications of the one (big) divine substance.

Rationalist that he is, Leibniz cannot help but feel some pull toward these extreme rationalist theses. Early in his career, Leibniz seems to have affirmed a straightforward necessitarian position which he explicitly tied to the PSR.[4] Further, despite his career-long rejection of monism—what he calls with Spinoza in mind "a doctrine of ill-repute"[5]—Leibniz does speak of finite individuals emanating from God (*Discourse*, §14) and as being generated "by continual fulgurations of the divinity from moment to moment" (*Monadology* §47). And, most strikingly, Leibniz says in a paper from 1676, "It seems to me that the origin of things from God is of the same kind as the origin of properties from an essence."[6] These claims suggest that some version of monism held some allure for Leibniz.

Nonetheless, Leibniz decisively rejected both necessitarianism and monism. One reason he does so is freedom. Although Leibniz

thought he saw how our freedom could be reconciled with determinism, he denied (apart from the early letter to Wedderkopf) that
freedom could be reconciled with necessitarianism.[7] Similarly, for
Leibniz, if monism were true and we were somehow modes of the
one substance, then we would not have any causal powers of our
own and so, once again, we could not be free.[8] Spinoza obviously
was not concerned to preserve our freedom, which was, after all,
partly illusory for him. Leibniz, though, did seek to preserve freedom and may have paid the price of spoiling the coherence of his
would-be rationalist system.

2. BAYLE AND HUME

The use of "Spinozism" as a term of abuse was perhaps solidified
by Pierre Bayle's typically ambiguous writing on Spinoza. Bayle
(1647–1706) portrayed Spinoza as a philosophic saint. But, at the
same time, he subjected Spinoza to trenchant criticism. This attack
found its most influential expression in Bayle's massive dictionary,
originally published in 1697. The dictionary's entry on Spinoza was
by far the longest in that work. Bayle made obligatorily disparaging
remarks about Spinoza's TTP ("a pernicious and detestable book,"
p. 293) and about his commitment to determinism and necessitarianism (which Bayle believed would render Spinoza's act of
writing the Ethics "ridiculous" [p. 313]). However, Bayle chose as
the focus of his attack another thesis at the heart of Spinoza's
rationalism: his substance monism. As Bayle puts it,

> I have confined myself to opposing what he clearly and precisely
> sets forth as his first principle, namely, that God is the only
> substance that there is in the universe and that all other beings
> are only modifications of that substance.
>
> (Bayle 1991: 304)

We saw in Chapter 2 how Spinoza's PSR dictates his monism. Thus
Bayle—who saw that Spinoza "had a mathematical mind and

wanted to find a reason for everything" (Bayle 1991: 290)—was, in effect, challenging the PSR in challenging Spinoza's monism. Bayle refers to this thesis as "the most monstrous hypothesis that could be imagined" (*la plus monstrueuse hypothèse qui se puisse imaginer*) (Bayle 1991: 296) and his challenges can be boiled down to three. First, by seeing all things as mere modes or mere states of the one substance, Spinoza undermines the immutability of God. (Changes in us are changes in God, but how could God change?) Second, Spinoza's monism thus makes God complicit in evil. (Because I am a mode of God, my evil actions are God's evil actions.) This is, in Bayle's eyes, another unacceptable challenge to the traditional conception of God. Finally, for Bayle, Spinoza's monism is logically incoherent, for it entails that a single subject—namely God—has contrary predicates. If you hate Emma Thompson movies and I love them, then, since you and I and our states are all modes of God, "it follows that God hates and loves, denies and affirms the same things at the same time" (Bayle 1991: 310). But this, says Bayle, is logically incoherent.

These objections can, I believe, be satisfactorily answered. Briefly: Spinoza does acknowledge that God is immutable (1p20c2), but when he does, he stresses that it is God's attributes in particular that are immutable. Spinoza may not be troubled by changes in God's modes. Evil, as we have seen, is a matter of perspective. Something may be bad and wrong for me, from my point of view, but good and right for you or for a larger whole that includes me and you. Good and evil are, for Spinoza, a matter of power, thus, from the divine point of view—which, of course, contains no passivity—each thing is right and good. The evil that Bayle is worried about is, for Spinoza, mere passivity and, as such, does not exist from the absolute, divine point of view. Finally, it would be a problem if God had contradictory properties. But it is not accurate to say simply that God loves and does not love certain movies, something that seems contradictory. Rather, for Spinoza, God, insofar as he constitutes me, loves those movies, and God, insofar as he constitutes you, does not love those movies. The different respects in which God is being considered—namely as me and as you—prevent any problematic contradictions from taking hold.

Perhaps Bayle's criticisms of Spinoza were most significant in the way that they helped to shape Hume's entire philosophical system. In many ways, Hume's system is the flip-side of Spinoza's. Whereas Spinoza sees the world as fundamentally one thing, Hume sees the world as a plurality of very many independent things, all "loose and separate."[9] Whereas Spinoza is not a skeptic, Hume arguably is. Whereas Spinoza reduces consciousness and all other mental features to representation, Hume does not. Whereas Spinoza recognizes only one kind of mental state—representation—which is by its nature active, Hume has two kinds of mental states: reasons or representations, on the one hand, and passions, non-representational mental states, on the other hand, which are the only source of activity in the mind. Underlying these differences is Hume's and Spinoza's fundamental disagreement over the PSR. Hume denied the PSR and that is why he was confident in rejecting monism and in embracing skepticism and in accepting a bifurcation of passions and actions in the mind. Spinoza accepted the PSR and so differed from Hume in all these ways. They agreed, though, in seeing the PSR as the linchpin of philosophy. Spinoza saw the results that the PSR would generate, and he embraced them; Hume recoiled. But for both of them, there was no middle-ground position of the kind that most philosophers are generally and unthinkingly happy to try to occupy.[10] In the final section of this chapter, I will offer an argument designed to force philosophers out of this unprincipled middle ground.

What is particularly significant about Hume for our purposes is that he has an argument against the PSR, an argument that stems directly from his encounter with Spinoza's monism. Hume's argument against the PSR is roughly the following. It is conceivable that a given event or object not have a cause that guarantees the occurrence or existence of that event or that object. In other words, it is conceivable that there be, in effect, no sufficient reason for that thing. That this is conceivable amounts to a denial of the PSR. But why is this conceivable? For Hume, each thing can be conceived as existing on its own: "all distinct ideas are separable from each other" (Hume 1978: 79). But why should this be so? We find a hint of an answer in Hume's only direct discussion of Spinoza in the *Treatise*, a discussion that is explicitly indebted to Bayle's criticism of Spinoza. (On p. 243 of the *Treatise*, i.e. Hume 1978, as he launches his own discussion of Spinoza, Hume cites Bayle's entry on Spinoza.) In this stretch of the *Treatise*, Hume says in effect: What would be the case if one thing could not be conceived to exist without another thing? In that case, Hume says, the first thing would be a mode of the other thing. For Hume, a mode is just a thing that depends on another thing ("a mode, not being any distinct or separate existence. ... " [Hume 1978: 243]). Thus if each thing must have a cause and so not be conceivable without something else, then each such thing is a mode of this something else, is a mode of its cause, which in turn is a mode of its cause, etc. Now, Hume firmly rejects the view that objects such as you, me, and the chair are modes of anything. In Hume's eyes, to hold that all such objects are modes would quickly lead to the view that all finite things are "nothing but modifications of that one, simple, and necessarily existent being, and are not possest of any separate or distinct existence" (Hume 1978: 240–41). But this would be Spinoza's substance monism, which Hume dismisses out of hand as "this hideous hypothesis" (Hume 1978: 241), in a phrase that echoes Bayle's talk of Spinoza's "monstrous hypothesis."

Obviously not all the steps of this attack on Spinoza and thus on the PSR are fully worked out in Hume, but we can see how deeply Hume is grappling with Spinoza and how he draws on the widespread sentiment against Spinoza in order to construct his entire anti-rationalist structure.

Thus Hume is, in effect, arguing from the denial of Spinoza's monism to the denial of the PSR. Spinoza, as we have seen, would run the argument the other way: from the affirmation of the PSR to the affirmation of monism. Again, Hume and Spinoza agree significantly on the conditionals linking the PSR to other theses; they simply have different starting points: Spinoza starts with the PSR and Hume with the denial of the hideous hypothesis.

It must be admitted that Hume's starting point—the denial of monism—has considerable intuitive appeal which Hume gladly marshals in this context. But what support can be given for Spinoza's starting point, for the PSR itself? This is a question that, it seems, Spinoza never directly takes up, and this failure seems to put his system at a severe disadvantage with regard to Hume and with regard to Spinoza's opponents generally. We face yet again the question of how Spinoza could justify the PSR, a question that we will take on directly in the final section of this chapter.

3. THE PANTHEISM CONTROVERSY

Although Spinoza's influence remained strong—mostly in a negative fashion—throughout the eighteenth century, it was not until the last 15 years of the century that Spinoza came to be accorded the kind of widespread, public respect that had so far eluded him. The change in Spinoza's philosophical fortunes was precipitated by an unlikely event: F. H. Jacobi's (1743–1819) account of conversations he had had with Gotthold Lessing (1729–81), an icon of the Enlightenment in Germany, shortly before Lessing's death. (Jacobi's account was originally offered in letters written to Mendelssohn in 1783 and was subsequently published in 1785.) In these conversations, astonishingly, Lessing allegedly expressed admiration for Spinoza's philosophy and affirmed that he was—in fact—a convert to Spinozism. According to Jacobi, Lessing said "there is no other philosophy than that of Spinoza" (Jacobi 1994: 187). Jacobi's report of Lessing's apparent conversion touched off an intellectual firestorm. Why?

Lessing (as reported by Jacobi), and also Jacobi in his own voice, cut to the very core of Spinozism and presented it in an extremely compelling fashion. Lessing and Jacobi saw—and rightly so, of course, in my opinion—that the PSR drives Spinoza's system. As Jacobi says when Lessing asks what he took to be the spirit of Spinozism: "It is certainly nothing other than the ancient *a nihilo nihil fit* [from nothing nothing is made]" (Jacobi 1994: 187). Jacobi later says (and here again I must agree):

> What distinguishes Spinoza's philosophy from all the other, what constitutes its soul, is that it maintains and applies with the strictest rigour the well known principle, *gigni de nihilo nihil, in nihilum nil potest reverti* [from nothing, nothing is generated; into nothing, nothing can return].
>
> (Jacobi 1994: 205)

The claim that nothing comes from nothing is certainly in the spirit of the PSR, but that Jacobi has the PSR specifically in mind in discussing Spinoza is also evident from the fact that, in explicitly rejecting Spinoza's position, Jacobi saw himself as led to "the perfect conviction that certain things admit of no explication" (p. 193). Spinoza is thus in Lessing's and Jacobi's eyes the most consistent rationalist, and Leibniz who, like Spinoza, was enamored of the PSR, was, according to Lessing (as reported by Jacobi), "a Spinozist at heart" (Jacobi 1994: 190).

Jacobi also saw the PSR as excluding causation between heterogeneous things (p. 208), as leading to monism (pp. 288–89), to the denial of the reality of temporal succession (pp. 288–89, 290, 342–44) and to the affirmation that existence comes in degrees (pp. 342–44). All of these results are, as we have seen, in keeping with Spinoza's views.

Lessing and Jacobi also stressed that Spinoza's PSR leads to fatalism—understood as the denial of human freedom—and to atheism. However, it's not so clear that it is appropriate to pin either of these conclusions on Spinoza. Although it is strictly true that the PSR leads Spinoza to deny that human beings are free, he does allow, as I have argued, that we are capable of degrees of freedom. Spinoza's account of human freedom may thus not be as starkly negative as Lessing and Jacobi indicate. Further, it is extremely misleading to characterize Spinoza as an atheist. Spinoza does, as I have stressed, insist on the existence of a being that he calls "God," a being that is necessary, omniscient, eternal, perfectly free, perfectly good, perfectly just. These are all features traditionally accorded to God (although, of course, Spinoza understands these features in very non-traditional ways), and Spinoza attributes them to God precisely because of the PSR. Spinoza's conception of God also attributes non-standard features to God: God acts necessarily, God doesn't create the world, finite things are states of God, God doesn't single out human beings or other creatures for special provident action. These non-standard aspects of Spinoza's conception of God may lead some, including Lessing and Jacobi, to characterize Spinoza as an atheist. But, given the rich overlap between Spinoza's conception of God and the traditional conception, to label Spinoza as an atheist is not entirely appropriate.

However, Spinoza's claims about human freedom and about the nature of God *were* troubling to dominant religious and traditional views, and what was so troubling about Jacobi's account of Spinoza was that Jacobi saw the PSR itself as having these odious implications. If the PSR—the principle of reason itself—leads to views that could naturally be construed as fatalistic and atheistic, then reason itself was under threat. If Lessing—one of the leading figures of the Enlightenment, who opposed dogmatism in all its forms and championed reason—should in the end succumb to Spinozistic fatalism and atheism, then people's worst fears not only about Spinoza but also about the Enlightenment and reason itself would be confirmed. As Beiser puts it,

> Jacobi was raising the very disturbing question, Why should we be loyal to reason if it pushes us into the abyss?
>
> (Beiser 1987: 80)

Jacobi—apparently unlike Lessing—was horrified by the abyss and refused what he saw as the vile cocktail of atheism and fatalism: "from fatalism I immediately conclude against fatalism and everything connected with it" (Jacobi 1994: 189). Jacobi proposed that we abandon reason entirely and make a leap of faith, a *salto mortale* [a mortal jump]. Jacobi claims (in a passage quoted in part already) that his encounter with Spinoza has led him to

> the perfect conviction that certain things admit of no explication: one must not therefore keep one's eyes shut to them, but must take them as one finds them. ... I must assume a source of thought and action that remains completely inexplicable to me.
>
> (Jacobi 1994: 193)

Only in this way, Jacobi claims, can we preserve belief in God and in our own freedom. Only in this way can we therefore preserve morality and all that Jacobi sees as valuable in the world.

Jacobi's abandonment of reason had the good effect of making Spinoza at last a respected philosophical figure. By recounting Lessing's conversion to Spinozism, Jacobi enabled Spinoza to be taken seriously. Beiser again:

> After 1785 public opinion of Spinoza changes from almost universal contempt to almost universal admiration, largely as a result of the publication of Jacobi's *Briefe*, in which he revealed Lessing's Spinozism. Lessing was the most admired figure of the *Aufklärung* [Enlightenment], and his credo automatically gave a stamp of legitimacy to every secret Spinozist. One after another the Spinozists could now come out of their closets and form a file behind Lessing. If Lessing was an honorable man and a Spinozist, then they could be too. Ironically, Jacobi's *Briefe* did not destroy Lessing's reputation, as Mendelssohn feared. It did the very opposite, making him a hero in the eyes of the nonconformists.
>
> (Beiser 1987: 59)

One might say on Spinoza's behalf: with enemies like Jacobi, who needs friends?

After Jacobi's opening salvo, others quickly became swept up in the controversy. Moses Mendelssohn (1729–86)—shortly before his own death—weighed in with Morning Hours, a broadly Leibnizian defense of reason and critique of Spinoza that accorded a privileged place to common sense. Kant stepped in as well with his essay, "What Does It Mean to Orient Oneself in Thinking?" He too wanted to trace a middle path between Spinoza (reason) and Jacobi, but he saw Mendelssohn's reliance on common sense as no less an abandonment of reason as Jacobi's irrationalism. Instead, Kant proposed that reason itself has two radically different modes of access to the truth, through knowledge and through (rational) faith. Thus Kant began to articulate the theme that reason itself can provide grounds for faith in the existence of God and in our own freedom, even though it cannot provide knowledge in these domains. As Kant says, rational faith "is not inferior in degree to knowing, even though it is completely different from it in kind".[11]

Spinoza, of course, would reject Kant's distinction between two fundamentally different kinds of access to the truth. For Spinoza, all belief is more or less rational, i.e. all representation has some degree of power. Faith, for Spinoza, is simply a less than fully adequate, a more confused, form of cognition. There is no difference in kind of the kind that Kant wants to draw between faith and knowledge. The Kantian bifurcation between faith and knowledge is one of many inexplicable bifurcations that Spinoza would see Kant's system as riddled with. (Thus consider, for example, the distinctions between phenomena and noumena, between intuition and concept, and between [as we saw in Chapter 5] determined objects and radically free objects.) Spinoza would reject all these Kantian chasms because of his more thoroughgoing commitment to the PSR.

4. HEGEL

Although Leibniz and Hume developed systems that engaged deeply with Spinoza's thought, they did not embrace Spinozism. Although

Lessing (apparently) saw the light and converted to Spinozism at the end of his life, he cannot be said to have developed a system that was Spinozistic in orientation. The development of a system that not only was a response to Spinoza but was also Spinozistic would have to wait for Hegel. Indeed, the system Hegel developed is, perhaps, more Spinozistic than Hegel himself realized.

Hegel's praise for Spinoza is explicit. He says in his lectures on the history of philosophy:

> thought must begin by placing itself at the standpoint of
> Spinozism; to be a follower of Spinoza is the essential
> commencement of all Philosophy.
>
> (Hegel 1996: 482)

And there is explicit and substantial overlap between Hegel and Spinoza. Thus, Spinoza and Hegel are, in one way or another, both monists. They agree that there is fundamentally only one thing and that this is God. So they also agree in rejecting the notion of a transcendent God-creator. They both hold, instead, that God is in some sense the world itself. Most fundamentally, they agree that reality is through-and-through intelligible, that the real is the rational. We have seen many expressions of this view in Spinoza; Hegel's most famous expression occurs in the preface to the *Philosophy of Right*: "What is rational is actual; and what is actual is rational" (Hegel 1967: 10; see also Hegel 1991: §6, p. 29). Hegel also says in his *Lectures on the History of Philosophy*, "nature and mind are rational" (Hegel 1996: 494). Thus Hegel, no less than Spinoza, is a big fan of the PSR.

But there are important differences between Hegel and Spinoza—or at least important perceived differences. Let me begin with some of the differences that are more apparent than real before turning to a genuine and extremely significant difference.

Like Bayle before him (whose critique of Spinoza Hegel cites in Hegel 1996: 496), Hegel is concerned about the implications of

Spinoza's monism, about the view that all finite things are merely modes of the one substance. But, apparently unlike Bayle, Hegel is basically in agreement with the idea of monism; Hegel merely objects to what he sees as devastating consequences of Spinoza's particular way of carrying out his monistic system. Hegel fears that Spinoza's ontology of substance and modes denies finite things any genuine reality. Spinoza's finite things or modes, for Hegel, are "cast into the abyss" of Spinoza's substance, and there is no such thing as finite modes (Hegel 1996: 506, 513). Hegel thus labels Spinoza's view "acosmism," the denial of finite reality (Hegel 1996: 506).

For Hegel, the denial of the finite is the real source of the greatest opposition to Spinoza. Hegel believes that, contrary to what some may think, Spinoza is not an atheist: "with [Spinoza] there is too much God," not too little (Hegel 1996: 507). What people really object to in Spinoza, Hegel holds, is not God's being out of the picture, but rather their own removal from the ranks of the real.

Not only does Hegel agree with those who see Spinoza as eliminating the reality of the finite, he deepens this criticism by seeing Spinoza as undermining the self-consciousness and the freedom that Hegel sees within the finite realm and in God as well. For Hegel, by failing to accord reality to the finite, Spinoza thus fails to allow for the kind of differentiation that is needed in order for self-consciousness and freedom to arise. As Hegel says, in Spinoza's system, "the 'I' disappears, gives itself altogether up, merely withers away" (Hegel 1996: 511). For Spinoza, according to Hegel, there is:

> an utter blotting out of the principle of subjectivity, individuality, personality, the moment of self-consciousness in Being. Thought has only the signification of the universal, not of self-consciousness.
>
> (Hegel 1996: 512)

Further, for Hegel, without self-consciousness on the part of human beings or God, there can be no genuine freedom:

"There is lacking the infinite form, spirituality and liberty" (Hegel 1996: 512).

There is a grain—or more than a grain—of truth to the claim that finite modes, for Spinoza, do not exist. But ultimately the claim is seriously inaccurate. It is true, as we saw in Chapter 7, that a finite mode, for Spinoza—insofar as it is passive, i.e. insofar as it is a state of something that is determined from without—does not fully exist. Nonetheless, a finite mode, so considered, does exist to some degree, i.e. to the limited degree that the thing this mode is a state of is active. Further, the same mode, considered as a state of God who is, of course, not externally affected at all, does fully exist.[12]

Hegel is right that there is a way of considering Spinozistic finite modes according to which they do not fully exist. But, contra Hegel, this does not mean that these modes—so considered—do not exist at all. Hegel has, it seems, mistaken the degree of non-existence to which Spinozistic modes are subject for a complete lack of existence, for "a complete abyss of annihilation" (Hegel 1996: 513).

Hegel's criticism that Spinozistic modes lack self-consciousness and freedom can be handled similarly. As we have seen (in Chapter 3), consciousness is simply the degree of activity of a thing insofar as that thing is considered under the attribute of thought. And since each thing has some degree of activity (1p36), each thing is conscious to some degree. This consciousness will involve some self-consciousness. The activity of each thing is simply a function of that thing's conatus, its striving. The striving of a thing—as Spinoza characterizes it—is a striving to preserve *itself* in existence. For Spinoza, each thing—considered as thinking—in some way represents *itself* and represents that which will preserve itself in existence. This conclusion applies to things in general—dogs, rocks, you name it—all of which have, for Spinoza, some degree of self-consciousness. This is simply a manifestation of Spinoza's panpsychism. So, far from the "I" withering away, the "I" is, in a way, pervasive in nature. And the one substance itself, the maximally active thing, has the highest degree of consciousness. Further, as a thing whose striving for *self*-preservation is always successful, it also has the highest degree of self-consciousness.

Similarly, Hegel's complaint about the loss of freedom in Spinoza also seems misguided. For Spinoza, finite things do, as we have seen, enjoy a degree of activity and thus a degree of freedom. And the one substance, in addition to being maximally self-conscious, is also maximally free. Hegel has mistaken a degree of a lack of freedom in finite things for a complete lack of freedom.

Nonetheless, there are important differences between Hegel and Spinoza, the most important of which, perhaps, is the following. Although both Spinoza and Hegel espouse the intelligibility of all things, for Spinoza this intelligibility is actual. Each thing, and of course God which comprises all these things, is, for Spinoza, already fully intelligible, even if we, from our limited point of view, cannot fully grasp the reasons of—the intelligibility of—all things. By contrast, for Hegel, the intelligibility of all things is an ideal toward which each thing and indeed God is striving. The more intelligible things become, the more real, the more perfect they become and the more perfect God becomes. Because, for Hegel, things are not yet fully intelligible, history has a direction; it is a process, and this process tends toward greater and greater intelligibility. Hegel says in the preface to the *Phenomenology of Spirit*:

> The True is the whole. But the whole is nothing other than the essence consummating itself through its development. Of the Absolute it must be said that it is essentially a *result*, that only in the *end* is it what it truly is; and that precisely in this consists its nature, viz. to be actual, subject, the spontaneous becoming of itself.
>
> (Hegel 1977: §20)

Spinoza would absolutely reject this view, for to see some temporal periods as more perfect than others is to introduce an objectionable asymmetry in the world. Just as, as we saw in Spinoza's critique of teleology, any privileging of one species or person or thing over another would be arbitrary and so rejected, so too any privileging of later times over earlier ones as more perfect would be arbitrary and rejected as well. Thus consider: for God to become more perfect, for Spinoza, would be for God to become more powerful. Spinoza would ask: if God does become more powerful, where would this greater degree of power come from? It cannot come from outside God, for there is nothing outside God. It cannot come from God himself because, if the greater degree of power came from God himself, then God would already have that greater degree of power and so would not need to (or be able to) become more powerful. If the greater degree of power came from nothing, i.e. if it just popped into existence, then we know what Spinoza would say: this greater degree of power would then be a brute fact, and like all brute facts should be rejected out of hand. Thus the PSR dictates that it is not the case that the world is becoming more perfect. To the extent that there is perfection (power, goodness, justice, value) in the world, it should be able to be found equally at this moment as at later ones. Value exists now as much as at any later time (or earlier time, for that matter). To look beyond to another time for more value in the world, as Hegel does, is, for Spinoza, to make the same mistake as those who seek to have an afterlife—separate from this one—in which perfection can reside. Spinoza's rejection of the progressive improvement of the world is thus of a piece with his rejection of all other attempts to find the value of a thing in a source outside that thing. We can once again see that, for Spinoza, value and perfection are radically intrinsic. This Spinozistic theme is the one, above all others, that brings Spinoza closest to Nietzsche.

5. NIETZSCHE

Nietzsche is conflicted about Spinoza. Why?

One of Nietzsche's main aims is to offer a critique of popular morality because—as Nietzsche sees it—popular morality is inimical to our nature as striving beings, beings who seek more and more power. Popular morality developed, according to Nietzsche's genealogical account, out of a desire by the weak—who were being oppressed by the stronger, more noble human beings—to gain power over their oppressors. This desire led the weak (somehow) to develop the tools of popular morality: free will, guilt, and conscience. These tools enabled the weak to condemn the expressions of power on the part of the strong and led the strong themselves to feel guilty and to restrain themselves. Thus developed a morality at odds with human nature because, for Nietzsche, the guiding principle of human beings—and indeed of things in general—is the striving for greater power. In denying the value of powerful expression, the weak—in a natural attempt to gain more power— came to thwart the guiding principle of human nature. The values of self-denial were thus contrary to what Nietzsche sees as the value of acting transparently out of one's nature. Nietzsche thus seeks a revaluation of values, an acknowledgement that the values of popular morality are not themselves valuable and should be replaced by his newer, more honest values which give pride of place to a transparent embrace of the will to power.

As Nietzsche sees it, one of the main devices developed by the purveyors of popular morality is reason itself. Reason—in its guise as the disinterested search for truth—is, for Nietzsche, opposed to the will to power. Reason, for Nietzsche, is too often employed to thwart our basic desire for power. Reason dictates that we should do certain things even if those things go against our basic nature as beings that strive for more and more power. That is why Nietzsche derisively says that Kant's categorical imperative—supposedly a moral principle dictated by reason itself—"smells of cruelty" (Nietzsche 1994: 45), i.e. does violence to our nature as striving beings.

For Nietzsche, then, reason goes against human nature and is in conflict with what is valuable in and for human beings. Instead of being guided by the will to truth which can only be a non-transparent way of expressing our power and can only, as non-transparent, do violence to ourselves, we ought—Nietzsche says—to guide ourselves openly by the will to power and discard our harmful will to truth. As Nietzsche says in criticizing the will to truth,

> those who are truthful in that audacious and ultimate sense that is presupposed by the faith in science *thus affirm another world* than the world of life, nature, and history; and insofar as they affirm this "other world"—look, must they not by the same token negate its counterpart, this world, *our* world?
>
> (Nietzsche 1974: §344; see also Nietzsche 1994: 119)

In some ways, as I have presented him throughout this book, Spinoza is the arch-rationalist, the paradigmatic defender of reason. Nietzsche recognized that Spinoza could be seen this way, and given Nietzsche's aversion to reason, he recoiled. For Nietzsche, Spinoza's use of reason is a classic expression of *ressentiment*, the animus that the weak feel toward the strong. For Nietzsche (sometimes), Spinoza uses reason as a cudgel to frustrate or even eliminate the expression of our affects, of our will to power. Thus, in *Beyond Good and Evil*, Nietzsche speaks of "that laughing-no-more and weeping-no-more of Spinoza" (Nietzsche 1966: §198). He elaborates this negative assessment in *The Gay Science*:

> The meaning of knowing.—*Non ridere, non lugere, neque detestari, sed intelligere!* [Not to laugh, not to lament, not to detest, but to understand, *Tractatus Politicus* I §4] says Spinoza as simply and sublimely as is his wont. Yet in the last analysis, what else is this *intelligere* than the form in which we come to feel the other three at once? ... we suppose that *intelligere* must be something conciliatory, just, and good—something that stands essentially opposed to the instincts, while it is actually nothing but a *certain behavior of the instincts toward one another.*
>
> (Nietzsche 1974: §333)

The charge that Spinoza uses reason in a harmful way and is, indeed, a purveyor of a kind of *ressentiment* appears pointedly in this passage from *Beyond Good and Evil*:

> These outcasts of society, these long-pursued, wickedly persecuted ones—also the compulsory recluses, the Spinozas or Giordano Brunos—always become in the end, even under the most spiritual masquerade, and perhaps without being themselves aware of it, sophisticated vengeance-seekers and poison-brewers (let someone lay bare the foundation of Spinoza's ethics and theology!).
>
> (Nietzsche 1966: §25)

Nietzsche goes so far as to deride Spinoza's use of the geometrical method as rigid and fearful and sick:

> Or consider the hocus-pocus of mathematical form with which Spinoza clad his philosophy—really "the love of *his* wisdom," to render that word fairly and squarely—in mail and mask, to strike terror at the very outset into the heart of any assailant who should dare to glance at that invincible maiden and Pallas Athena: how much personal timidity and vulnerability this masquerade of a sick hermit betrays!
>
> (Nietzsche 1966: §5)

Spinoza as a rationalist seems to be on the wrong side, as far as Nietzsche is concerned.

But all I can say is that Nietzsche should know better. Far from thwarting the will to power, Spinozistic reason is an expression of it. Spinoza extols the will to power as much as (perhaps more than) Nietzsche does. Spinoza does not seek the "destruction of the affects"; rather, he seeks to purify them, i.e. to make them more powerful, more active. Indeed, for Spinoza, the operations of reason are affective and can constitute our greatest joy and activity. Far from being an expression of timidity and weakness, Spinoza's use of the geometrical method is meant to be just the opposite. In fact, Spinoza's view of reason as joyful and affective mirrors Nietzsche's own view of the right kind of understanding. As we just saw, in Nietzsche 1974: §333, Nietzsche contrasts what he sees as Spinoza's notion of understanding as inflexible and as opposed to the instincts with a proper notion of understanding as nothing but a "certain behavior of the instincts toward one another." Arguably, Spinoza's view is much closer to Nietzsche's than Nietzsche himself supposes in these passages.

Just as Hegel saw Spinoza's substance as too rigid in its apparent elimination of the finite, so, too, Nietzsche saw Spinoza as eliminating the affective. But in each case, the negative assessment of Spinoza is simply mistaken. As I said, Nietzsche should know better. And in many ways, Nietzsche did know better. He appreciated the similarity between himself and Spinoza precisely with regard to the affective value of reason, and he praised Spinoza for this similarity. Most famously he does so in a postcard to a friend in 1881 (i.e. *before* the anti-Spinozistic passages I have just quoted):

> I am utterly amazed utterly enchanted. I have a *precursor*, and what a precursor! I hardly knew Spinoza: that I should have turned to him just *now*, was inspired by "instinct." Not only is his overall tendency like mine—making knowledge the *most powerful* affect—but in five main points of his doctrine I recognize myself; this most unusual and loneliest thinker is closest to me precisely in these matters: he denies the freedom of the will, teleology, the moral world order, the unegoistic, and evil. Even though the divergencies are admittedly tremendous, they are due more to the difference in time, culture, and science. *In summa*: my lonesomeness, which, as on very high mountains, often made it hard for me to breathe

and made my blood rush out, is now at least a twosomeness.
Strange.

(Nietzsche 1974: 92)

Notice here how—in direct opposition to §333 of *The Gay Science* and other passages—Nietzsche acknowledges that, for Spinoza, knowledge is the most powerful affect. Nietzsche acknowledges that Spinoza recognizes—in Nietzschean terms—that reason is a good expression of the will to power. As I said, Nietzsche is conflicted about Spinoza.

Spinoza and Nietzsche both reject what I have called a bifurcation between will and intellect. The rejection of this bifurcation is of a piece with the rejection of other bifurcations, rejections that are central to the thought of both philosophers, who can now be seen as kindred spirits after all. Thus, consider that Nietzsche—like Spinoza—rejects the belief in freedom of the will. For Nietzsche, the idea that there could be a radical freedom to do otherwise was merely a device invented by the weak in order to be able to blame the strong and to subvert their power.

> Might it not be the case that that extremely foolhardy and fateful philosophical invention, first devised in Europe, of the "free will," of man's absolute freedom to do good or evil, was chiefly thought up to justify the idea that the interest of the gods in man, in man's virtue, *could never be exhausted*.
>
> (Nietzsche 1994: 48–49)

Thus, for Nietzsche, there is no freedom of the will; there is no self, there is no locus of moral responsibility. More generally, there is no doer behind the deed. Thus Nietzsche says:

> Just as the common people separates lightning from its flash and takes the latter to be a *deed*, something performed by a subject, which is called lightning, popular morality separates strength

> from the manifestations of strength, as though there were an
> indifferent substratum behind the strong person which had the
> *freedom* to manifest strength or not. But there is no such
> substratum; there is no "being" behind the deed, its effect and
> what becomes of it; "the doer" is invented as an afterthought—the
> doing is everything.
>
> (Nietzsche 1994: 28)

Thus Nietzsche's rejection of free will stems from his rejection of the bifurcation between doer and deed.

Spinoza also rejects this bifurcation—as we have seen, what we are, for Spinoza, is just a collection of states of God, i.e. certain actions of God. I am intelligible and fully exist insofar as I can be seen as certain actions of God. Spinoza and Nietzsche agree that there is nothing more to me than certain actions. Spinoza and Nietzsche would both see these actions as somehow actions of mine, but Spinoza makes an important departure from Nietzsche by seeing these actions as also and more fundamentally actions of God. We'll return to this difference shortly. But for now, I want to stress Spinoza's and Nietzsche's shared view that I am nothing more my actions. In Spinoza this point of agreement leads to the view, also shared by Nietzsche, that there is no free will. Precisely because, for Spinoza, there is nothing more to me than certain actions, and because these actions are all determined by other things outside me, none of my actions is free, is something for which I can be held morally responsible, as popular morality would have it. Thus Spinoza's and Nietzsche's shared rejection of a bifurcation between the doer and the deed leads to their denial of free will.

Similarly, as we have seen, Nietzsche, like Spinoza, rejects any bifurcation between a thing to be evaluated and the source of that evaluation. For Nietzsche, as for Spinoza, the source of value must be within the nature of the thing to be evaluated, if those evaluations are to be at all legitimate.

These denials of bifurcation and this immanence of value come to a head in Nietzsche with his remarkable doctrine of eternal recurrence. Thus Nietzsche famously asks:

> What, if some day or night a demon were to steal after you in your loneliest loneliness and say to you: "This life as you now live it and have lived it, you will have to live once more and innumerable times more; and there will be nothing new in it, but every pain and every joy and every thought and sigh and everything unutterably small or great in your life will have to return to you, all in the same succession and sequence—even this spider and this moonlight between the trees, and even this moment and I myself. The eternal hourglass of existence is turned upside down again and again, and you with it, speck of dust!"
>
> Would you not throw yourself down and gnash your teeth and curse the demon who spoke thus? Or have you once experienced a tremendous moment when you would have answered him: "You are a god and never have I heard anything more divine." If this thought gained possession of you, it would change you as you are or perhaps crush you. The question in each and every thing, "Do you desire this once more and innumerable times more?" would lie upon your actions as the greatest weight. Or how well disposed would you have to become to yourself and to life *to crave nothing more fervently* than this ultimate eternal confirmation and zeal?
>
> (Nietzsche 1974: §341)

For Nietzsche, the truly powerful individual, the individual who transparently expresses and exerts his will to power, is one who at each moment finds value in that moment, who in order to find value does not have to look beyond that moment, does not have to look to another life that will redeem the present, defective life (as in some forms of Christianity) and does not have to look to a future time that will improve and render finally intelligible this moment (as in Hegel). Rather, the maximally powerful individual is one who says "yes" to each moment and is willing to live each moment over and over again just as it is. Such willingness reveals that one has passed the test, the test of whether one values for the right reasons, for the reasons most in keeping with one's natural will to power.

Spinoza would find this test very congenial because it presupposes that the value of things is inherent in them. In Spinoza's eyes, as well as Nietzsche's, to look elsewhere for value is to do violence to our nature and this is something both philosophers—disdainers of illegitimate bifurcation—abhor.

Because, for both philosophers, our nature consists in the striving for power, they agree that in all inquiry our beliefs, our judgments, are liable to be skewed by our desires. Indeed, for both Spinoza and Nietzsche, there is no sense to be made of an affectless intellectual inquiry. For Spinoza, this means that, because our intellects are not perfect, because they are limited, our inquiries achieve only a relative truth and not the genuine article. As we saw, for Spinoza we are inevitably subject to inadequate and confused ideas in which the truth is obscured by our limited perspective. Nietzsche also sees all human perspectives, all human inquiries, as partial and not able to grasp any absolute truth precisely because each inquiry is a manifestation of one individual's will to power which is—very often—opposed to another individual's will to power. For Spinoza and Nietzsche both, human inquiry is affective and thus self-interested, and thus the truth we arrive at is not absolute truth, but truth from the perspective of a certain locus of power.

But here we run up against a real and not exaggerated difference between Nietzsche and Spinoza. While the two philosophers agree that each human being has a necessarily limited and not fully objective, not fully true hold on things, Nietzsche also holds that there is no standpoint from which there is truth full-stop, absolute truth, to be had. Nietzsche says:

> There is *only* a perspective seeing, *only* a perspective "knowing";
> the *more* affects we allow to speak about a thing, the *more* eyes,
> various eyes we are able to use for the same thing, the more
> complete will be our "concept" of the thing, our "objectivity." But
> to eliminate the will completely and turn off all the emotions
> without exception, assuming that we could: well? would that not
> mean to *castrate* the intellect?
>
> (Nietzsche 1994: 92)

But for Spinoza, of course, there is objective truth, and God grasps it. Indeed, for Spinoza, we cannot make sense of our limited perspective unless we invoke the objective, divine perspective. Further, we can, for Spinoza, have access to this objective perspective when we enjoy adequate ideas. And although we inevitably have very many inadequate ideas, we can know that there is an absolute perspective from which ideas are true absolutely (and things exist absolutely).

Nietzsche emphatically rejects Spinoza's commitment to absolute truth. For Nietzsche, such a commitment is simply a pernicious manifestation of *ressentiment* and does violence to—it "castrates"— the intellect. And because this objective perspective that Spinoza endorses is, of course, God's perspective, Nietzsche objects to Spinoza's notion of God. Yes, Spinoza's God is not transcendent and— from Nietzsche's point of view this is a virtue of Spinoza's conception of God—nonetheless, Spinoza's talk of God and objective truth betrays—according to Nietzsche—Spinoza's sickness, his being in the grip of *ressentiment*.

Here we return to Nietzsche's misplaced criticisms of Spinoza. As the passage just quoted from the *Genealogy* makes clear, Nietzsche's worry when it comes to objective truth is that it "eliminate[s] the will completely and turn[s] off all the emotions." But this is precisely what the absolute perspective that Spinoza endorses does *not* do (and Nietzsche *knows* this). Like Nietzsche (as Nietzsche, in effect, acknowledges), Spinoza identifies the will and intellect.

Thus Spinoza does not, in affirming that there is an absolute grasp of reality, turn off all the emotions. Spinoza merges the desire for objective truth with the desire to realize more fully the power of the affects, at least the power of active affects.

Still Nietzsche would deny that we can make sense of the objective, fully active perspective. Why should Nietzsche grant that there is such a perspective in which reason is fully active? How could Spinoza convince Nietzsche (and us) that it makes sense to speak, as Spinoza does, of this fully active and objective and true perspective? Answer: by invoking the PSR, of course. To see how this answer might proceed, consider what would be the case if there were only the finite, limited perspective that Nietzsche allows. What would be wrong with this scenario? In such a situation, there would be no perspective from which everything is fully intelligible. If a limited perspective, as Nietzsche would agree, can render only so much intelligible, then if the only perspectives were, as Nietzsche holds, limited, then there would be no perspective from which everything is intelligible. But this result would certainly go against the PSR, which demands the intelligibility of everything, i.e. demands that each thing and everything can be explained, can be made clear to an intellect. Spinoza would thus—because of the PSR—reject Nietzsche's claim that there are only limited, non-objective perspectives, and Spinoza's most fundamental criticism of Nietzsche would be that he is in violation of the PSR.

But so what? This violation of the PSR would be a badge of honor for Nietzsche. He would regard the PSR as simply another manifestation of the bad kind of reason, a manifestation of reason as a cudgel, as a fear-ridden suit of armor that rationalists hide behind. Nietzsche thus joins Hume in opposing Spinoza by opposing the PSR.

Perhaps Nietzsche is free to reject the PSR on these grounds. But there is a problem. We saw that Nietzsche, like Spinoza, wants to get rid of illegitimate bifurcations. But what's so bad about such bifurcations? Perhaps Nietzsche just doesn't like these bifurcations and that's all there is to say on the matter. I suspect that this is all we can say on Nietzsche's behalf. But if so, his position does not seem very satisfactory; we seem to want there to be a reason why the bifurcations should be rejected. I think Nietzsche's rejection of bifurcations does have more pull on us than this response would admit and that they have pull on us precisely because we (and perhaps Nietzsche at some level) are motivated by a perhaps limited version of the PSR. As we have seen, the PSR does dictate the rejection of these bifurcations and thus the PSR is well-suited for underwriting the rejection of the bifurcations Nietzsche joins Spinoza in rejecting. Without affirming the PSR, Nietzsche may be left without a ground for his entire approach to morality and the world. Again, such groundlessness may not trouble Nietzsche (but who knows?); nevertheless, it certainly can seem troubling to us. Here then is a hint of an internal tension in Nietzsche's position, a tension between his steadfast rejection of the PSR and his equally steadfast rejection of divisions within nature. In the next and final section of this chapter, I want to explore in general terms this kind of conflict that faces not just Nietzsche, but any philosopher who wants simultaneously to reject the PSR and also to reject certain problematic gaps in reality. If it can be shown to be real, this internal conflict facing positions that reject the PSR can perhaps provide the kind of support for the PSR—and thus for Spinoza's entire system—that we have not yet been able to find.

6. PROSPECTS OF SPINOZISTIC RATIONALISM

In the twentieth century and today, it is rare for a philosopher to structure his system around a response to Spinoza in the way that, say, Leibniz and Hegel did. There are important recent cases in which a philosopher is very deeply guided in one or more aspects of his system by Spinoza and Spinozistic themes. Davidson's anomalous monism is a notable example of a view which draws on Spinoza to develop a new (but really not-so-new) take on the mind–body problem.[13] More generally, we see philosophers today still struggling to avoid an extreme rationalism of the kind that Spinoza espoused, and struggling to do so with or without explicit attention to Spinoza. Further, through Spinoza's impact on the likes of Leibniz, Hume, Kant, the German idealists, Nietzsche and others, Spinoza's philosophical influence is permanent. To chart the ways in which—through Leibniz and company—Spinoza's philosophy ramifies throughout twentieth- and twenty-first-century philosophy would be to write the entire history of philosophy in this period, and this, fortunately, is not a task we can or need to take on here.

What we can do, however, is this: we can try to make good on the promise of Spinozism. And to do this, the most important thing we can do—by far—is to make good on the PSR, to show how it can be justified, for. as I have argued throughout this book, very much of what Spinoza has to say rises and falls with the PSR. If we cannot demonstrate the power of the PSR, then Spinoza's philosophy can have no pull on us.

Most philosophers, of course, simply refuse to accept the PSR in its unrestricted—Spinozistic—form, and in most cases they do so without argument. Hume who did, as we saw, offer an argument against the PSR is an exception in this regard, whether or not Hume's argument is effective. What we find when we canvass contemporary philosophy is the prevalent presupposition that some facts are simply given and have no explanation. For example, in recent debates over the metaphysics of identity, it seems to be taken for granted on all or nearly all sides that there can be cases in which two things are distinct but in which their non-identity is primitive, without explanation. A commitment to primitive identity and non-identity is central to the otherwise widely divergent metaphysical views of David Lewis and Saul Kripke. Kripke and Lewis agree about little when it comes to the metaphysics of identity, but when the bandwagon of primitive identity comes through, both Kripke and Lewis jump readily on board. If it is pointed out to those many who philosophize in this general vein that this acceptance of primitive identity is an acceptance of a brute fact, a violation of the PSR, the purveyors of primitive identity don't bat an eyelid. "Of course we have to accept some primitives," they might say, or, to revert to Wittgenstein's locution which I invoked in Chapter 1, "Here my spade is turned." To try to defend the PSR, and so to defend Spinozism, in this climate seems at best futile.

Nonetheless, we owe it to Spinoza and really to philosophy itself to see if we can go further. In this final section, I want to go against the grain of philosophy today and offer a sketch of a defense of the PSR, a principle whose denial so many philosophers are happy simply to take for granted. My argument here will develop a strategy adumbrated in my criticism of Nietzsche at the end of the previous section.

Perhaps one justification of the PSR is that—by employing it—one is able to develop the most coherent overall system. Certainly Spinoza has a marvelously interconnected system in which metaphysics, epistemology, philosophy of mind, moral philosophy, philosophy of religion, and political philosophy are all linked in a seamless, internally coherent way. The PSR—as we have discovered—makes possible many of these links, and this productiveness itself provides indirect support for the PSR. One is inclined to say: "if the PSR can lead to this broad and elegant system, we should accept it."

Nonetheless, Spinoza's system as a whole—however internally coherent and elegant it may be—may still seem wildly implausible (not to me any longer, but I do know how it can seem). After all, Spinoza's system offers us (among other horrors) necessitarianism, the equivalence of right and power, degrees of existence, etc. Internal coherence is nice, but one can be forgiven for running away from a system as shocking as this one and for rejecting the PSR which plays such a large role in generating that system.

Fair enough. But matters begin to look different and better once we realize that any opposing system—i.e. one that denies the PSR—is likely to be fraught with internal incoherence of a kind from which a system that incorporates the PSR is exempt. This relative incoherence of systems hostile to the PSR may provide the best support for the PSR. After all, who wants an internally incoherent system? I should say at the outset that the considerations I am about to offer in defense of the PSR (and thus of Spinoza) are certainly in need of further development, which I hope to offer elsewhere. But I do aim to provide enough of an indication here to convince you that there is an argument for the PSR that ought to be taken very seriously.

I want to begin by bracketing the PSR and turning to certain local cases in which we—or at least many of us—would endorse a kind of argument I will call an explicability argument. Thus consider a simple example from Leibniz. "[Archimedes] takes it for granted that if there is a balance in which everything is alike on both sides, and if equal weights are hung on the two ends of that balance, the whole will be at rest. That is because no reason can be given why one side should weigh down rather than the other."[14] This certainly seems like a sensible inference. Absent any relevant difference between the sides of the balance, one must conclude that the whole will be at rest. Leibniz (or Archimedes) here rejects a certain possibility—namely that the balance is not at rest—because this possibility would be inexplicable: given the equal weights and the lack of any other relevant difference, there could be no reason for the whole not to be at rest and so the whole is at rest. I'm not necessarily endorsing this inference, but merely pointing out that it is extremely plausible.

This is an example of what I call an explicability argument. In such an argument, a certain state of affairs is said not to obtain simply because the existence of that state of affairs would be inexplicable, a so-called brute fact. Here the state of affairs rejected because of its inexplicability is the motion of the balance. The Archimedean scenario illustrates the power that explicability arguments can have. It remains to be seen whether such arguments have force more generally. If explicability arguments are legitimate generally, then it follows directly that the PSR is true, for the PSR is simply the rejection of inexplicability in general. But, it seems, one can accept the Archimedean scenario which concerns physics without thereby being committed to the PSR, which purports to have universal applicability. Perhaps explicability arguments work in some cases, but not in others.

Well, let's see. Let's take another extremely plausible example: brute dispositions. Imagine two objects categorically exactly alike. They each have (qualitatively) the same molecular structure and have all the same categorical physical features. If one of these objects has the disposition to dissolve in water, could the other one fail to have that disposition? It would seem not: given their exact categorical similarity, nothing could ground this dispositional difference between the two objects, and so we reject the scenario in which there is such a difference.[15]

Once again, this conclusion is enormously intuitively plausible. Here we reject brute dispositional differences, differences that would be inexplicable. This is another explicability argument: the state of affairs rejected because of its inexplicability is the one in which the objects have different dispositional properties. Again, this explicability argument does not by itself force us to embrace the PSR, the denial of inexplicability in general. But this case and the previous one can give us pause, for now we wonder just how extensive this embrace of explicability is. There's no cause for alarm just yet, merely a question that we are naturally led to pursue.

There are other similarly uncontroversial explicability arguments, but let's turn now to a more controversial argument, one which nevertheless has considerable intuitive appeal. For a reductionist about causation, there must be something in virtue of which a causal relation obtains. Why is it that these events are causally related and those are not? What is it that *makes* them causally related? To deny that there is any deeper fact that can explain why a causal relation obtains in a given situation is to treat causation as primitive or inexplicable, and such inexplicability does seem rather unpalatable. It would seem odd for causation to be a primitive fact, for there to be nothing one could say in answer to the question: What is it in virtue of which these events are causally related and those not? Similarly, brute causation would seem to be as unwelcome as brute dispositions, as the view that one thing is soluble and another thing not despite their categorical exact similarity, and so on for other cases. The reductionist about causation seems to be relying on the rejection of inexplicability in this case, just as inexplicability was rejected in the other cases. And my point here—shared by many other philosophers—is that this rejection of the inexplicability of causation does have considerable intuitive appeal.

Notice that to accept the demand for an explanation is not by itself to put forward a specific account of causation. More important than a specific account is the general demand that causation not be inexplicable. This demand generates the explicability argument in this case. And notice also that accepting this demand does not by itself commit one to the general PSR. Rejecting inexplicability in this case does not by itself require rejecting inexplicability in all cases.

We are now in a position to turn to the final explicability argument that I want to consider here, one that concerns existence. Just as we may (or may not) demand an account of what causation is, just as we may (less contentiously) demand an account of why it is that the balance in the Archimedean case moves or does not move, an account of what it is in virtue of which things have the dispositions they do, so too it can come to seem natural to demand an account of existence, of what it is for a thing to exist. What is it in virtue of which things that exist enjoy existence? Just as, when we have a case of causation, we might ask what explains why this case is a case of causation, what is it in virtue of which there is a causal relation here, so too it seems natural to ask what explains why this case is a case of existence? What is it in virtue of which this thing exists? If we take this path, then we advance an explicability argument here: the existence of each thing that exists must be explicable, just as the presence of a causal relation in a given situation must be explicable. Exactly what the account of existence is, is a separate issue, one that we need not resolve here. We have, of course, seen that, for Spinoza, existence is intelligibility, but I am not relying here on that claim because that claim derives from the PSR itself. Here I am interested in motivating a general demand that existence be explained, a demand that stems from other more or less intuitive cases in which we embrace explicability arguments. It is this demand that existence be explained that leads, as we will see, to the PSR.

The point so far is just that the more or less uncontroversial use of explicability arguments in these other cases can make it seem natural to advance an explicability argument in the case of existence. In other words, the use of explicability arguments in these other cases puts pressure on us to accept an explicability argument here in the case of existence—unless, of course, one can draw a line between this explicability argument and others. To insist on such a principled difference is not to presuppose the full-blown PSR; rather, it is simply yet another plausible and local appeal to explicability.

And, indeed, the need to draw a line is urgent because the explicability argument in the case of existence differs from the previous ones in one crucial respect: while the other explicability arguments do not by themselves commit one to the full-blown PSR, the explicability argument concerning existence does, for to insist that there be an explanation for the existence of each existing thing is simply to insist on the PSR itself. So the explicability argument concerning existence, unlike the other explicability arguments, is an argument for the PSR itself, and it is our willingness to accept explicability arguments in other, similar cases that puts pressure on us to accept the explicability argument in the case of existence, i.e. puts pressure on us to accept the PSR itself.

In light of this pressure, a non-rationalist needs to draw a principled line between the explicability arguments he accepts and those he does not. To draw an unprincipled, arbitrary line is not legitimate in this context in which the truth of the PSR is the very point at issue. To appeal to an arbitrary line here is to appeal to a brute fact—the alleged fact that there is no explanation as to why the line between legitimate and illegitimate explicability arguments is to be drawn here; it just is drawn here. To appeal to a brute fact in this dialectical context is simply to presuppose that the PSR is false, and this is the one thing that a non-rationalist may not do in this context.

How might such a principled line be drawn? It's not at all clear.[16] But until such a line is found, there is genuine and unrebutted pressure—stemming from one's acceptance of relatively uncontroversial explicability arguments—to accept the PSR itself. Thus we can see that there is at least the threat of internal incoherence in a position that denies the PSR. For let's say that one denies the PSR (and thus rejects the explicability argument concerning existence), but also accepts at least some other explicability arguments, such as the arguments concerning dispositions, causation, etc. The explicability arguments one accepts naturally put pressure on one to accept other similar explicability arguments, including the explicability argument concerning existence. Unless one can resist this pressure in a principled way, i.e. unless one can draw a non-arbitrary line between explicability arguments, one has no good way to maintain one's denial of the PSR. Thus a position which combines an acceptance of certain, perhaps plausible, explicability arguments with a rejection of the PSR threatens to be at odds with itself and to be, for this reason, internally incoherent. By contrast, a position that accepts a full-blown PSR does not threaten to be incoherent in this way. This threat of incoherence facing positions that reject the PSR promises to provide strong support for the PSR itself. And so the explicability arguments we tend to accept may, surprisingly perhaps, commit us already to the PSR itself. Developing this line of thought is, I believe, the best prospect for establishing the PSR and validating the kind of system that Spinoza aimed to develop.

Until we find a principled line, therefore, between explicability arguments, we must regard the PSR and, indeed, Spinozism itself as very much live options in philosophy and as options to which we may, in fact, already be committed. Spinoza could not ask for anything more.

SUMMARY

Spinoza's influence on subsequent philosophy has been and continues to be enormous. His model of an extreme and extremely consistent rationalism is a challenge for all philosophers, most of whom seek to avoid Spinoza's rationalist conclusions. But whether one can consistently avoid Spinoza's rationalism is an open question. His influence on Leibniz was immediate and pervasive. Leibniz met Spinoza and was perhaps uniquely well-suited to understanding his philosophy. Leibniz was as much a fan of the PSR as Spinoza was, but Leibniz did not apply the PSR as thoroughly as he might have. For example, Leibniz's rejection of Spinoza's necessitarianism and monism does not sit well with Leibniz's commitment to the PSR. Leibniz may have been led into this perhaps incoherent combination of views out of his desire to provide room for a meaningful kind of human freedom.

Bayle's influential critique of Spinoza was directed at Spinoza's monism and his view that finite things are merely modes of God. It is this criticism that resonated with Hume, who structured his philosophy to avoid the denial of Spinoza's monism. Because Hume saw correctly that the PSR leads to something like Spinoza's monism, Hume rejects the PSR. Hume and Spinoza agree on the link between the PSR and many counterintuitive metaphysical positions. But whereas Spinoza embraces those metaphysical claims because of the PSR, Hume rejects them and so denies the PSR.

For most of the eighteenth century, Spinoza was publicly treated as a philosopher to be scorned, although there was much underground Spinozism. Spinoza was able to come out of the closet, however, with the pantheism controversy in Germany in the

1780s. Lessing and Jacobi correctly saw that Spinoza's system was structured around the PSR. Jacobi in particular argued that the only consistent philosophy was Spinozism. For this reason, Jacobi abandoned philosophy, but the way Jacobi saw the issues set the agenda for a generation of philosophers in Germany, many of whom, including Kant and Mendelssohn, sought to find a consistent and non-Spinozistic middle ground for philosophy to occupy. A German idealist who appreciated the power of Spinozism was Hegel. He too embraced monism and the intelligibility of all things, but Hegel thought—wrongly—that Spinoza denies the reality of finite modes, and he sought to distance himself from Spinoza in this regard. However, for Spinoza the finite is real, though not fully real, and this is more or less Hegel's position too. Where Hegel and Spinoza genuinely differ is with regard to Hegel's view that history is a temporal procession of increasing perfection, a process heading toward a final goal of full intelligibility. The developmental and teleological character of Hegel's philosophy is incompatible with Spinoza's rejection of teleology. For Spinoza, any privileging of one temporal period over another would be objectionably arbitrary: why should any stage be privileged above any other?

Nietzsche, like Hegel, is more similar to Spinoza than he perhaps always realizes. Nietzsche often presents himself as the opponent of reason and inveighs against rationalists like Spinoza for downplaying the affective aspect of life. But, as Nietzsche often recognizes, there is nonetheless a deep affinity between the two thinkers. Both deny that there is anything more to me than certain actions: I am what I do. Both reject any absolute freedom of the will, and, most significantly, both reject a source of evaluation that is outside the thing to be evaluated and both see that source of value in the power of the individual. Where Nietzsche and Spinoza differ, however, is in Nietzsche's rejection of an absolute, unlimited perspective on the truth. For Spinoza, the unlimited perspective that God enjoys is the locus of absolute truth. This difference between Nietzsche and Spinoza stems from the fact that

Nietzsche is not committed to the PSR in anything like the way Spinoza is.

Finally, because the success of Spinoza's system rides so heavily on the PSR, we need to investigate whether the PSR itself can be justified. Perhaps the most promising route is to focus on ordinary and very plausible arguments that certain states of affairs are to be rejected because they would be inexplicable. Such arguments may be able to lead to a more general rejection of inexplicability and a more general defense of the PSR.

FURTHER READING

Frederick C. Beiser (1987) *The Fate of Reason: German Philosophy From Kant to Fichte*. (Engaging account of the pantheism controversy touched off by the conversations between Lessing and Jacobi.)

Jonathan Israel (2001) *Radical Enlightenment: Philosophy and the Making of Modernity 1650–1750*. (Monumental work on the varieties of underground and not-so-underground Spinozism.)

Harold H. Joachim (1901) *A Study of the Ethics of Spinoza*. (Significant Hegelian reading of Spinoza.)

Alexander R. Pruss (2006) *The Principle of Sufficient Reason: A Reassessment*. (Recent book that defends a watered-down, no-necessitarianism version of the PSR.)

Matthew Stewart (2005) *The Courtier and the Heretic: Leibniz, Spinoza, and the Fate of God in the Modern World*. (Lively narrative about the personal encounter between Spinoza and Leibniz.)

Peter van Inwagen (2002) *Metaphysics*, 2nd ed., chap. 4. (Rejects the PSR because it leads to necessitarianism.)

Yirmiyahu Yovel (1989) *Spinoza and other Heretics*, vol. 2. (Chapter 2 on Spinoza and Hegel, and chapter 5 on Spinoza and Nietzsche, offer good overviews.)

Glossary

Acosmism   The view that finite individuals lack all reality. Hegel misleadingly charges Spinoza with acosmism.

Adequate Idea   An idea that is not caused from outside the mind and is, as such, completely clear and unconfused.

Affect   (noun) An emotion, a state of the mind or body in which the mind's or body's power of acting is increased or diminished.

Attribute   A fundamental property of a substance, a property that constitutes the essence of a substance.

Brute Fact   A fact that has no explanation.

Conatus   Striving. For Spinoza, each thing strives to preserve itself.

Conceptual Truth   A claim that is true simply by virtue of the concepts contained in the claim, such as, e.g., "all bachelors are unmarried."

Cosmological Argument   An argument that attempts to establish the existence of God from the PSR together with the fact that there are or can be dependent beings, i.e. beings whose existence is explained by something other than themselves.

Determinism   The thesis that each event or state is determined by prior events or states.

Dualism   Descartes's view that the mind and body are distinct substances.

Egoism   The thesis that each individual is morally obligated only to do what is in his or her self-interest.

Eliminativism   The view that some commonly accepted phenomenon does not in fact exist. Thus some philosophers are eliminativists about consciousness or morality, etc. Spinoza, by contrast, tends not to eliminate ordinary phenomena but to understand them in radically different, often reductionist ways.

Epistemology   The theory of knowledge.

Final Cause   The purpose for which a certain state is brought about.

Idealism   The view that all things that exist are mental and that the mental is more fundamental than the physical or any other way of being.

Identity of Indiscernibles   Leibniz's and Spinoza's view that any two things that share all the same properties (i.e. things that are indiscernible) are therefore identical. The converse of Leibniz's Law.

Inherence   The relation whereby one thing is a state or property of another. Thus the squareness of the table inheres in the table, my thought that today is Wednesday inheres in my mind.

Leibniz's Law   The principle that if two things differ with regard to some property, then those things are not identical.

Marranos   A derogatory term, meaning "swine," for Jews in Spain and Portugal who were forced to convert to Christianity.

Materialism   The thesis that all that exists is the material or physical and that the material or physical is more fundamental than the mental or any other way of being.

Metaphysics   The study of the nature of reality and of the relations among things that are real.

Mode   Traditionally a property of a substance. There is a controversy about whether Spinoza understands this term in its traditional sense or, instead, sees modes simply as effects of a substance and not as properties of it.

Monad   Leibniz's term for a simple thinking substance. Spinoza's one substance is, in some respects, like a Leibnizian monad.

Monism   The view that reality is one thing. In Spinoza, this view takes the form of a substance monism.

Naturalism   The thesis that everything in the world plays by the same rules or laws; there are no anomalous phenomena. Naturalism can be seen as derived from the PSR.

Necessitarianism   The thesis that all truths are necessary and that each thing that exists necessarily exists.

Ontological Argument   An argument for the existence of God that proceeds from the claim that existence belongs to the very nature of God. The proof originated with Anselm in the eleventh century, and Spinoza produces a version of it in 1p11.

Panpsychism   The thesis that all beings are thinking beings. Spinoza and Leibniz are panpsychists.

Pantheism   The thesis that God is the whole of reality. Most commentators interpret Spinoza as a pantheist.

Parallelism   The thesis that for each physical state there is a corresponding mental state and that the mental states are connected among each other in the same way that the physical states are connected among each other. Spinoza's parallelism appears most prominently in 2p7.

Prime Matter   A concept deriving from Aristotle according to which bodily substances consist in part in an intrinsically propertyless basis for a substantial form to inhere in.

PSR (the Principle of Sufficient Reason)   The principle that each truth has an explanation or that for each thing that exists there is an explanation of its existence.

Rationalism   On one construal, this is the view that there is a reason for everything, i.e. that the PSR is true. Another, related version of rationalism is the view that sense perception is a less valid form of cognition than reason.

Reductionism   The view that some commonly accepted phenomenon is nothing but some other, perhaps more fundamental phenomenon. Thus, for Spinoza, consciousness is nothing but active representation, virtue is nothing but power, etc. Spinoza thus doesn't eliminate these phenomena.

Representation   A state of mind that is about or of a given thing.

Representational Theory of Mind The view that all mental states are fundamentally representational.

Skepticism The claim that we lack knowledge in a given domain or in general.

Substance Traditionally, a thing that has properties or states and is not itself a property or state of anything. Alternatively, a substance is a thing that is independent of all other things. These conceptions of substance come to the same thing for Spinoza.

Substantial Form In Aristotelian philosophy, the essence of a substance, that which—when combined with prime matter—makes for the existence of a substance of a certain kind.

Utilitarianism The thesis that what it is right to do is what will maximize utility or overall happiness.

Will to Power Nietzsche's view—similar to Spinoza's—that all activity is simply a manifestation of the striving to increase one's power.

Notes

ONE SPINOZA'S UNDERSTANDING AND UNDERSTANDING SPINOZA

1 Wittgenstein 1958: §217.
2 See, in particular, how Spinoza moves naturally from claims about the way in which substance is conceived to claims about the way substance is explained (1p10s, 1p14d, 2p5). See also the way in which conceiving a thing is identical to understanding it or finding it intelligible (1ax5). For further discussion, see Della Rocca 1996a: 3–4.
3 For more on Spinoza's method, see Aaron Garrett 2003.
4 Bergson 1975: 113.
5 And he outlines this strategy in the TdIE.
6 Goldstein 2006.
7 Thus Lucas relates: "He had such a great propensity not to do anything for the sake of being regarded and admired by the people, that when dying he requested that his name should not be put on his *Ethics*, saying that such affectations were unworthy of a philosopher" (in Wolf 1970: 62).
8 See Nadler 1999. Lucas's biography (in Wolf 1970) was written in 1677 or 1678 and first published in 1719. Colerus' biography was first published in 1705.
9 On this aspect of Spinoza's thought, Yovel 1989, vol. 1, is very good.
10 Colerus 1880: 416; see also Bayle 1991: 292.
11 Hereafter "TTP."

TWO THE METAPHYSICS OF SUBSTANCE

1 Curley also, especially in Curley 1988, argues that Spinoza's position on substance is simply the Cartesian position taken to its logical extreme. Curley's development of this theme is very illuminating, but quite different from mine.
2 See CSM III 207/AT III 502, CSM II 157, 159/AT VII 222, 226, CSM I 297/AT VIII-2 348, and for discussion see Rozemond 1998: 7.

3 This account applies only to corporeal substances. Spiritual substances do not have prime matter as a constituent.

4 There's a controversy over whether Descartes does indeed allow for genuine causal interaction between minds and bodies. I think it is clear that he does allow both minds to act on bodies *and* bodies to act on minds. For some discussion, see Della Rocca 2008a.

5 See Della Rocca 2008a.

6 For Spinoza, affections are modes, as 1def5 makes clear.

7 See Leibniz, "On the Ethics of Benedict de Spinoza," in Leibniz 1969: 198–99.

8 Spinoza makes clear in 2p5d and elsewhere that for one thing to express another is for the first to be sufficient for conceiving of the second. See Della Rocca 2002: 20–21.

9 See "Meditations on Knowledge, Truth, and Ideas" in Leibniz 1989: 25–26, and *Discourse on Metaphysics* §23 in Leibniz 1989.

10 For more on these issues, see Della Rocca 2006.

11 For Spinoza, the definition of a thing states its essence, as Spinoza says in a number of places; see, e.g., 3p4 and Letter 9 (G IV 43).

12 This notion of modal dependence has its origin in the Aristotelian-scholastic notion of the way in which accidents (such as whiteness and being eight feet tall) depend on substances. For a good discussion of these traditional notions as they figure in Descartes and Spinoza, see Carriero 1995. For an account of the transition from the talk of accidents to the talk of modes, see Garber 1992: chap. 3.

13 This kind of conceptual dependence of modes on substance goes back to the Aristotelian *definitional* dependence of accidents on substance. See Carriero 1995: 248.

14 Carriero 1995: §2.

15 Compare 3pref: "nature is always the same, and its virtue and power of acting are everywhere one and the same."

16 For this reason, we can see that, when Spinoza says that substance is in itself, this simply amounts to the claim that substance is dependent only on itself or is conceived only through itself.

17 TTP, p. 50 (G III 60); see also KV II, chap. 26, G I 111; I am grateful to Yitzhak Melamed for calling the relevance of these passages to my attention.

18 Spinoza's interpreters have given conflicting answers to this question. See, e.g., Garrett 1991; and Curley and Walski 1998.

19 Curley and Walski, however, do make this claim.

20 Spinoza argues similarly that any such mode must also be eternal.

21 There is some unclarity as to whether the mediate infinite modes can be said to follow from God's nature absolutely. The account I gave above of the nature of following absolutely from God suggests that they do not, for the mediate infinite modes follow from God only because something else (namely an immediate infinite mode) also follows from God. And 1p23 does indicate that the mediate infinite modes do not follow from the absolute nature of God. However, in 1p23d, Spinoza seems to allow mediate infinite modes to follow absolutely from God as well (see Giancotti 1991). I believe, in light of what I take to be the natural interpretation of Spinoza's line of reasoning in 1p21d, that the locution in 1p23 is to be favored over the locution in 1p23d.

22 See especially TdIE §101. For a classic statement of the relation between infinite modes and laws of nature, see Curley 1969: 58–62. As Curley explains, it would be more accurate to say that the infinite modes are not themselves the laws of nature, but are rather the facts within extension or thought that correspond to the laws. The laws are, as it were, statements of these facts. As Spinoza puts it in TdIE §101, the laws are inscribed in the "fixed and eternal things."

23 See 2def6 for the equivalence or reality and perfection, and 4pref (G II 208) for the equivalence of perfection and power. Spinoza also links power and reality in 2p49s (G II 133).

24 For such a connection between the PSR and necessitarianism, see van Inwagen 2002: chap. 7, and Bennett 1984: 115. Curley and Walski object to using PSR to justify a necessitarian reading of Spinoza. They base this objection on the claim that the totality of particular facts cannot be explained because "if the totality really does contain all the particular facts … the only facts available for explaining that totality are those wholly general facts described by the laws of nature, and you cannot deduce any particular facts from general facts alone" (Curley and Walski 1998: 258). Curley and Walski seem to assume that the laws of nature and thus the attributes are wholly general facts. To assume this is really to beg the question because the necessitarian reading involves the claim that attributes are sufficient explanations for particulars and thus attributes may be seen as not mere general facts.

25 There are some worries here about whether a mental intention can give rise to a physical action, but we will bracket these worries for now and return to this matter in the next chapter when we discuss Spinoza's parallelism.

26 See note 23.

THREE   THE HUMAN MIND

1 See Descartes's definition of thought in the *Replies to the Second Objections* (CSM II 113, AT VII 160).

2 I am indebted here to Yitzhak Melamed for convincing me that the parallelism between modes of two non-thinking attributes does not follow directly from the parallelism between things and ideas stated in 2p7 itself.

3 For some discussion, see Della Rocca 1996a: 23.

4 For other such passages, see TdIE §§36, 51; TTP, p. 48, chap. 4 (G III 58), Ethics 4pref (G II 208), 5ax2.

5 See Aaron Garrett 2003.

6 See also 1p8s2, G II 51.

7 I will present a different derivation of this claim in Chapter 7.

8 Actually, of course, there are, given the infinity of attributes, infinitely many different ways of explaining the same things.

9 The classic statement of Davidson's position is in Davidson 1980. I have analyzed the similarities between Spinoza and Davidson in Della Rocca 1996a: chap. 8. Davidson has expressed his indebtedness to Spinoza in Davidson 1999.

10 This is a fully general account of individuality, applying to extended things and to thinking things. In the next chapter, we will consider in detail a compatible account of individuality for bodies in particular. I am here treating being a singular thing as equivalent to being an individual, or at least I see Spinoza as drawing no sharp line here.

11 Indeed, for Spinoza, the idea of the body is a representation of the body only in virtue of the ideas of the affections of the body: "The human mind does not know the human body itself, nor does it know that it exists, except through the ideas of affections by which the body is affected" (2p19). (Spinoza understands affections of the body very broadly as any constitution of the body (3da1exp).) I think that in 2p19 Spinoza expresses the view that, unlike a substance, the human body is not prior to its affections or constitutions. For example, it, unlike substance, is divisible into its parts. Thus the representation of the body is posterior to the representation of the affections of the body, as 2p19 indicates.

12 Wilson 1999: 130.

13 Bennett advances a similar argument (Bennett 1984: 135–39).

14 See Simmons 2001. For my understanding of consciousness in Leibniz and in early modern philosophy in general, I am indebted to Jorgensen 2007.

15 See the way Spinoza invokes 2p23 in 3p9d.

16 For a helpful exploration of the issue of the human mind's ability to have fully adequate ideas, see Marshall forthcoming.

17 See, e.g., Tye 1997. Leibniz also holds a fully representational theory of mind; see Simmons 2001.

18 It's also often the view of the philosopher on the street, e.g. Descartes.

19 Cf. KV II App. §§5–6. Guéroult 1974: 33.

20 See the definition of thought in the Second Replies (AT VII 160, CSM II 113); see also *Principles* I 9; AT III 273, CSMK 165 66; AT VII 246, CSM II 171

21 Spinoza makes this point in various places, including 1a5, 1p3, 2p7s, 3p2, 5pref.

22 For further evidence, see Della Rocca 2003b: 220–24.

23 See, e.g., Descartes, *Passions* I §17, CSMK 182/AT III 372.

24 Spinoza's focus on essences is due, I believe, to Spinoza's view, already discussed, that one represents a thing by representing its essence.

25 See TTP, chap. 2, p. 21: "Imagination by itself, unlike every other clear and distinct idea, does not of its own nature carry certainty with it." This passage indicates that certainty is simply a function of clear and distinct representation and that lack of certainty is a function of confusion or lack of clarity.

FOUR PSYCHOLOGY

1 See also the reference to 3p4d in 4p17s. Spinoza also sees the related claim that bodily states persist by their very nature as self-evident in 2le3c and in PPC 2p14. See also 4p20s.

2 For Spinoza's discussion of suicide, see, e.g., 4p20s. For the candle, see TdIE §57.

3 In reading 3p5 as invoking degrees of being in, I am much indebted to Garrett 2002. However, I part company with Garrett in allowing that, for Spinoza, if *x* is partly caused by *y*, then *x* is to that extent in *y*. I do not see how one can deny this and still maintain the equivalence—on which Spinoza insists—between causation and the in-relation. For further discussion, see Della Rocca 2008b.

4 Similarly, Hoffman speaks of a stripped-down notion of final causation in Descartes and Aquinas in Hoffman unpublished.

5 See also *Principles* II 37, where Descartes does not use the term "strives" and instead uses "tends." But it seems clear from this passage that the notion he is concerned with is equivalent to the notion of striving. (For a contrary view, see Hoffman unpublished.) It's not clear how Descartes would account in these terms for the striving of minds. This is, as we will see presently, a major difference from Spinoza. For further discussion and a limited defense of Descartes' extremely subtle views on striving and causation in the extended realm, see Della Rocca 1998 and 2008a.

6 Garber discusses this objection in Garber 1992: 363n39, and in Garber 1994: 47–48.

7 See PPC 2p17, 3d3. A similar account of striving is found in CM I.6.

8 I have preferred the more literal translation of *quantum in se est* as "insofar as it is in itself" to Curley's "as far as it can by its own power" because the former translation makes clear the connection between Spinoza's conatus doctrine and his definition of substance as that which is in itself. Spinoza thus says, in effect, in 3p6 that a thing strives to persist to the degree to which it is a substance. Lucretius, Descartes, and Newton also make use of the phrase *quantum in se est*. In giving this account of the meaning of the phrase as Spinoza uses it, I do not presuppose that any of these other thinkers use the term in precisely this sense. For a wonderful account of the term in Lucretius, Descartes, and Newton, see Cohen 1964.

9 See 2le3 and its corollary.

10 How does calling the proportion of motion and rest the essence of a complex individual cohere with Spinoza's view that a thing's essence consists in having certain causes? Spinoza does not take up this question directly, but it is clear what the general line of his response would be: the causes of a body cause its parts to bear this relation to one another and, in this way, the relation directly follows from the causes. Perhaps, then, it is the having of these causes that is strictly the essence and the relation among the parts is a derivative feature. Perhaps so, but Spinoza does not develop his notion of essence far enough in order for us to be confident that he would embrace this more nuanced account.

11 I say "apparently non-living" because, as you will recall, Spinoza insists that all bodies are animate to some degree.

12 And because these parts have a tendency to preserve this overall relation, the parts have many affects jointly in common. Thus this account of being a complex corporeal individual in this definition is compatible with the more general, attribute-neutral account of being a singular thing in 2def7, an account that we discussed briefly in the previous chapter.

13 Leibniz himself, however, may not be well placed to reject this response because there are indications in Leibniz that he is sympathetic to the equivalence of causal and conceptual relations.

14 Or at least strive to have those ideas insofar as it can. This qualification plays, I believe, the same role as the qualification "insofar as it is in itself."

15 See 3da25 and 4p52.

16 For a vivid discussion of this passage, see Frankfurt 1999.

17 Plato accounts for irrational action in similar terms in the *Protagoras*.

18 Hobbes explicitly derives the striving to increase one's power from the ability to anticipate. See *Leviathan* Part I, chap. 11 (Hobbes 1994).

FIVE THE ETHICS OF THE *ETHICS*

1 Indeed, the notion of epistemic justification can be seen as already turning on the notion of goodness; it is the notion of a good reason to believe.

2 Here I differ from Garrett who sees virtue, unlike goodness, as applying only to persons and their behavior and states of character (Garrett 1996: 292). But Spinoza's definition of virtue insofar as it is related to man suggests strongly that Spinoza is making room for the notion of virtue insofar as it is related to things generally: if there can be virtue insofar as it is related to man, there can, it seems, be virtue insofar as it is related to other things. Indeed, if as Spinoza says in 4def8 virtue is just power, then since things in general have some degree of power, things in general have some degree of virtue.

3 4p28. Notice that Spinoza's equivalence between good and virtue is on display.

4 See also KV II 12 §2. Praise and blame are thus in the same category as other affects such as humility and repentance (3da 26, 27), hate, mockery, disdain, and pity (4p50s, KV II 11 §1), all of which turn on a mistaken belief in the freedom of others.

5 Garrett 1990 insightfully articulates this line of thought.

6 Kant explicitly bites this bullet in "On a Supposed Right to Lie because of Philanthropic Concerns" contained in Kant 1981.

SIX THE STATE, RELIGION, AND SCRIPTURE

1 Hobbes 1994: part I, chap. 13, §9.

2 Spinoza's willingness to consider promises invalid absent an enforcement mechanism may be more robust than Hobbes's. See Hobbes 1994: part I, chap. 14, §27; and Curley 1996: 323. See also the beginning of Spinoza's Letter 50, where he draws a similar contrast to Hobbes.

3 See Deuteronomy 4:24 and 9:3.

4 Popkin 1996: 388.

5 Hobbes 1994: part III, chap. 33.

6 Popkin 1996.

SEVEN FROM PSR TO ETERNITY

1 In the Ethics he does speak of the immortality of the mind (5p41) but only while deriding the views of others. However, see KV I, chap. 23.

2 Nadler, for example, develops this line of thought in Nadler 2001: chap. 5.

3 As we saw in Chapter 2, note 16, the relation of being in itself is coextensive with the relation of being conceived through itself.

4 Perhaps Kant is making this point in his criticism of the ontological argument when he says, "when I think a thing, through whichever and however many

predicates I like, ... not the least bit gets added to the thing when I posit in addition that this thing is" (Kant 1997, *Critique of Pure Reason* A600/B628). Perhaps Hume makes the same point: "the idea of existence is nothing different from the idea of any object, and when after the simple conception of any thing we wou'd conceive it as existent, we in reality make no addition to or alteration of our first idea" (Hume 1978, *A Treatise of Human Nature*, p. 94).

5 The idea also seems to be caused by certain infinite modes which follow— directly or indirectly—from God's absolute nature. But this intermediate step between God and the ideas can be passed over here because the problem that I want to raise emerges more clearly from considering the apparent infinite cause, God.

6 See 2p36d.

7 And, of course, given Spinoza's parallelism, if our mind becomes more powerful and exists more fully, then our bodies too will enjoy greater power and greater existence.

8 Yovel 1989 also emphasizes that, for Spinoza, eternality is immanent in this life.

EIGHT THE AFTERMATH OF SPINOZA

1 Spinoza has also had a broad impact on literature (e.g. Malamud, Borges, George Eliot, etc.). I will, though, focus in this chapter on certain lines of Spinoza's influence within philosophy.

2 For a wonderfully rich account of the lengths to which many philosophers went to avoid Spinoza's conclusions, and of the often surprising extent to which other philosophers (secretly or not) accepted some of Spinoza's main views, see Israel 2001.

3 An engaging account of their meeting can be found in Stewart 2005.

4 See especially the letter to Wedderkopf (May 1671) in Leibniz 1969: 146–47 and the discussion in Adams 1994: 10–12.

5 "On Nature Itself," in Leibniz 1989: 160.

6 "On the Origins of Things from Forms," in Leibniz 1992: 77. For some helpful discussion of monism in Leibniz, see Cover and O'Leary-Hawthorne 1999: chap. 7. Mercer 1999 argues, however, that such passages do not point to Spinozism.

7 See "On Freedom" in Leibniz 1969: 263–66.

8 See the argument against monism, in "On Nature Itself," where the connection to freedom is explicit in Leibniz 1989: 161.

9 Hume 1975, *Enquiry Concerning Human Understanding*, section 7, part 2, p. 74.

10 Someone who sees the contrast between Hume and Spinoza in precisely these terms is Goldstein 2006.

11 Kant 1998: 10.

12 However, as we saw in the previous chapter, there may be reason to think that there is not a strict identity between the mode considered as a state of God and the mode considered as a state of some less than fully active thing. The modes in question may approximate being identical without being fully identical.

13 See Davidson 1980.

14 Leibniz to Clarke, p. 321; also "Primary Truths," p. 31, in Leibniz 1989.

15 See Sider 2001: 40.

16 I canvass some possible strategies in Della Rocca unpublished.

Bibliography

Adams, Robert M. (1994) *Leibniz: Determinist, Theist, Idealist*, New York and Oxford: Oxford University Press.

Bayle, Pierre (1991) *Historical and Critical Dictionary*, Richard H. Popkin (trans.), Indianapolis: Hackett.

Beiser, Frederick C. (1987) *The Fate of Reason: German Philosophy from Kant to Fichte*, Cambridge, Mass.: Harvard University Press.

Bennett, Jonathan (1984) *A Study of Spinoza's Ethics*, Indianapolis: Hackett.

Bergson, Henri (1975) "Philosophical Intuition," in Bergson, *The Creative Mind*, Totowa, N.J.: Littlefield, Adams, and Co., 107–29.

Carraud, Vincent (2002) *Causa sive Ratio: La Raison de la Cause, de Suarez à Leibniz*, Paris: Presses Universitaires de France.

Carriero, John (1995) "On the Relationship between Mode and Substance in Spinoza's Metaphysics," *Journal of the History of Philosophy* 33, 245–73.

———. (2005) "Spinoza on Final Causality," *Oxford Studies in Early Modern Philosophy* 2, 105–47.

Cohen, I. B. (1964) "'*Quantum in Se Est*': Newton's Concept of Inertia in Relation to Descartes and Lucretius," *Notes and Records of the Royal Society of London* 19, 131–55.

Colerus, John (1880) *The Life of Benedict de Spinosa*, in Frederick Pollock, *Spinoza: His Life and Philosophy*, London: C. Kegan Paul and Co., 411–43.

Cover, J. A. and Mark Kulstad (eds.), *Central Themes in Early Modern Philosophy*, Indianapolis: Hackett.

Cover, Jan and John O'Leary-Hawthorne (1999) *Substance and Individuation in Leibniz*, Cambridge: Cambridge University Press.

Curley, Edwin (1969) *Spinoza's Metaphysics: An Essay in Interpretation*, Cambridge, Mass.: Harvard University Press.

———. (1973) "Spinoza's Moral Philosophy," in Marjorie Grene (ed.), *Spinoza: A Collection of Critical Essays*, Garden City, N.Y.: Anchor Books, 354–76.

———. (1975) "Descartes, Spinoza, and the Ethics of Belief," in Eugene Freeman and Maurice Mandelbaum (eds.), *Spinoza: Essays in Interpretation*, LaSalle, Ill.: Open Court, 159–89.

————. (1988) *Behind the Geometrical Method: A Reading of Spinoza's Ethics*, Princeton, N.J.: Princeton University Press.

————. (1990) "Notes on a Neglected Masterpiece (II): The Theologico-Political *Treatise* as a Prolegomenon to the *Ethics*," in J. A. Cover and Mark Kulstad (eds.), *Central Themes in Early Modern Philosophy*, Indianapolis: Hackett, 109–59.

————. (1991) "On Bennett's Interpretation of Spinoza's Monism," in Yirmiyahu Yovel (ed.), *God and Nature: Spinoza's Metaphysics*, Leiden, The Netherlands: E. J. Brill, 35–51.

————. (1996) "Kissinger, Spinoza, and Genghis Khan," in Don Garrett (ed.), *The Cambridge Companion to Spinoza*, Cambridge: Cambridge University Press, 315–42.

Curley, Edwin and Gregory Walski (1998) "Spinoza's Necessitarianism Reconsidered," in Rocco Gennaro and Charles Huenemann (eds.), *New Essays on the Rationalists*, New York: Oxford University Press, 241–62.

Damasio, Antonio (2003) *Looking for Spinoza: Joy, Sorrow, and the Feeling Brain*, New York: Harvest/Harcourt.

Davidson, Donald (1980) "Mental Events," in Davidson, *Essays on Actions and Events*, Oxford: Clarendon Press, 207–25.

————. (1999) "Spinoza's Causal Theory of the Affects," in Yirmiyahu Yovel (ed.), *Desire and Affect: Spinoza as Psychologist*, New York: Little Room Press, 95–111.

Deleuze, Gilles (1992) *Expressionism in Philosophy: Spinoza*, Martin Joughin (trans.), New York: Zone Books.

Della Rocca, Michael (1996a) *Representation and the Mind-Body Problem in Spinoza*, New York: Oxford University Press.

————. (1996b) "Spinoza's Metaphysical Psychology," in Don Garrett (ed.), *The Cambridge Companion to Spinoza*, Cambridge: Cambridge University Press, 192–266.

————. (1998) "'If a Body Meet a Body': Descartes on Body-Body Causation," in Rocco Gennaro and Charles Huenemann (eds.), *New Essays on the Rationalists*, New York: Oxford University Press, 48–81.

————. (2002) "Spinoza's Substance Monism," in Olli Koistinen and John Biro (eds.), *Spinoza: Metaphysical Themes*, New York: Oxford University Press, 38–59.

————. (2003a) "A Rationalist Manifesto: Spinoza and the Principle of Sufficient Reason," *Philosophical Topics* 31, 75–94.

————. (2003b) "The Power of an Idea: Spinoza's Critique of Pure Will," *Nous* 37, 200–31.

————. (2004) "Egoism and the Imitation of Affects in Spinoza," in Yirmiyahu Yovel and Gideon Segal (eds.), *Spinoza on Reason and the "Free Man,"* New York: Little Room Press, 123–47.

————. (2006) "Explaining Explanation and the Multiplicity of Attributes," in Michael Hampe and Robert Schnepf (eds.), *Ethik in Geometrischer Ordnung Dargestellt*, Berlin: Akademie Verlag, 17–36.

————. (2007) "Spinoza and the Metaphysics of Scepticism," *Mind* 116, 851–74.

————. (2008a) "Causation without Intelligibility and Causation without God in Descartes," in Janet Broughton and John Carriero (eds.), *The Blackwell Companion to Descartes*, Oxford: Blackwell, 235–50.

————. (2008b) "Rationalism Run Amok: Representation and the Reality of Affects in Spinoza," in Charles Huenemann (ed.), *Interpreting Spinoza*, Cambridge: Cambridge University Press, 26–52.

————. (unpublished) "PSR."

Descartes, René (1984–91) *The Philosophical Writings of Descartes*, 3 vols., ed. and trans. J. Cottingham, R. Stoothoff, D. Murdoch and A. Kenny, Cambridge: Cambridge University Press.

Donagan, Alan (1988) *Spinoza*, Hertfordshire, U.K.: Harvester Wheatsheaf.

————. (1996) "Spinoza's Theology," in Don Garrett (ed.), *The Cambridge Companion to Spinoza*, Cambridge: Cambridge University Press, 343–82.

Doney, Willis (1975) "Spinoza on Philosophical Skepticism," in Eugene Freeman and Maurice Mandelbaum (eds.), *Spinoza: Essays in Interpretation*, LaSalle, Ill.: Open Court, 139–58.

Frankfurt, Harry (1999) "Two Motivations for Rationalism: Descartes and Spinoza," in Frankfurt, *Necessity, Volition, and Love*, Cambridge: Cambridge University Press, 42–54.

Garber, Daniel (1992) *Descartes' Metaphysical Physics*, Chicago: University of Chicago Press.

————. (1994) "Descartes and Spinoza on Persistence and Conatus," *Studia Spinozana* 10, 43–67.

Garrett, Aaron (2003) *Meaning in Spinoza's Method*, Cambridge: Cambridge University Press.

Garrett, Don (1979) "Spinoza's 'Ontological' Argument," *Philosophical Review* 88, 198–223.

————. (1990) "'A Free Man Always Acts Honestly, Not Deceptively': Freedom and the Good in Spinoza's *Ethics*," in Edwin Curley and Pierre-François Moreau (eds.), *Spinoza: Issues and Directions*, Leiden, The Netherlands: E. J. Brill, 221–38.

————. (1991) "Spinoza's Necessitarianism," in Yirmiyahu Yovel (ed.), *God and Nature: Spinoza's Metaphysics*, Leiden, The Netherlands: E. J. Brill, 191–218.

————. (1996) "Spinoza's Ethical Theory," in Don Garrett (ed.), *The Cambridge Companion to Spinoza*, Cambridge: Cambridge University Press, 267–314.

————. (1998) "Teleology in Spinoza and Early Modern Rationalism," in Rocco Gennaro and Charles Huenemann (eds.), *New Essays on the Rationalists*, New York: Oxford University Press, 310–35.

————. (2002) "Spinoza's *Conatus* Argument," in Olli Koistinen and John Biro (eds.), *Spinoza: Metaphysical Themes*, New York: Oxford University Press, 127–58.

Giancotti, Emilia (1991) "On the Problem of Infinite Modes," in Yirmiyahu Yovel (ed.), *God and Nature: Spinoza's Metaphysics*, Leiden, The Netherlands: E. J. Brill, 97–118.

Goldstein, Rebecca (2006) *Betraying Spinoza: The Renegade Jew Who Gave Us Modernity*, New York: Schocken.

Guéroult, Martial (1968, 1974) *Spinoza*, 2 vols., Paris: Aubier-Montaigne.

Gullan-Whur, Margaret (1998) *Within Reason: A Life of Spinoza*, New York: St. Martin's Press.

Hegel, G. W. F. (1967) *Hegel's Philosophy of Right*, London: Oxford University Press.

————. (1977) *Phenomenology of Spirit*, A. V. Miller (trans.), Oxford: Oxford University Press.

————. (1991) *The Encyclopaedia of Logic* (with the *Zusätze*), T. F. Geraetsz, W. A. Suchting, and H. S. Harris (trans.), Indianapolis: Hackett.

————. (1996) *Lectures on the History of Philosophy*, E. S. Haldane and Frances H. Simson (trans.), abridged student edition, New Jersey: Humanities Press.

Hobbes, Thomas (1994) *Leviathan*, edited and with an introduction by Edwin Curley, Indianapolis: Hackett.

Hoffman, Paul (unpublished), "Does Efficient Causation Presuppose Final Causation? Aquinas vs. Early Modern Mechanism."

Hume, David (1975) *Enquiries Concerning Human Understanding and Concerning the Principles of Morals*, 3rd ed., Oxford: Clarendon Press.

————. (1978) *A Treatise of Human Nature*, 2nd ed., Oxford Clarendon Press.

Israel, Jonathan (2001) *Radical Enlightenment: Philosophy and the Making of Modernity 1650–1750*, New York: Oxford University Press.

Jacobi, Friedrich Heinrich (1994) *The Main Philosophical Writings and the Novel Allwill*, Montreal and Kingston: McGill-Queen's University Press.

James, Susan (1997) *Passion and Action: The Emotions in Seventeenth-Century Philosophy*, Oxford: Clarendon Press.

Joachim, Harold H. (1901) *A Study of the Ethics of Spinoza*, Oxford: Clarendon Press.

Jorgensen, Larry (2007) "Continuity and Consciousness in Leibniz's Philosophy of Mind," dissertation, Yale University.

Kant, Immanuel (1981) *Grounding for the Metaphysics of Morals* with "On a Supposed Right to Lie because of Philanthropic Concerns," James W. Ellington (trans.), Indianapolis: Hackett.

————. (1997) *Critique of Pure Reason*, Paul Guyer and Allen W. Wood (trans. and eds.), Cambridge: Cambridge University Press.

————. (1998) "What Does It Mean to Orient Oneself in Thinking?," in Kant, *Religion within the Boundaries of Mere Reason*, Allen Wood and George di Giovanni (eds.), Cambridge: Cambridge University Press.

Leibniz, Gottfried Wilhelm (1969) *Philosophical Papers and Letters*, Leroy Loemker (ed.), Dordrecht, The Netherlands: D. Reidel.

———. (1985) *Theodicy*, E. M. Huggard (trans), LaSalle, Ill.: Open Court.

———. (1989) *Philosophical Essays*, Roger Ariew and Daniel Garber (trans.), Indianapolis: Hackett.

———. (1992) *De Summa Rerum: Metaphysical Papers, 1675–76*, G. H. R. Parkinson (trans.), New Haven, Conn.: Yale University Press.

Marshall, Eugene (forthcoming) "Adequacy and Innateness in Spinoza," *Oxford Studies in Early Modern Philosophy*.

Matheron, Alexandre (1969) *Individu et Communauté chez Spinoza*, Paris: Les Editions de Minuit.

Matson, Wallace (1969) "Death and Destruction in Spinoza's *Ethics*," *Inquiry* 20, 403–17.

———. (1990) "Body Essence and Mind Eternity in Spinoza," Edwin Curley and Pierre-François Moreau (eds.), *Spinoza: Issues and Directions*, Leiden, The Netherlands: E. J. Brill, 82–95.

Melamed, Yitzhak (forthcoming) "Spinoza's Metaphysics of Substance: The Substance-Mode Relation as a Relation of Inherence and Predication," *Philosophy and Phenomenological Research*.

Mercer, Christia (1999) "Leibniz and Spinoza on Substance and Mode," Derek Pereboom (ed.), *The Rationalists: Critical Essays on Descartes, Spinoza and Leibniz*, Lanham, Md.: Rowman and Littlefield, 273–300.

Nadler, Steven (1999) *Spinoza: A Life*, Cambridge: Cambridge University Press.

———. (2001) *Spinoza's Heresy*, New York: Oxford University Press.

Neu, Jerome (1977) *Emotion, Thought and Therapy: A Study of Hume and Spinoza and the Relationship of Philosophical Theories of the Emotions to Psychological Theories of Therapy*, Berkeley and Los Angeles: University of California Press.

Nietzsche, Friedrich (1954) "Postcard to Overbeck," in *The Portable Nietzsche*, Walter Kaufmann (ed. and trans.), Harmondsworth, U.K.: Penguin, 92.

———. (1966) *Beyond Good and Evil*, Walter Kaufman (trans.), New York: Vintage Books.

———. (1974) *The Gay Science*, Walter Kaufman (trans.), New York: Vintage Books.

———. (1994) *On the Genealogy of Morality*, Carol Diethe (trans.), Cambridge: Cambridge University Press.

Parkinson, G. H. R. (1954) *Spinoza's Theory of Knowledge*, Oxford: Clarendon Press.

Popkin, Richard (1996) "Spinoza and Bible Scholarship," Don Garrett (ed.), *The Cambridge Companion to Spinoza*, Cambridge: Cambridge University Press, 383–407.

Pruss, Alexander R. (2006) *The Principle of Sufficient Reason: A Reassessment*, Cambridge: Cambridge University Press.

Radner, Daisie (1971) "Spinoza's Theory of Ideas," *Philosophical Review* 80, 338–59.

Rozemond, Marleen (1998) *Descartes's Dualism*, Cambridge, Mass.: Harvard University Press.

Sider, Theodore (2002) *Four-Dimensionalism: An Ontology of Persistence and Time*, New York: Oxford University Press.

Simmons, Alison. (2001) "Changing the Cartesian Mind: Leibniz on Sensation, Representation, and Consciousness," *Philosophical Review* 110, 31–75.

Stewart, Matthew (2005) *The Courtier and the Heretic: Leibniz, Spinoza, and the Fate of God in the Modern World*, New York: Norton.

Strauss, Leo (1988) "How to Study Spinoza's *Theologico-Political Treatise*," in Strauss, *Persecution and the Art of Writing*, Chicago: University of Chicago Press, 142–201.

Tye, Michael (1997) *Ten Problems of Consciousness*, Cambridge, Mass.: MIT Press.

van Inwagen, Peter (2002) *Metaphysics*, 2nd ed., Boulder, Col.: Westview.

Wilson, Margaret (1999) "Objects, Ideas, and 'Minds': Comments on Spinoza's Theory of Mind," in Wilson, *Ideas and Mechanism: Essays on Early Modern Philosophy*, Princeton, N.J.: Princeton University Press, 126–40.

Wittgenstein, Ludwig (1958) *Philosophical Investigations*, G. E. M. Anscombe (trans.), New York: Macmillan.

Wolf, A. (1970) *The Oldest Biography of Spinoza*, Port Washington, N.Y.: Kennikat Press.

Yovel, Yirmyahu (1989) *Spinoza and other Heretics*, 2 vols., Princeton, N.J.: Princeton University Press.

Index of Passages from the *Ethics*

1def2 72
1def3 42, 93
1def4 43, 56, 261
1def5 46, 62, 93, 262, 319n6
1def6 51, 56
1def8 257, 259
1ax1 260
1ax2 4–5, 70, 76
1ax4 44, 91–99, 112, 134, 233
1ax5 322n21
1p1 47
1p3 322n21
1p4d 47, 61
1p5 46, 49, 52, 53
1p5d 47
1p6c 44, 50
1p7 46, 49–53
1p7d 50
1p8s2 321n6
1p10 43, 53
1p10s 49, 52, 54, 318n2
1p11 50–53, 257
1p11d2 4, 52
1p12 63
1p14 52, 57
1p14d 318n2
1p15 260
1p15d 62
1p15s 63–64
1p16 67–8, 76–7, 92, 257

1p16d 67–8
1p17s 84
1p20 261
1p20c2 280
1p21 70
1p21d 70, 320n21
1p23 85, 320n21
1p23d 70, 320n21
1p24 62
1p25 81
1p25d 44
1p25s 263
1p25c 61
1p26 62
1p28 71, 84, 98
1p28d 74
1p29 77
1p31 84
1p33 77
1p36 84, 85, 142
1app 80, 81, 83–4, 176, 177–8,
   181, 190
2ax1 257
2ax2 120
2ax3 119–20
2ax4 105–8
2ax5 105–8
2def3 224
2def6 320n23
2def7 127, 323n12

2p1 57
2p1s 58
2p2 57
2p3 92, 97
2p3d 92
2p5 97–8, 318n2
2p5d 97–8, 319n8
2p6 44
2p7 90–1, 92, 321n2
2p7c 104
2p7s 57, 91, 100, 102, 122,
    322n21
2p8c 255
2p10c 120
2p11d 120
2p11c 74, 105, 114
2p12 109
2p12d 109
2p13d 106
2p13s 110, 115, 116, 147
2ax1" 94, 265–66
2ax2" 148
2def 148
2le3 323n9
2le3c 73, 322n1, 323n9
2le4 148, 149
2le5 149
2le6 149
2le7 149
2le7s 74
2p15 109, 225
2p16 112
2p16c2 112
2p17c 172
2p17s 245, 259
2p18 164
2p18d 165
2p18s 259
2p19 321n11
2p23 321n15
2p28 114
2p29s 113–14
2p36d 325n6
2p40s1 113
2p40s2 258
2p43s 133
2p44c2 257

2p48d 257
2p49 123
2p49c 123
2p49s 126–7, 320n23
3pref 5, 9, 73 319n15
3def2 155
3p2 322n21
3p3 114
3p4 135–43, 144, 147
3p4d 137–43, 322n1
3p5 144
3p5d 144
3p6 137, 144–5, 147–52, 155,
    323n8
3p6d 147
3p9d 321n15
3p9s 176
3p11s 158
3p12 155, 158
3p13s 160
3p15 165
3p16 165
3p18s1 168
3p18s2 168
3p21 161
3p22 161
3p22s 161, 167
3p24s 161
3p27 166
3p27s 167
3p29 168
3p29s 190
3p30 168
3p31c 228
3p31s 228, 229
3p32s 167
3p35 162
3p35s 162–3
3p39s 181
3p40s2 101
3p46 165–6
3p57s 110
3da1exp 321n11
3da2 156
3da3 156
3da3exp 156
3da25 323n15

3da26 324n4
3da27 324n4
3gen.def 158
4pref 81–2, 156, 176–7, 180, 189,
 320n23, 321n4
4def8 181–2, 185, 324n2
4ax 85, 142–3, 188
4p4 188
4p9 169
4p9d 170
4p9s 169
4p10 171
4p17s 171, 322n1
4p18s 182, 185, 196, 199
4p20s 141, 322n12
4p26 186
4p27 186
4p28 324n3
4p31c 199
4p32 195
4p34 195
4p35c1 193–4
4p35c2 195
4p37 193, 198
4p39s 259

4p50s 324n4
4p52 323n15
4p63cs 192
4p66 171
4p67d 189
4p68s 189
4p72 199, 201
4p72d 199
4p72s 199, 202
4app30 171
5pref 123, 322n21
5ax2 321n4
5p3 191
5p17 156
5p18 191
5p21 259
5p22 257
5p23 254
5p35 157
5p38d 258
5p38s 200, 258
5p39s 116
5p41 324n1
5p42 256

Index

absolute truth 300–1, 312–13
acosmism 289, 314
Adams, Robert 325n4
affects 153–73; power over 190–1; as representational 119–20, 157–9, 160, 173
ambition 167–8, 229
anger 161
Anselm, Saint 51
anticipation 156, 168–72
appetite 153–4
Aquinas, Saint Thomas 4, 38
Archimedes 306
aristocracy 221
Aristotle 34, 38, 275
association of mental states 163–7
atheism 284–6, 289
attribute: as conceptually independent 39–40, 42–4, 49, 54–5; Descartes' conception of 36–41; as essence of substance 43, 56, 314; infinitely many 43, 45–6, 51; and intellect 43, 56; not shared 46–9; Spinoza's conception of 42–58

Bayle, Pierre 20, 32, 279–81, 288–9, 311
Beiser, Frederick 313
Bennett, Jonathan 32, 88, 274, 320n24, 320n13

Bergson, Henri 9–10
Bible: divine authorship of 21; interpretation of 25, 27, 237–44, 244; truth of 241–2, 243, 248–9, 252
bifurcation 6–8, 23, 131, 135, 232–3, 237, 265, 273, 281, 287, 297–300, 302–3
Borges, Jorge Luis 325n1

Carraud, Vincent 32
Carriero, John 62, 67–8, 88, 319nn12, 13, 14
Cartesian circle 127, 130
Casearius, Johannes 24
causation 1, 7, 8, 30, 307–8; adequate 155, 187; between mind and body in Descartes 40; between modes generally 68–9; and conceptual dependence 43–4, 50, 150–2, 179; and inherence 62–9
Cohen, I.B. 323n8
Colerus, Johan 15, 20, 22, 32
Collegiants 20–1, 22
conatus see striving
consciousness 7–8, 30, 90, 110–11, 115–18, 121, 126, 134–5, 154, 179, 277, 281
conversos 15, 218
Cover, Jan 325n6

Curley, Edwin 61–9, 88, 135, 204, 221–3, 252, 319nn18, 19, 320nn22, 24, 323n8, 324n2

Da Costa, Uriel 17–19, 254
Damasio, Antonio 173
Davidson, Donald 57, 103–04, 135, 303, 326n13
Deleuze, Gilles 88
Della Rocca, Michael 32, 88, 136, 173, 204, 274, 318n2, 319nn 4, 5, 8, 321nn3, 9, 322n22, 322n3, 326n16
democracy 21, 221
Descartes, René 3, 5, 9, 23–4, 33–46, 72, 79, 87, 90, 93, 99–100, 110, 118, 135, 137, 173, 255, 321n18, 323n8; and belief 123–7; and modes 36–41, 59–61; and naturalism 35–6; as non-rationalist 44–5, 55, 152; and ontological argument 51; and principal attributes 36–41, 56, 59; and skepticism 127–34; and striving 145–7, 150; and substance 33–41, 48, 66; and unintelligible causal relations 40, 44–45, 152; and weak conceptual barrier 55
determinism 70, 74–77, 87, 232, 277, 279, 314
desire 154–60, 173; and judgments of goodness 176–7
de Volder 146
De Witt, Cornelis 27
De Witt, Johan 26–7
dispositions 307–8
Donagan, Alan 32, 247, 252
Doney, Willis 136

egoism 159–60, 192–200, 203–4, 314
Eliot, George 325n1
emotions *see* affects
envy 161, 167
epistemic standards 128–35; analogous to moral standards 185–7

essence: and causation 92–6, 134, 139; and definition 93, 262; and self-destruction 138–43; of substance 36–37, 49–50; and rights 209; as unique 94–95, 114; and virtue 181–2
eternity 254–73; degrees of eternality 270–1, 273
existence 8–9, 37, 134; as conceivability or intelligibility 50, 261–3, 267, 273; degrees of 263, 267–71, 273, 284, 290, 305, 312; God's 261
extension: as attribute 36, 57–8; conceptually independent of thought 40, 54, 90, 96–9, 103–04, 121

Fabritius, Johann Ludwig 27–8
face of the whole universe 74
faith 234–6, 287
favor 161
fear 168
Fisher, Samuel 244
Frankfurt, Harry 324n16
freedom 21, 31, 75–6, 124–5, 187–92, 248, 251, 284–5, 289–91, 297–8; of action 219–25; degrees of 188–90, 200–4, 230–2; to philosophize 235–6; of speech 217–19, 223–25, 235; of thought 215–17, 223–25, 235
free man 189, 196, 200–1
Freud, Sigmund 191

Garber, Daniel 173, 319n12
Garrett, Aaron 318nn3, 32, 321n5
Garrett, Don 52–3, 75, 88, 173, 205, 319n18, 322n3, 324nn2, 5
geometrical method 9–11, 295–6
Guéroult, Martial 88, 322n19
Giancotti, Emilia 320n21
God 2, 3, 9; and acting for an end 78–87, 124–25, definition of 10, 30–1, 46, 51–3, 55, 257, 262; determines all 76–8; essence and existence identical 261–2;

existence of and miracles 232–4; following absolutely from 70–2; freedom of 188–9; as good 182; immutability of 280; knowledge of 186–7; modes inhering in 61–9; necessary existence of 51–3; as striving 152–3, 154, 182; will of 84, 124–5

Goldstein, Rebecca 12, 325n10

good 8, 12–14, 175–83, 187, 189, 203, 239

Gullan-Whur, Margaret 32

hate 160–3

Hawthorne, John 325n6

Hegel, G.W.F. 287–92, 296, 312, 313

helping others 192–9

Hobbes, Thomas 137, 196, 210–11, 221, 227, 244, 323n18, 324n2

hope 168

Hume, David 3, 45, 275, 281–3, 287, 302, 304, 311, 325n4

Huygens, Christiaan 25

ibn Ezra 243

idealism 58, 103–4, 315

ideas; as active 124–7, 135, 224; adequate/inadequate 114–15, 133, 158, 186, 187, 189, 224, 245–8, 258–9, 265–7, 273, 287, 300–1; as beliefs 123–7, 215–7; confusion of 112–15, 133; of ideas 90–1; as inherently certain 131–4, 245, 264; parallel to things 90–2; as representational 89, 118–27

identity: degrees of 269, 326n12

identity of indiscernibles 47–8, 87, 100–1, 134, 196, 197, 277, 315

imitation of affects 166–8, 198–9, 228–9; and anticipation 169

immortality: Descartes on 102; Jewish thought on 17–18, 21

in see inherence

indignation 161

individuals 107–8, 137, 148–50, 211, 213

infinite modes 70–4, 325n5

inherence 7, 34, 38, 42, 59, 144, 260, 265–73, 315; and conceptual dependence 60–1, 65–9; degrees of 69, 144

insofar as it is in itself 145, 147, 152, 323n8

intelligibility see principle of sufficient reason

irrational action 170–1

Israel, Jonathan 313, 325n2

Jacobi, F.H. 283, 312

James, Susan 174

Jesus 245–8, 252

Joachim, Harold H. 274, 313

Jorgensen, Larry 321n14

joy 156–60

justice 211–13, 225, 255–6

Kant, Immanuel 3, 57, 183, 200, 202–4, 29, 275, 287, 304, 312, 324n6, 324n4

Karl Ludwig, Elector of Palatine 27

Kripke, Saul 304

La Peyrere, Isaac 244

laws of nature 70–4, 226, 232–3

Leibniz, Gottfried Wilhelm 4, 25, 30, 49, 52, 76, 85, 111, 146, 150–2, 275, 276–9, 284, 287, 303, 304, 306, 311, 321n17

Lessing, Gotthold 283, 288, 312, 313

Lewis, David 304

lies 199–204, 212

Locke, John 3

love 160–3; intellectual 157

Lucas, Jean-Maximilian 318nn7, 15, 21

Lucretius 323n8

Maimonides, Moses 18, 241–2

Malamud, Bernard 325n1

Marranos 16, 31, 315

Marshall, Eugene 321n16

Matheron, Alexandre 253

Matson, Wallace 174, 273

Melamed, Yitzhak 88, 319n17

memory 259
Mendelssohn, Moses 283, 286–7,
  312, 313
Mercer, Christia 325n6
Meyer, Lodewijk 24, 25
mind: as collection of ideas 64, 104,
  134; eternality of 68–9, 200, 250,
  254–73; as idea of body 104–8,
  134–5, 257; identical to body
  99–104; mineness of my 108;
  representational theory of 89,
  118–27; thought as essence of 36
miracles 232–4, 245
mode: caused by God 62; conceived
  through substance 59–60, 319n13;
  Descartes' conception of 36–41,
  58; essence of 93; infinite/finite
  70–4; inhering in God 61, 63–9,
  77; Spinoza's conception of 46–8,
  58–69, 315
monarchy 220–1
Moses 240, 243–4, 245
motion-and-rest 72–3

Nadler, Steven 15, 16, 17, 18, 19,
  20, 22, 24, 25, 26, 32, 277,
  324n2
naturalism 4, 5–7, 11, 14, 18, 21,
  23, 42–4, 65–9, 80–1, 85–7, 117,
  120–2, 134–5, 152–3, 154, 156,
  158–9, 189, 207, 208, 232–4,
  237, 248–50, 256, 265, 272–3, 316
nature see essence
necessitarianism 7, 69–78, 87, 257,
  278–9, 305, 316
Neu, Jerome 174
Newton, Isaac 323n8
Nietzsche, Friedrich 9, 292–303,
  305, 312–13

obedience 231–2, 234–5
Oldenburg, Henry 25, 28
ontological argument 51–2, 316

panpsychism 109–18, 134–5, 224,
  290, 316
Parkinson, G.H.R 136

Parmenides 4
parallelism 90–2, 98–9, 100–3, 107–
  8, 134, 153, 157, 164–5, 255,
  257, 316, 325n7
personal identity 259
philosophy vs. faith 235–6
physicalism 57–8, 103–4
piety 234, 249, 252
pity 167
Plato 323n17
Popkin, Richard 243, 324n6
popular morality 292–4
power 8, 133; of acting 154–60,
  171–2, 180; and freedom 188; and
  knowledge 185–7, 191; and rights
  206–10; and virtue 182
prime matter 38, 48, 316, 319n3
primitives 3, 8, 11, 131–3, 159, 304
principle of sufficient reason 4–5, 6–
  9, 11, 23, 24, 30–2, 42–3, 47, 50,
  54–5, 58, 67, 109, 117–8, 134–5,
  140, 142, 143, 170, 173, 187,
  264, 273, 275–6; and belief 123–
  7, 215, 316; and certainty 127–34;
  and consciousness 117–8; and
  content of ideas 105; and
  determinism 70, 75; and divine
  teleology 84–7; and eternality of
  the mind 261; and goodness 177–
  83; and Hegel 288–92; and Hume
  281–3; and individuals 107; and
  interpretation of scripture 239,
  250; justification of 11, 133, 272,
  277–8, 283, 303–11, 313; and
  Leibniz 276–9; and Lessing and
  Jacobi 284–7; and lying 202–3;
  and mind-body identity 100; and
  mineness of my mind 108; and
  miracles 232–4; and
  necessitarianism 77–8; and
  Nietzsche 302–3; and ontological
  argument 51–2; and panpsychism
  110; and representational theory of
  mind 120–2, 159; and right 183–
  5, 202; and rights 208; two-fold
  use of 8, 30, 45, 68, 89, 95–6,
  107, 108, 119, 126–7, 151–2,

159, 183, 185, 192–3, 208–9,
  250, 263, 265, 272, 277; and self-
  destruction 139–40; and striving
  138, 153; and uniqueness of
  essences 94–5
prophecy 244–50
Pruss, Alexander 313
PSR see principle of sufficient reason
punishment 191–2, 211–12

quantum in se est see insofar as it is in
  itself

Radner, Daisie 136
ratio of motion and rest 148–50
rationalism 21, 23, 41, 44, 67, 134,
  138, 152–3, 159, 208, 239, 256,
  316; see also principle of sufficient
  reason
religion: should be subservient to
  sovereign 225–7, 251–2;
  threatening to state 225, 227–30,
  251–2; useful to state 230–6, 251–2
representation 8, 277, 281, 316–17;
  and essence 92–9, 134, 322n24; as
  essence of mind 89, 118–27; and
  explanation 98–9, 150, 264; and
  parallelism 89–92, 98–9
responsibility 190, 204, 297
ressentiment 294, 301
Rieuwertsz, Jan 24, 26, 28, 29
right 8, 159, 175, 183–5, 187, 189,
  201, 203, 208
rights 206–25, 250–1
Rozemond, Marleen 38, 88, 318n2

sadness 156–9, 173
scripture: interpretation of 237–44;
  truth of 241–2, 243, 248–9
self-consciousness 289–91
self-destruction 138–45, 173, 214
shame 168
Sider, Theodore 326n15
Simmons, Alison 136, 321nn14, 17
skepticism 23, 127–35, 263–4, 317
Spinoza, Baruch de: biography 12–29;
  Compendium of Hebrew Grammar 27;

Descartes' Principles of Philosophy 24;
  Ethics 9–10, 23–4. 25. 28–9, 31–2;
  excommunication 20–2, 254;
  Metaphyiscal Thoughts 24; motto 15,
  225; Political Treatise 29, 32; Short
  Treatise 23–4; Tractatus Theologico-
  Politicus 25–6, 31; Treatise on the
  Emendation of the Intellect 12–15, 23, 31
Spinoza, Gabriel de 19
Spinoza, Hanna de 19
Spinoza, Michael de 19
state 206–8, 211–35, 250–2
Stewart, Matthew 313, 325n3
Stoics 4
Strauss, Leo 225, 238, 246–8, 253
striving 137, 144–53, 173, 203,
  290–1, 293, 300, 314; and power
  of acting 154–6, 180–1
substance: conceived through itself
  42, 50; Descartes' conception of
  33–41; exists by nature 49–50; as
  explanatory engine 38;
  individuation of 39, 46–8; in
  itself 319n16, 323n8; monism of
  46–58, 278–83, 288; prior to
  modes 36, 47–8; as self-caused
  50; Spinoza's conception of 42–
  58, 317
substantial form 38, 317
suicide 138, 141
superstition 227–30, 231–2

teleology 78–87, 177–8, 226, 291–2,
  312
thought: as attribute 36, 57–8;
  conceptually independent of
  extension 40, 54, 90, 96–7; 103–
  4, 121
time bomb 138, 140–3
transference 165
Tschirnhaus, Ehrenfried Walther von
  25, 72
Tye, Michael 136, 321n17
universals 60–2

van den Enden, Clara 22
van den Enden, Franz 19, 21, 22

van Inwagen 88, 313, 320n24
virtue 181–2, 255–6, 324n3

Walski, Greg 319nn18, 19
Wedderkopf, Magnus 279, 325n4
will: and belief 123–7, 131, 135; of
    God 84; as striving of mind 153

will to power 293–300, 317
Wilson, Margaret 109, 136
Wittgenstein, Ludwig 1, 57, 305
Wolf, Abraham 32

Yovel, Yirmiyahu 32, 313, 318n9,
    325n8

Related titles from Routledge

Metaphysics Third Edition
Michael J. Loux

'An excellent, pellucidly clear and well constructed introduction.' – E.J. Lowe, Durham University, UK

'Excellent… It is well written and meets the need for something harder than first year texts. Students and teachers will like it.' – Frank Jackson, Australian National University

'Loux has done a masterful job.' – Mark Timmons, Memphis State University

'Very good…It goes into a lot of detail while always keeping the reader's eyes on the main issues. The chapters are well-structured and well-written.' – Tim Crane, Times Higher Education Supplement

Metaphysics: A Contemporary Introduction is aimed at students of metaphysics who have already completed an introductory philosophy course. This third edition of the successful textbook provides a fresh look at key topics in metaphysics and includes two new chapters on time and causation.

Wherever possible, Loux links contemporary views to their classical sources in the history of philosophy. This new edition also keeps the user-friendly format, the chapter overviews summarizing the main topics and examples to clarify difficult concepts.

ISBN 10: 0-415-40133-X (hbk)
ISBN 10: 0-415-40134-8 (pbk)

ISBN 13: 978-0-415-40133-3 (hbk)
ISBN 13: 978-0-415-40134-0 (pbk)

Available at all good bookshops
For ordering and further information please visit:
www.routledge.com

Related titles from Routledge

Classical Modern Philosophy
by Jeffrey Tlumak

"This is the ideal text for undergraduate courses in early modern philosophy. Tlumak's account of these philosophers is accurate, thorough, and concise, and written in a clear and accessible style." – *James Baillie, University of Portland*

"The book is impressively researched and rich in detail. There are no books on the market that rival this in terms of breadth and depth. It will be crucial reading for those encountering the philosophy of the modern period for the first time, as well for more advanced students."– *Andrew Chignell, Cornell University*

Classical Modern Philosophy introduces students to the key philosophers of the seventeenth and eighteenth centuries, and explores their most important works. Jeffrey Tlumak takes the reader on a chronological journey from Descartes to Kant, tracing the themes that run through the period and their interrelations. The main texts covered are:

- Descartes' *Meditations on First Philosophy*
- Spinoza's *Ethics*
- Locke's *Essay Concerning Human Understanding*
- Leibniz's *Discourse on Metaphysics and Monadology*
- Berkeley's *A Treatise Concerning the Principles of Human Knowledge* and *Three Dialogues between Hylas and Philonous*
- Hume's *An Enquiry Concerning Human Understanding* and *Dialogues Concerning Natural Religion*
- Kant's *Critique of Pure Reason*

Classical Modern Philosophy: A Contemporary Introduction is the ideal textbook to accompany a course in the history of modern philosophy, but each chapter can also be studied alone as an introduction to the featured philosopher or work. Jeffrey Tlumak outlines and assesses prominent interpretations of the texts, and surveys the legacy of each great thinker.

Jeffrey Tlumak is Associate Professor of Philosophy at Vanderbilt University.

Series editor: Paul K. Moser, Loyola University of Chicago

ISBN 13: 978-0-415-27592-7 (hbk)
ISBN 13: 978-0-415-27593-4 (pbk)

Available at all good bookshops
For ordering and further information please visit:
www.routledge.com

Related titles from Routledge

Leibniz
By Nicholas Jolley

'Nicholas Jolley's Leibniz is an excellent volume in the new Routledge Philosophers series. High marks are in order for its clarity, accessibility and acumen, as well as for the pace and style of its prose... a serious, freestanding study of the philosopher for the non-specialist and a stimulating, enjoyable read for the specialist – in a word, recommended reading. And highly recommended at that.' – *Samuel Levey, Notre Dame Philosophical Reviews*

'... full, thoughtful, lucid and interesting, and it can be recommended without hesitation both to those who are new to Leibniz's philosophy and to those who are well acquainted with it.' *G.H.R. Parkinson, British Journal for the History of Philosophy*

'Jolley has done a fabulous job, and the result is perfectly suited for its intended purpose and audience. The work is very clearly written; the organization is excellent; and the coverage comprehensive. The needs of students and beginners are indeed well-served here, but the result is not bland.' – *Vere Chappell, University of Massachusetts*

'The best introduction available.' – *Glenn Hartz, Ohio State University*

'Reading this gave me great pleasure – it is interesting, illuminating, systematic, thorough and above all pleasantly, smoothly and accessibly written. A splendid book.' – *Roger Woolhouse, University of York, UK*

'An excellent work. It will clearly establish itself as the best introduction to the thought of Leibniz, and I would recommend it to students wrestling with this difficult philosopher for the first time.' – *Brandon C. Look, University of Kentucky*

Gottfried Wilhelm Leibniz (1646– 1716) was hailed by Bertrand Russell as 'one of the supreme intellects of all time'. A towering figure in seventeenth-century philosophy, his complex thought has been championed and satirized in equal measure, most famously in Voltaire's *Candide*.

In this outstanding introduction to his philosophy, Nicholas Jolley introduces and assesses the whole of Leibniz's philosophy. Beginning with an introduction to Leibniz's life and work, he carefully introduces the core elements of Leibniz's metaphysics: his theories of substance, identity and individuation; monads and space and time; and his important debate over the nature of space and time with Newton's champion, Samuel Clarke.

He then introduces Leibniz's theories of mind, knowledge, and innate ideas, showing how Leibniz anticipated the distinction between conscious and unconscious states, before examining his theory of free will and the problem of evil. An important feature of the book is its introduction to Leibniz's moral and political philosophy, an overlooked aspect of his work.

The final chapter assesses legacy and the impact of his philosophy on philosophy as a whole, particularly on the work of Immanuel Kant. Throughout, Nicholas Jolley places Leibniz in relation to some of the other great philosophers, such as Descartes, Spinoza and Locke, and discusses Leibniz's key works, such as the *Monadology* and *Discourse on Metaphysics*.

Nicholas Jolley teaches philosophy at the University of California, Irvine. He is author of *Locke: His Philosophical Thought* and editor of *The Cambridge Companion to Leibniz*.

ISBN 13: 978-0-415-28338-0 (hbk)
ISBN 13: 978-0-415-28337-3 (pbk)

Available at all good bookshops
For ordering and further information please visit:
www.routledge.com

CPSIA information can be obtained
at www.ICGtesting.com
Printed in the USA
FFOW02n1918040614
5761FF

9 780415 283304